HOW TO BE YOUR
BEST
WHEN YOU FEEL
YOUR WORST

HOW TO BE YOUR
BEST
WHEN YOU FEEL
YOUR WORST

CASEY TREAT

BERKLEY PRAISE, NEW YORK

BERKLEY PRAISE
An Imprint of The Berkley Publishing Group
Published by the Penguin Group
Penguin Group (USA) Inc.
375 Hudson Street, New York, New York 10014, USA
Penguin Group (Canada), 90 Eglinton Avenue East, Suite 700, Toronto, Ontario M4P 2Y3, Canada
(a division of Pearson Penguin Canada Inc.)
Penguin Books Ltd., 80 Strand, London WC2R 0RL, England
Penguin Group Ireland, 25 St. Stephen's Green, Dublin 2, Ireland (a division of Penguin Books Ltd.)
Penguin Group (Australia), 250 Camberwell Road, Camberwell, Victoria 3124, Australia
(a division of Pearson Australia Group Pty. Ltd.)
Penguin Books India Pvt. Ltd., 11 Community Centre, Panchsheel Park, New Delhi—110 017, India
Penguin Group (NZ), 67 Apollo Drive, Rosedale, North Shore 0632, New Zealand
(a division of Pearson New Zealand Ltd.)
Penguin Books (South Africa) (Pty.) Ltd., 24 Sturdee Avenue, Rosebank, Johannesburg 2196,
South Africa

Penguin Books Ltd., Registered Offices: 80 Strand, London WC2R 0RL, England

Copyright © 2008 by Casey Treat.
Scripture references can be found on page 299.
Interior text design by Tiffany Estreicher.

PRINTING HISTORY
Berkley Praise hardcover edition / January 2008
Berkley Praise trade paperback edition / January 2009

Berkley trade paperback ISBN: 978-0-425-22565-3

The Library of Congress Cataloging-in-Publication Data

Treat, Casey.
  How to be your best when you feel your worst / Casey Treat. — 1st ed.
    p. cm.
  ISBN 978-0-425-21920-1
  1. Self-actualization (Psychology) —Religious aspects—Christianity.   2. Christian life.   I. Title.
  BV4598.2.T74 2008
  248.4—dc22
                                                                          2007038010

PRINTED IN THE UNITED STATES OF AMERICA

10 9 8 7 6 5 4 3 2 1

PUBLISHER'S NOTE: Neither the publisher nor the author is engaged in rendering professional
advice or services to the individual reader. The ideas, procedures, and suggestions contained in this
book are not intended as a substitute for consulting with your physician. All matters regarding your
health require medical supervision. Neither the author nor the publisher shall be liable or responsible
for any loss or damage allegedly arising from any information or suggestion in this book.

The publisher does not have any control over and does not assume any responsibility for author or
third-party websites or their content.

*I've had many occasions to practice what I preach
and Wendy Treat has always been my greatest inspiration.
I never want to disappoint or fail her. I strive to have her
discipline and courage. She is my hero; a great friend,
wife, mother, and pastor.
Thank you, Wendy.*

Contents

Contents

Preface

I spent my first twenty years of life developing and overcoming several addictions, convictions, and miseries. It was a terrible way to start a life. I ruined some important relationships and made those years much more difficult than they needed to be. While my friends were off to college and careers, I was wasting time and energy on foolishness and lawlessness.

I've spent the last thirty years making up for lost time: building a marriage, raising a family, growing an organization to over 150 employees and some assets. The last thirty years have been much better than the first twenty. However, I can't say they've all been fun and easy. Some of those "good years" were very difficult and I think I foresee a few more tough times up ahead. I know they are coming because I have goals, dreams, and visions I have not accomplished yet; and whenever you strive to reach new heights, there are bound to be some difficult situations to face, struggles to deal with, and obstacles to overcome. You must realize I'm a very optimistic person; I will attack hell with a squirt gun. But even us smart guys can learn a lesson after we live through challenges a few times.

Success in life is not about all the fun times or easy paths we take. In fact, success in life may be defined by the challenges we live through and overcome. If you only take the easy paths and avoid all the difficult roads, you won't get where you want to go. Every good part of life brings its own hard parts with it. For instance, having children, one of our most rewarding and fulfilling experiences in life, is also one of the hardest. You can choose to avoid the challenge but you will also miss the reward. And when the negatives of life come upon you unexpectedly, your success is not thwarted; in fact, it may be more assured because of the problems you must face. Facing the hard things means you are alive and moving forward to your goals and dreams. You are facing your giants and getting ready for your victories. Throughout the next chapters you'll read about relational battles, financial wars, mountains to climb, diseases to overcome, disappointments, and despairs; but you'll also read of victories and celebrations.

Getting married and having children started a series of difficult situations that I'm still praying my way through. It also started the most rewarding relationships and events of my life. I doubt that anything, other than going to heaven, will compare with the joy and fulfillment I get from my wife, Wendy. Caleb, Tasha, and Micah have added more to my life than any other people on earth. They bring out the best in me (and maybe the worst at times). The difficulties of making family work have been well worth the effort, and the rewards are far beyond.

Climbing Mount Rainier three times caused a lot of strain and pain. Training, preparing, and spending days on the highest mountain in the continental United States are not what I call fun. But it was rewarding and added so much to my life. Building three major ministry facilities brought a few sleepless nights, but has also made me a better person and brought growth and success to the organization. It's not all easy, but it's all good.

Along the way I was given a few challenges that I didn't choose— a life-threatening disease, for one. It was no fun enduring eleven months of chemotherapy, or giving myself shots and daily medication. But even then I was getting better and stronger from the inside out. I wouldn't want to do that again, though, and I wouldn't wish it on anyone else. But I am glad I went through it. It's kind of like drug and alcohol rehabilitation; you should avoid it if at all possible, but it will make you a better person if you need it.

The message of this book is that even when you face life's greatest challenges you can overcome problems, make decisions, and get to your most fulfilling place in life. If you're looking for a quick and easy way, give this book to someone else now. If you want to be a victim and find an excuse for your issues, I can't help you. But if you're looking for your summit and want to overcome your obstacles, we'll have some fun in the next pages.

I'm for you succeeding, and I believe you can have a great life. I'll give you all my heart, soul, experience, and truth in the chapters of this book. I hope and pray it will grow up in you and produce more success in life than you've ever known.

Introduction

There are times and seasons in every person's life that are challenging and difficult. Major or minor, they happen to us all: health issues, relationship issues, financial issues, and others. It is simply a part of life. We all experience "stuff." "Stuff happens."

I have learned that the things I believe God for do not always happen right away—or when I want them to. And so I start to wonder: *When's it gonna happen?* I hear the glowing testimonies of others and I think, *What's up with that? It seems like it's working easier for them. Why isn't it happenin' for me?* I'm following what I feel God has called me to and praying for God to bring new things to my life, but God usually does not act on my timetable. I want everything quickly, but God sees a bigger purpose for my life.

I went through one of those times (it has actually been several years ago now) when I learned I had a serious medical condition. After hearing the diagnosis, I had some choices to make. I'll tell you more about them as we move through this book, but early on

I decided to live by faith as I had always done and trust God for the strength and stamina I knew I needed.

My experience reinforced for me the truth that we all have to learn how to find our best and be our best when we feel our worst. For help, I did what I always do: I turned to God's Word, the Bible, for direction and truth. That's what we'll be doing throughout this book. Everything I'm about to say to you has its roots in the Word—and what it says can sometimes surprise us.

DO GOOD THINGS ALWAYS HAPPEN TO GOOD PEOPLE?

Somehow, many of us believe that if we are doing God's will, then life will be a "bed of roses." We think that if we are doing what God wants us to do, then we are going to be blessed and prosperous and nothing bad will ever happen to us. And if it does, we must be out of God's will. Somehow we have the idea that if we're walking with God the way God wants us to, everything is always going to be good.

But that's just not true. We can be in God's will, fulfilling and finishing His will—and yet still have bad stuff going on in our lives. The world hated Jesus even though He only did good and fulfilled all of God's will. Religious people stoned Stephen for being full of the Holy Spirit and doing good things. You may be trying to improve your life, giving up addictions and resisting temptation, but your old friends complain that you're no longer fun and try to sabotage your efforts. We live in a world that does not always applaud the good performances.

Even in the midst of the bad, however, God is still God. He is so wise and loving and mighty that He uses even the bad to make us into better people.

If you put the wrong ingredient into your food, it's going to taste terrible; but for those of us in the kingdom of God, the world can put the wrong ingredients into our food and God will turn it around and still make it taste good! So you and I have to learn some of the same lessons that the apostle Paul learned long ago:

- When we are weak, we can still be strong.

- When we're under the greatest stress and facing the greatest challenge, it may be the best day of our lives, for God is working to make us into the people He wants us to be.

- When we don't know how to pray, the Holy Spirit helps us and prays through us.

- When the world is against us, God is still for us.

- When people try to push us down, God can still lift us up.

God has a plan and purpose for every life on earth. This plan comes to our hearts in the form of desires, visions, and dreams. As we try to walk them out, the enemy—the spirit of the world—is against us. It is obvious in our world that Satan is alive and well. His goal is not just to do evil, but to stop God's purposes. He started this rebellion in heaven, continued it in the Garden of Eden, and he persists with it today. As we begin to live in God's will and purpose for our life, we soon become a target.

The enemy is always trying to keep you from your purpose and from your vision. Sometimes we forget that, don't we? Peter told us to be "sober, be vigilant; because your adversary the devil walks about like a roaring lion, seeking whom he may devour" (1 Peter 5:8).

You have to know that there *is* a devil out there who does not want you to win. He doesn't want you to have a great marriage. He doesn't want your kids to grow up godly. He doesn't want you to prosper and tithe and give to the kingdom of God. He doesn't want you to win your neighbor to Christ. He doesn't want you to invite your coworker to church. He doesn't want you to fulfill the purposes of God in your life.

And he is relentless.

Just about the time you get your bills paid, you have a teenager who goes crazy on you. Just about the time your family is flowing together and everyone is doing pretty well, you get fired from your job. Just about the time you get your company going or you get your job up to where you want it to be, someone gets into a car accident. Just about the time you get your car taken care of, you throw your back out for two weeks.

It's one thing after another!

How can you be your best when you feel your worst? How can you seize your destiny when it feels as if everything is falling apart? That's what I want to explore with you in this book.

A TIME FOR FAITH

We all know there are times when we all feel that our visions and dreams are not coming to pass. We feel as though we don't have what we need to overcome the challenges of life. *Those* are the times when our faith needs to kick in! *That's* when our understanding of God's plans and purposes needs to be clear.

We need to say, "This is a great time for God to show up. When I can't change the circumstances, now is the time for God to show Himself strong." Rather than pulling us away from God, problems and challenges should push us to Him. In the midst of our greatest battle, let's have our greatest relationship with our Lord. Let's call on

Him, trust Him, lean on Him, and see His will be done on earth as it is in heaven. The very things that the enemy sends to destroy us can make us stronger because they cause us to draw near to our Creator. James 4:8a says, "Draw near to God and He will draw near to you."

How many of us settle into a life that we really don't want because of unexpected and hurtful things that happen along the way: wounds, failures, stresses, anxieties, problems, and pressures? We accept a world that we really don't like and give up on the dream that God put in our hearts.

I'll never forget talking to a man, about forty years old, who told me, "I started a job in my twenties just to make enough money to get through college. I've been there eighteen years now, and I've hated it every day."

If you're going to move on and run your race to destiny, you have to deal with how you face adversity. If problems cause you to quit and draw back in life, you will not see God's purposes come to pass. But if problems cause you to seek God and get stronger on the inside, you will see many successes and God's plan unfold. The Lord says to us through the prophet Isaiah,

Have you not known?
Have you not heard?
The everlasting God, the LORD,
The Creator of the ends of the earth,
Neither faints nor is weary.
His understanding is unsearchable.
He gives power to the weak,
And to *those who have* no might He increases strength.
Even the youths shall faint and be weary,
And the young men shall utterly fall,
But those who wait on the LORD

Shall renew *their* strength;
They shall mount up with wings like eagles,
They shall run and not be weary,
They shall walk and not faint.

(Isaiah 40:28–31)

What an awesome passage! God is overseeing the whole universe and dealing with all of us here on earth. He has a lot going on—and yet He doesn't faint, He's not weary, He's not stressed out about anything. He's just chillin' and thrillin'.

You and I are supposed to be like Him. We must not shy away from the visions, dreams, and the destiny of a great life God has given us, even as we face big challenges that threaten to make us feel overwhelmed or stressed out.

Hey, haven't you heard? The Creator of the ends of the earth neither faints nor is weary! And those who wait on the Lord *renew* their strength. They move. They don't quit. They don't give up. They run and they don't get weary.

You can be one of them. You can run your race to destiny. Even when you feel your worst, you can be your best. And in the pages to come, I want to show you how.

PART I

Finding Your Course

Let the Truth Be Known

It was disgusting and it was sad. I could have died, lying on that filthy floor with a needle hanging out of my arm.

Back in those days, I was committed to partying and running around. Like my friends, I had lost track of what I was doing to my body. At that point in my life, I'd given up any care, any concern at all. I was just trying to stay high, however and whenever I could.

I remember waking up and seeing blood all over the floor. Who knows whose blood covered that bathroom? Who knows who else used the needle I had in my arm? It's a wonder I didn't die in those gross conditions. In fact, I believe it was only the grace of God that kept me alive. But it was probably there, in that grimy bathroom, that I set the course for a difficult drama to unfold in my life many years later.

WHAT DO YOU DO?

What do you do when you're believing God for good things...and something really bad happens instead? How do you respond when disease or disaster blows into your life, without warning and without your permission? Where do you turn? What do you do?

I found myself asking exactly those kinds of questions a few years ago, when I took an exam for a life insurance policy. When I got the results back, I was surprised to learn I had some problems with my blood work. Immediately we started a process to find out what was going on. I'll tell you more about this part of my story later, but for now, I want you to know how shocked I felt when I heard the diagnosis. I'll never forget it.

"Pastor Treat," the doctor said, "you have hepatitis C, and if something doesn't change, you'll die young."

What? No *way!* As someone who has believed for more than thirty years that healing is available to all Christians through faith in the work of Jesus on the cross, the news stunned me. How could *I* have hepatitis C? And what is it, anyway?

Basically, hepatitis C is a slow-moving disease that gradually destroys the liver. The virus that causes it can be in your system for many years without causing any symptoms. The doctors think I probably picked it up as a teenage drug user. Since I got saved at age nineteen and had stayed off alcohol and drugs ever since, the virus must have been in my body all those years, lying dormant. For all that time it waited to do its slow, destructive work—and I never knew.

That's why the news stunned me. And yet, despite my shock, I never asked, "Why, God?" Instead, I went straight to Him and said, "All right, Lord. It looks like we have some battles to fight, some giants to defeat...and one day soon, some good stories to tell." I think I was able to respond to negative news this way because I have spent the last thirty years walking with God, learning His Word and His ways, and putting Him to the test almost every day of my life. In my family, business, and ministry I have walked by faith and seen God do great things.

When we casually believe in God and nonchalantly walk with Him through life we can get overwhelmed when bad news comes. But when God is the core of our life and faith is used every day, we are ready for anything.

THE TRUTH ABOUT GOD

As I tell my story and try to encourage you in this book, the very first thing I want to say to you is this:

God is for you, not against you.

So many times kids come up to me and say, "I'm going to be like you, Pastor. I'm gonna go out and party. I'm gonna go do my thing and have my fun, and then I'll get saved later."

"You can do that if you want to," I usually reply, "but you should remember that if you do get saved later—*if* you get saved—you may take some nasty stuff with you that you didn't bargain for. If you really do turn your life to God and choose to walk with Him, He will always be there for you, but are you sure you will turn to Him? Many people never do go back to the faith of their childhood. In the midst of having your fun, you may pick up some demons along the way. I probably contracted hepatitis C as a teenager using drugs."

I've learned that God is always willing to forgive us our bad choices—but He doesn't always remove the consequences.

"If God *is* for us," wrote the apostle Paul, "who *can be* against us? He who did not spare His own Son, but delivered Him up for us all, how shall He not with Him also freely give us all things?" (Romans 8:31–32). God is not the problem! He never is.

Unfortunately, we tend to get emotionally agitated over things like a negative medical diagnosis. We go into crisis mode over financial problems. We get all wrapped up in relationship dramas. So when we get into the midst of the disease or disaster, we say things like, "Why did You let this happen, God? What are You trying to say? Why don't You stop it? Why don't You turn it around? Why me, God?"

Do you see the problem with questions like these? Such an accusatory tone says, "God, *You* let this happen." And that tone very often leads to another accusation: "God, You are *making* this happen."

You know what we're really saying when we speak this way, don't you? We're actually blaming God for putting us in the bad spot. We're accusing Him of evil.

"You should have done something to make sure this didn't happen!" we cry—revealing a subconscious attitude that the Lord is the problem. He isn't.

God is for you, not against you. He is not your problem. And if you've made God the reason for your difficult circumstances, then you're going to find it very hard to trust Him for healing or for help.

So don't let your thoughts go in that direction. Don't run from God; run to God. Bathe your mind in the truth of Romans 8:31–32:

If God *is* for us, who *can be* against us? He who did not spare His own Son, but delivered Him up for us all, how shall He not with Him also freely give us all things?

With that thought in mind, let me give you a second thought. I have to warn you, though, you may need to brace yourself for what I'm about to say. What follows may be hard for you to read—especially if you listen a lot to Christian radio or watch a lot of Christian television. Are you ready? Here it is:

God is not in control.

How many times have you heard one preacher or another say, "God is in control"? You've probably lost count. But I'm telling you, on the authority of God's Word, that God is *not* in control. Now, before you misunderstand me, I believe that there is nothing that is outside of God's control. God is all-powerful. But everything that happens is not necessarily caused by God. Some believe if something happens, it must be God's will. Not so. Many things happen because of human will, nature, or even Satan's will. God is *not* behind every event that happens in this world. He is *not* a puppet master, pulling all the planet's strings to force everyone who lives here to dance exactly as He intends.

God didn't cause a tsunami to kill 250,000 guiltless people in Asia. When terrorists kill innocent men, women, and children, that's not God. He did not cause 25 percent of the Zambian population to be infected with AIDS. He does not cause millions of babies to be aborted every year around the world. God is not the reason evil turns our world upside down.

"But doesn't Psalm 47:2 say that God is 'King over all the earth'?" someone asks. "Doesn't the Bible say 'He rules over all'?" (Psalm 103:19). "Doesn't the book of Daniel say about God, 'His dominion is an eternal dominion; / his kingdom endures from generation to generation. / All the peoples of the earth / are regarded as nothing. / He does as he pleases / with the powers of heaven / and the peoples of the earth. / No one can hold back his hand / or say to him: 'What have you done?'" (Daniel 4:34–35, New International Version).

Yes, that's exactly what the Word says. I know all of those verses and I'm glad for them. I believe God is all-powerful and it thrills me to know that God ultimately wins and that God's plan most certainly will be fulfilled. But it's a very different thing to say that God causes everything, every day! If He did, then that must mean He was the reason for every disease and every disaster, as well as every sin—and that is simply not true.

Let me ask you, does temptation exist in this world? Have you ever been tempted to do something you knew was wrong? Do you know of anyone who has been tempted to sin? If you answer "yes" (and you're lying if you don't), then that means temptation exists in this world. But what does the Word of God say about temptation? Listen:

> When tempted, no one should say, "God is tempting me." For God cannot be tempted by evil, nor does he tempt anyone. (James 1:13, NIV)

We are tempted, though, aren't we? Temptation exists in this world, even though God has no part in it. So that must mean that God does not control everything that happens on planet Earth.

Do yourself a big favor and stop telling yourself that God is behind everything that happens. He can certainly *use* everything that happens, but He doesn't necessarily cause it. Things exist in this world that God does not like, cause, or approve of—and that means you'll have to walk through some dangerous minefields in your lifetime. You have some battles to face! And yet the Bible declares that if you will walk with God, looking to Jesus for strength and guidance, then He will help you to make it safely through those minefields to reach the place of blessing He has for you.

Think of it like this: God uses *everything* in life to make us better people, just as we parents use everything at our disposal to help our kids grow up to be strong, healthy, godly, and mature adults. I don't think God prefers to use bad things to help us grow up spiritually. In fact, I rebel against the concept that God would *rather* have something bad happen to us in order to make us better, even if He could accomplish the same thing by making good things happen to us. I think God would rather use good things to teach us—like His teaching, His Word, His promises, His Spirit, and His guidance. He'd rather we learn from the good than from the bad.

Unfortunately, many times we don't. We miss it. So we end up in crises, either of our own accord (by ruining our marriages or destroying our health through alcoholism or drugs or bad health habits) or accidentally (through problems that arise from the natural world). God wants to do us good, however, so He uses everything at His disposal to bless us. If bad is the only thing He has to work with—and if that's the only way we'll hear it—then He'll use it. But I don't believe God ever sends something bad my way just to teach me something I could have learned in some other way.

I just can't see Jesus putting cancer on somebody and then saying, "Now, when you get spiritually strong and when you get enough faith, then come back and I'll heal you." I don't see Jesus taking his staff, beating some guy upside the head, and saying, "Now, when you wake up, get back into my next sermon and I'll tell you what to do about it."

Jesus didn't run around Israel kicking people in the groin. He healed them; He didn't afflict them with nasty diseases. Paul strongly condemned those who taught the idea "Let us do evil that good may come" (Romans 3:8)—and yet, that's exactly what some teachers say God loves to do. He doesn't! He is a good God who wants to do you good. It is "the goodness of God [that] leads you to repentance" (Romans 2:4b).

The trouble is, we live in this world, where Satan is called "the god of this age" (2 Corinthians 4:4) and "the prince of the power of the air" (Ephesians 2:2). There is also a divine curse on our planet (Genesis 3:14–19). "For the creation was subjected to futility, not willingly, but because of Him who subjected *it* in hope; because the creation itself also will be delivered from the bondage of corruption into the glorious liberty of the children of God. For we know that the whole creation groans and labors with birth pangs together until now. Not only *that*, but we also who have the firstfruits of the Spirit, even we ourselves groan within ourselves, eagerly waiting for the adoption, the redemption of our body" (Romans 8:20–23). So the whole earth groans and travails until the redemption of the sons of God (which I believe refers to the return of the Lord). Will Jesus come back pretrib, midtrib, or posttrib? Don't know, don't really care; I just know it'll all work out in the way He wants it. But until that day, we have to deal with the curse.

We see the results of the curse in what happened in Hurricane Katrina in Louisiana. We see its influence in the latest killer earthquake, the deadly tsunami, and the natural forces that sometimes bring destruction. The curse is behind the ugly stuff that engulfs us, like disease. Unlike some people, I don't believe that every disease comes directly from Satan. I suppose we could say it all comes indirectly from the devil, since he's the one who instigated the first human sin that prompted the curse, but I don't think the devil directly causes every car wreck, every heart attack, every plane crash, and every incidence of postnasal drip. To hear some Christians talk, Satan is directly behind every bad thing that happens. "The devil wrecked my car!" they'll say. But I doubt it. Probably, they're just lousy drivers.

But we do live in a world suffering under a curse and subject to the power of the evil one. That's why bad stuff happens. And when it happens, God uses even that—just as you do when your kid falls down. You didn't make your child fall down. You didn't want him to fall down. But you use even an unfortunate event like that for his good: "Okay, were you watching where you were going? Were you running too fast? Did you run when I asked you to walk?"

I think God uses everything at His disposal, both the bad and the good, to help us and to encourage us and to cause us to grow. I think of Paul once again and of the great question he asked: "What shall we say to these things [that is, the negative things in life]?" And I remember his answer: "If God is for us, then who can be against us?"

The truth is a lot of things can be against you: wrecked cars, broken bones, angry bosses, despicable neighbors, murderers, terrorists, plagues—the list goes on. None of those things are good in and of themselves. But God loves us so much, He can use even those negative things for our ultimate good. That's why Paul also says, "And we know that in all things God works for the good of those who love him, who have been called according to his purpose" (Romans 8:28, NIV).

If we're listening, if we're teachable, if we genuinely want to walk with God, then He helps us get better—regardless of the challenges we face.

And there will be challenges!

A THORN IN THE FLESH

No one has ever worked more effectively to spread the Good News of life in Jesus than the apostle Paul. If anyone ever knew and fulfilled the call of God on his life, it was Paul. He received revelations that would boggle our minds. And yet Paul knew a thing or two about pain and difficulties. Listen to his testimony:

And lest I should be exalted above measure by the abundance of the revelations, a thorn in the flesh was given to me, a messenger of Satan to buffet me, lest I be exalted above measure. Concerning this thing I pleaded with the Lord three times that it might depart from me. And He said to me, "My grace is sufficient for you, for

My strength is made perfect in weakness." Therefore most gladly I will rather boast in my infirmities, that the power of Christ may rest upon me. Therefore I take pleasure in infirmities, in reproaches, in needs, in persecutions, in distresses, for Christ's sake. For when I am weak, then I am strong. (2 Corinthians 12:7–10)

Although Paul certainly accomplished God's will and purposes for his life, things were certainly not always fun or easy for him. In fact, his life overflowed with challenges, but through them, he became his best.

At some point, Paul made an uncomfortable discovery. He found that as he did what God called him to do, he continually faced a powerful opponent. Paul called it a "thorn in the flesh," a "messenger of Satan" to buffet him. Many commentators over the years have speculated about what this "thorn in the flesh" might have been.

One writer said that Paul's "thorn" was that he was really ugly. Wherever the apostle went, people would make "ugly comments"— and it was these hurtful comments that buffeted him.

Another writer said that Paul had a bad back that made him hunch over slightly. This hindered him from traveling and preaching as he would have liked to, and he always had to deal with his back pain.

Still another writer said Paul had bad eyes. In the book of Galatians, Paul wrote that his friends in the church there would pluck out their eyes and give them to him if they could. So the writer extrapolated from that little tidbit that Paul had eye problems.

Someone else said that Paul's "thorn" was some other kind of sickness or disease, and that he wasn't a good speaker (see Acts 17:18; 1 Corinthians 2:1).

All very interesting interpretations. But what if we just go with what Paul said? I think we'll get some great insight here.

Paul said this thorn in the flesh had been given to him, a messenger of Satan—a demonic spirit assigned to Paul to do whatever it could do to hinder and buffet him from preaching the gospel.

Sometimes Paul *was* physically attacked (see Acts 14:19; 16:22; 21:27). Probably at other times he had to deal with the pain of back problems or some other kind of sickness or disease. On yet other days, Jewish religious authorities rose up against him, threw him in prison, and beat him with thirty-nine lashes. On another day it could be the Gentiles who got mad because he turned people away from their false gods. The next time it was a violent storm and a shipwreck. Some think that wild beasts chased him (see 1 Corinthians 15:32). It was one thing after another, making life hard for the apostle.

Now, Paul was a pretty spiritual guy. In fact, he was way more spiritual than we are, and yet he still faced big challenges. He still had to overcome sickness, anger, resentment, pain, and other problems.

But Paul came to a crucial revelation in the midst of it all. He said that this thing sent to buffet him—the word "buffet" comes from a word that describes the waves continually slapping the sides of a ship—never quit, never gave up, always hindered, always hassled, and always smacked him. All kinds of things continually tried to stop him from fulfilling his mission.

Paul says, "Concerning this thing I pleaded with the Lord three times." That's very interesting to me. He didn't just pray over and over about the problems in his life. He said, *"Three times* I talked to God about this."

Can you remember how many times you've talked to God about the problems you're facing? Many of us would probably say more than three. That tells you a lot about Paul's prayer life, doesn't it? He prayed very specifically and with focus. And this is what God said to him: "My grace is sufficient for you, for My strength is made perfect in weakness."

Sometimes religious people interpret these words to say that God told Paul to keep the thorn in his flesh, that he'd just have to learn to live with it and suffer with it. But that's not what God said at all! It's not even close to what the Lord said to him. The Lord said (my paraphrase), "Paul, you have what you need to overcome this thing. You have my grace." The grace of God is the favor of God, the power of God, at work in your life—the grace, the favor, and the power of God that you can't earn and you don't deserve. That grace is sufficient for you to win in life and fulfill His will.

God said it to Paul, and Paul is passing it on to us.

YOU HAVE WHAT YOU NEED

Many people who face a crisis feel as though they don't have what they need to make it through. I've seen it happen over and over again. Some calamity befalls them and they frantically grasp for something to save them: "I need more power! I need someone to pray for me! I need a new anointing! I want to call Brother What's-his-name's prayer line, and maybe if I call enough people and get enough people praying, then I'll get through this!"

But what about the person who can't call all the prayer lines? Does he not have a chance, simply because he can't get dozens of people praying for him? Or what about the person who lives in a small town, who attends a small church? At our church, we have all kinds of elders who are full of faith and who believe in healing. But the person from the small church has very few prayer partners to choose from. Does that mean he does not have a chance?

Once you have that attitude—"I don't have what it takes. I need more prayer partners. I need more elders. I need more power. I need a new anointing. I need a double, triple portion"—you've entered into unbelief. In fact, you're saying that your relationship with Christ is not enough.

Don't get me wrong; we thank the Lord for the prayer lines! And if you feel that they will support and stand with you, that's good. But at the end of the day, what do you and Christ have? Who's your daddy? Who do you believe? Who do you trust? Are you a Christian, or not?

If you're a Christian, then you have Christ—and that's all the power in the universe. That's the creative power of the world. And if you know Him, that settles it.

Paul said, "our sufficiency *is* from God" (2 Corinthians 3:5). He said he could do all things through Christ who strengthened him (Philippians 4:13). Can you? Not through 47 different prayer lines, 23 different elders, and 114 believers laying hands on you, shaking you until you don't need your chiropractor anymore. No, *you* can do all things through Christ who strengthens you. That means you are self-sufficient through *His* sufficiency.

I thank God for the Body of Christ. I thank God for churches of all sizes. But when you think that your relationship with Christ is insufficient, then you've been tricked. Now you're letting the devil rip you off.

You have to trust and know that you have a real, genuine, dynamic relationship with God. You have to confess Him as your Lord and Savior. You must commit and dedicate your life to Him, surrender everything you are to Him. You are there with Him and He infuses you with power. "And my God will liberally supply (fill to the full) your every need according to His riches in glory in Christ Jesus" (Philippians 4:19, Amplified Bible).

Your relationship, through faith, with God is more than a vague, mystical, ethereal concept. It is the ability to draw strength and wisdom from the Creator of the universe. Believe He is with you, He will never leave you or forsake you. And while He will not live your life for you, He walks through life with you and if you trust Him and make a place for Him, He will help you in every practical need.

There will be days when you'll have to go into a meeting where you'll have to say to yourself, "Whatever is on the other side of that door—whatever negotiations are taking place, whatever salesmen I have to deal with, whatever buyer or vendor I have to deal with, whatever new client I have to face, whatever challenge or difficulty waits for me there—I am ready for and equal to it, because Christ infuses me with inner strength."

There will be times when your family will be going through challenges, when your children are testing all the boundaries, or your wife is upset about something you said or did (or forgot to do). Maybe through some misunderstanding you feel like you have lost a close friend. That's when you'll need to decide and say: "I can handle this because God gives me strength and patience and wisdom. I walk in peace."

Don't allow your Christian life to be a secondary part of your way of life. Make your faith real, central, and valuable to you every day. Don't trivialize what you believe with faith that doesn't translate into everyday life. Believe your faith is real and it is working for you. The Bible is real, believe it. God is real and He is walking and working with you every day no matter what you face.

You must have the attitude that, if you walk with God and trust Him, you are going to win that battle, regardless of how weak you feel. You are going to get that contract. You're going to have a happy and loving family. You're going to overcome that disease. You're going to overcome that financial pressure. You're going to land that new job. You're going to receive that new position. You're going to build that company.

You're going to prosper!

If you'll stay with Jesus, walk with Jesus, and trust Jesus, then you're going to win.

2

You Can Change Your World

All over the world, people come up to me before or after a service and say, "Pastor, my name is Bob. Pray for me."

"Okay," I usually say, "what should I pray?"

"Well, just pray for me."

That request sounds religious and Christian, but it really makes no sense, does it? What am I praying *for*? Am I praying for you to get a new wife? Am I praying for you to get a new job? Am I praying for your health? What am I praying for?

The request "Just pray for me" seems spiritual and religious in a vague, nonspecific kind of way. The only problem is it's just not scriptural.

PRAY SPECIFICALLY

Sometimes these folks are surprised when I stop and pray for them right there. In fact, they did not really want prayer; they were just making religious conversation. They were following their tradition and saying something they had heard others say.

Nobody ever came to Jesus and said, "Jesus, pray for me!" They always came to Jesus and said, "Heal me!" Or cried out for whatever they needed.

In Mark 10, a man was crying out, "Jesus, Son of David!" and Jesus said, "What do you want Me to do for you?" It was obvious to everyone he was blind; but still Jesus said, "What do you want?"

The man told Him he wanted to see.

"Go your way;" Jesus answered, "your faith has made you well" (Mark 10:52). Jesus healed the man once he got specific, once he said, "Here's what I want. Here's what I'm believing for." Only then did Jesus say, "Your faith has made you well."

One of my missions in life is to help people to stop praying meaningless religious prayers that amount to little more than spiritual whining. Start believing what the Bible says and start believing what God has put in your heart!

A vague, religious prayer—as opposed to a scriptural or spiritual prayer—helps people to ease their conscience, to feel as though they're doing "God stuff," but there is no power there and no real results. So when we pray, let's pray specifically. Ask for something in particular and believe God hears and answers your prayers. And if you believe He's heard you, there's no sense in begging. Jesus says in Mark 11:24, "Therefore I say to you, whatever things you ask when you pray, believe that you receive *them*, and you will have *them*." After we ask God for what we need, thank Him for hearing and answering. First John 5:14–15 says, "Now this is the confidence that we have in Him, that if we ask anything according to His will, He hears us. And if we know that He hears us, whatever we ask, we know that we have the petitions that we have asked of Him." We must continue to confess the promises of God, pray with the Spirit, and thank God for the answer, but we aren't beggars, we are children of God.

I'm not trying to be legalistic here; I don't want to try to forbid someone from ever asking for the same thing twice. I'm just saying, let's be scriptural in our conversations with God. I don't go to my wife every day and repeat the same things to her, routinely begging her for love or for something else. We have a real relationship, so I try to keep it on that level.

You also need to stop praying for stuff you already have. Stop praying for strength when you have the strength. You don't have to pray for grace; you *have* grace. You don't have to pray for the Holy Spirit; you *have* the Holy Spirit. If you don't have Him, then get Him! You don't have to pray for more power; use the power you already have! What sense would it make for God to give you more power if you don't use the power you already have?

I once heard a friend praying, "Lord be with me, send your Holy Spirit to me, Lord be with me, send your Holy Spirit to me." I stopped him and asked when God had left Him. He was a little surprised but said he wasn't sure. Then I asked when the Holy Spirit had gone back to heaven. Again, he didn't know. I showed Him how the Bible says God will never leave you (Hebrews 13:5b) and that He has poured out His Spirit for all people (Acts 2:17). My final question for him was, "Do you believe the Bible?"

He was emphatic. "Yes, of course."

I responded, "Then stop asking God for things He says you already have. You are praying like you do not believe what God has said."

John tells how Jesus spoke to His Father about His dead friend, Lazarus. "Father," He said, "I thank You that You have heard Me. And I know that You always hear Me, but because of the people who are standing by I said *this*, that they may believe that You sent Me" (John 11:41–42). And then He called Lazarus to come forth. He didn't ask God twice for Lazarus's life; He'd already prayed. Now He's just there, walking it out, so to speak.

That's a spiritual prayer, rather than a religious, repetitious, and begging prayer. If we really are sons and daughters of God, we should never approach our Father as if we were poor beggars. I don't want my three kids to do that with me!

One morning, as my eighteen-year-old son, Micah, and I were getting ready for the day, I stuck my head in the bathroom. "I gotta get to a class at school early," I said. "See ya after school."

"Hey, Dad!" he hollered out of the bathroom. "Can I get some money for lunch?"

He didn't have to beg or cry or plead or cajole. He didn't have to throw himself at my feet and beg, "O merciful father! Do you have any extra money for a poor wretch like me? Oh, do you care? Oh, if only you could meet this need of mine!"

None of that! It was more like, "Dad, I need some money for lunch."

"Okay, I'll put it on your desk."

That's a real father-son relationship. He's my son. *Of course* I want to give him money for lunch! But I'm glad he asked, because I didn't know he didn't have any.

I think our heavenly Father's a lot like that. He's not an ogre in heaven withholding His loot, while we're down here begging, just hoping that if we say it right and suffer enough, He might just let a little lunch money go. No! He's already decided to bless us with all spiritual blessings, which tends to produce material blessings.

PRAY WITH THANKSGIVING

Once you pray for something specific and believe that God has heard you and granted you your request, then thank God for His provision.

Jesus, Paul, and John all instructed us to pray (Philippians 4:6). If you know that He hears you, whatever you ask, you know that you have it (1 John 5:14–15). So the Amplified Bible translates the passage in 1 John, "we also know [with settled and absolute knowledge] that we have [granted us as our present possessions] the requests made of Him."

So let's believe that and say, "Thank you, God. You heard my prayer. You're healing me; you're helping me with my finances. Thank you, Father." Much better than going through a begging routine every morning!

PRAY TO MAKE THINGS HAPPEN

As I said, part of my life mission is to help people stop being religious and start being spiritual. Don't do things that have never worked; instead, do meaningful things that are scriptural, productive, and that make positive things start happening in your life.

Wendy and I recently visited Rome. We were there among thousands of pilgrims to see the Vatican. The Pope needs a lot of security these days, so as we went through the screeners, we heard people talking. One lady in front of me said to her friend, "The first thing I want to do is buy some blessed jewelry!"

"Oh," her friend replied, "you mean you can buy it here?"

"Yes," said the first lady, "you can buy jewelry blessed by the Pope."

That got the other lady thinking. "Well," she asked, "can you buy any other kinds of blessings?"

"Sure," the first lady said, "there are lots of blessings we can buy. Crosses, Bibles..." She gave a long list.

I couldn't help myself; I started laughing. *This is the money changers at the temple,* I thought. It doesn't bother me that they're selling crosses and books; they should sell all of that stuff to raise money for the church to help it pay its bills. But to say it's "blessed" or somehow "spiritual"? I think that adds to people's religion without improving their spirituality—and the problem with that is that religion won't help a bit when you run into the really tough challenges of life. Nothing helps then, except God.

To help pull this all together here is a simple prayer plan:

- Pray clearly what you desire God to do. (Mark 11:24)

- Believe that God hears and answers your prayers. (1 John 5:14–15)

- Be patient. Give it time to come to pass. (Hebrews 10:35–36)

- Give thanks and praise for God in your life. (Philippians 4:6)

My first step to overcoming hepatitis C was to get a full diagnosis. I took several blood tests and a biopsy that was no fun. To do a liver biopsy you must lie on your side and be still for four hours. They take a piece of your liver out and see how much effect the disease has actually had. Doctors need to know exactly what they're dealing with before they can begin treating you. Similarly, you need to know what you really need from God before you can move forward and ask for it.

LET GOD STEP UP

It's when you don't have an answer for the tough issues you're facing that God's strength is made perfect in your weakness. It's when you don't know what to do that it's time to smile and say, "Thank you, Father. Since I've come to the end of myself—*tag*—you're it!" Time for God to step up and help us through.

God's grace is sufficient and His strength is made perfect in your weakness. But you have to open yourself to His blessings. That means you have to lay aside your pride, admit you need help, and turn to God. If you never get to the place where you feel weak and unable, you'll never come to the place where you need His strength. And so you'll never get it.

Don't forget that you're created to be like God, which means you're not designed merely to survive and exist. God calls you to achieve, to create things like marriages and families and businesses and homes and churches. I think He intends that for all of us, which gives birth to the challenge and the adventure of life. Every time we take on a challenge or adventure, we stretch ourselves—and at some point, we're going to get to a place where we don't think we can do it.

I asked Wendy to marry me when I was twenty years old and she was eighteen. Right after she said yes—can you guess my next thought? I warn you, it's not very spiritual. I thought, *I wonder if we can make this thing work?*

I'll bet that's probably true for every young person who gets married. Love? Sure! Excitement? Yeah! Sex? That's good! But I bet there are still those thoughts: *Gosh, I don't want to go through a divorce. And I don't want to have to struggle with a lousy marriage. I hope I can make this thing work!*

Anytime you set a significant or meaningful goal for yourself, you'll have a feeling of inadequacy. That's part of the process of living instead of merely existing or surviving. And the bigger the challenge we face, the more we probably feel inadequate—which should cause us to look to God, seek God, and rely on God.

More than a few times in my fifty-plus years, I've felt inadequate for some task ahead of me. Many of these challenges came in my marriage and family life, but lots of others had to do with ministry: trying to raise money, trying to create a healthy church. As I write this book, we're building a five-thousand-seat sanctuary. When we started out, we hoped we could do it for $25 million; now we're in over $50 million. I wasn't sure I could raise $25 million, so I have a lot of anxiety over $50 million! But I believe God has given me the vision and directed my steps and is going to help me.

Still, I have this helpless, weak feeling—and I think that's what Paul felt when he described all of his problems. He endured shipwrecks and beatings and all kinds of things, described in 2 Corinthians 11. And that's precisely when he says, "When I am weak, then I am strong." Because in those moments of helplessness, he knew he had the greatest power of all.

Challenges and problems cause us to come to the end of ourselves, and only there can we really see what an almighty God can do with us. And that's when we think, *Thank you, Lord, because that sure wasn't me.*

I never want to lose that. I never want to live a life where I don't need God. I often say to our church, "I doubt you're where God wants you if you've got it all budgeted, all figured out, and you feel comfortable that you can handle everything on your own." If that's you, then you're probably not living up to your full God-given potential.

If, however, you're living a life where you're not sure *how* to do it and you're not sure if you *can* do it—but you're believing God will help you—you're probably right where God wants you to be.

PROBLEM? NO PROBLEM

The apostle Paul had more than his share of challenges. In 2 Corinthians 12:10, he wrote, "Therefore I take pleasure in infirmities, in reproaches, in needs, in persecutions, in distresses, for Christ's sake. For when I am weak, then I am strong." Think for a moment about the kinds of challenges he mentioned in this passage. *None* of them sounds fun.

"Infirmities" literally means sicknesses, diseases, feebleness, or weakness. We rebuke illness. We pray against it. We believe God to be healed from it. But when we get sick anyway and are forced to deal with our physical infirmity, we may find our greatest strength. We may find our grandest faith. We may find our deepest character. We may find a phenomenal relationship with God that we never knew we could have.

"Reproaches" means insults and injuries. It's no fun when people don't like us—and yet that kind of rejection may cause us to examine what we truly believe in and what we stand for. Does it really matter what someone thinks about us? Are we trying to please people, or please God? Are we here to make people like us, or are we here to obey our Father in heaven? You may find more strength if you quit being a people-pleaser and instead see reproaches for what they are: opportunities to grow stronger.

What did Paul mean by "needs" (or necessities) and "distresses"? Remember, this is the apostle Paul, who had been to the third heaven, to Paradise. This believer had been in the very throne room of God and there saw things he couldn't even tell us about—and yet here he is, back on earth, with needs and distresses.

Just because Paul had needs, however, didn't mean he was outside of God's will. His needs simply gave him an opportunity to get stronger. In the same way, your own needs can help you to find greater strength and a richer relationship with God. Allow your needs to drive you to God, not away from Him. Remember that Jesus told us, "your Father knows what you need before you ask him" (Matthew 6:8, NIV). He knows your need. He does not despise you for it. And yet it's still true that "you do not have, because you do not ask God" (James 4:2, NIV). Let your needs help you to find greater strength in God and a deeper relationship with your Father.

Paul also mentioned "persecutions." Remember that Jesus said we'd receive a hundredfold when we give to the kingdom—but that it would come with persecution (Mark 10:30). We like the hundredfold increase, but not so much the persecution! We want to be filled with the Spirit, but we don't like it when people talk about us because we pray with the Spirit. We want to be a part of something that changes the spiritual landscape of our land, but then we get nervous when people persecute us because of what we believe.

But in the persecution, Paul tells you, you'll find a greater relationship with God. If they hated his Lord, they're going to hate you, too. If they crucified the Lord, they're going to take a few shots at you—but before you die, you can take a few to heaven with you. You have a decision to make: are you a Christian because it's nice, or because you love God?

The last word Paul mentions here is "distresses." Paul said that he found his greatest strength in distress and in the pressures of life. Who of us learns much through our victories? We just celebrate, have fun, and think we're cool. But in our hard times? In our losses and in our difficulties? That's where we learn more, we change more, and we become better people. When everything is going well, we don't think much about praying and seeking God and changing. But when things go bad, sometimes we get *really* spiritual. Let's walk with God all the time—in the good times and the bad.

When you're weak, you'll find your greatest strength. When you're down, you'll find your highest high. When you face your worst battle (and they're never fun), *that's* when you'll find your greatest victory.

WHAT DO YOUR CHALLENGES SAY ABOUT YOU?

It seems almost heretical today, but the members of the church in ancient Corinth had the audacity to question the apostle Paul's ministry. Two thousand years down the road, we all see Paul as one of the greatest ministers who ever lived; but when Paul preached, they questioned him.

Many people during his lifetime didn't even believe he was an apostle. They wrote letters that asked, "What does anyone follow *him* for? He doesn't have a clue! He doesn't know what he's talking about."

(I have to admit, this all makes me feel a little better, since I also have received a few letters like that.)

Once they actually demanded of Paul, "How do we know that you're an apostle?" Paul gave his response in 2 Corinthians 11:22–23:

Are they Hebrews? So *am* I. Are they Israelites? So *am* I. Are they the seed of Abraham? So *am* I. [That's where a lot of the prejudice came from.] Are they ministers of Christ?—I speak as a fool—I *am* more: in labors more abundant, in stripes above measure, in prisons more frequently, in deaths often.

Now notice, Paul didn't say, "Think of all the books and tapes that I've sold." No, he said, "labors more abundant...stripes above measure...prisons more frequently...deaths often."

What does any of *that* have to do with being in the ministry? How does *that* prove you're an apostle? Notice what Paul says. "The proof of my ministry is not in all the good things that have happened," he insisted, "but in all the challenges that I have faced and overcome."

Are you serving God? Are you in God's will? If you are, then let me tell you something: you are going to face some tough challenges. Maybe even challenges like those Paul faced:

From the Jews five times I received forty *stripes* minus one. [Thirty-nine lashes!] Three times I was beaten with rods; once I was stoned; three times I was shipwrecked; a night and a day I have been in the deep. (vv. 24–25)

Man! The brother needs to change his travel agent! I've whined if my flight got delayed. I've been angry because I had to take off my shoes at the security checkpoint. But here, Paul tells us his boat sank and he spent a whole day and night bobbing in the ocean. Talk about losing your luggage! And then it gets even worse:

in journeys often, *in* perils of waters, *in* perils of robbers, *in* perils of *my own* countrymen, *in* perils of the Gentiles, *in* perils in the city, *in* perils in the wilderness, *in* perils in the sea, *in* perils among false brethren; in weariness and toil, *in* sleeplessness often, *in* hunger and thirst, *in* fastings often, *in* cold and nakedness—besides the other things [*Other* things? What else could there *be*?], what comes upon me daily: my deep concern for all the churches. Who is weak, and I am not weak? Who is made to stumble, and I do not burn *with indigation*?

If I must boast, I will boast in the things which concern my infirmity. The God and Father of our Lord Jesus Christ, who is blessed forever, knows that I am not lying. (vv. 26–31)

Come on, people! Compared to what Paul has been through, we don't have much to complain about. And yet, somehow, Paul used the word "light" to describe his afflictions (2 Corinthians 4:17). Now, if *Paul's* afflictions were "light," then what are yours and mine? He was beaten so many times that he could barely count the stripes on his back. If his was a light affliction, then what are you and I whining about? If he had *light* afflictions, we have zero-calorie afflictions.

I think it also helps to remember that these light afflictions of ours last for only a moment, according to 2 Corinthians 4:17: "For our light affliction, *which is but for a moment*..." (emphasis added). I know they feel very real to us, but sometimes we let our challenges and difficulties and the pressures of life grow too big in our minds. We forget they are just "for a moment." They don't last forever. The coming blessing lasts forever, but not the discomfort and the pain of the challenge. The pain of losing a job is real, but it will pass as you get to your next position and another step of destiny. The pain and problems of sickness or disease in a family are real, but we know God heals. Even if we have lasting problems with our body, we will be free from physical limitation for eternity in heaven. Our time in these bodies is short compared to our time in heaven with God.

In the short time that the pain of the challenge lasts, though, it does an amazing work. Paul says our light affliction "is working for us a far more exceeding *and* eternal weight of glory." The test that is coming against you is working *for* you. The devil that is trying to hinder the building of your home is working *for* you. The person who is trying to stop the growth of your company is working *for* you.

You have to believe this. There is your true test. There is your faith.

Do you believe God? No matter what has come against you, it is working for you. No matter what the enemy throws at you, it's working for you. No matter how bad the sickness, the pain, or the problem, can you believe it's working for you?

In fact, we can't even comprehend how much that "light afflic-tion" is working for us. So Paul tells us that "the sufferings of this present time are not worthy *to be compared* with the glory which shall be revealed in us" (Romans 8:18).

Not worthy even to be compared! So do you think that might mean they're not really worthy of whining about, either?

IT'S NOT ABOUT BEING COMFORTABLE

Both Jesus and Paul remind us that the life of a genuine believer is not about being comfortable and being blessed. Rather, it's about obeying God and fulfilling His will, reaching people and changing our world.

Being blessed and comfortable is a great benefit along the way, but our goals in life should have more to do with helping others, making a positive impact on our world, being salt on the earth, and being a light in the darkness. And if we get blessed and experience some comfort as we're doing those things, that's good.

Our purpose in life is not to be doing only what's easy. If the point was to do only what's easy, then I have some advice for you: Don't get married. Don't have kids. Don't start churches. Don't help people. Just make enough money to feed yourself and get by—an option that a lot of people choose.

But that's not how I choose to live. My goal is to make a differ-ence in the world. And that oftentimes means taking on challenges and feeling uncomfortable.

I'll never forget when Wendy gave birth to our first son, Caleb. We decided to deliver the baby at home. We had a friend with us who had given birth, as well as a nurse who attended our church, but that was the sum total of our little delivery team. Caleb arrived in this world at almost eleven pounds, so Wendy really had to work hard, but what an awesome experience! As I bathed my first son in the sink, Wendy ate lasagna on the bed. That night, both of us were thinking the same thing as we were lying in bed with the baby: *This is amazing!*

But it wasn't easy, especially for her! She experienced discomfort, anxiety, and a great deal of physical pain. Caleb is twenty-two years old now, and through the years, raising our son has not always been a piece of cake. There are days when you struggle as a parent, just trying to keep your kids on track. But I'd never say, "I don't want kids. I wish I'd never had any." The pain of labor and delivery is just the first salvo in the pain of parenting. It's part of having kids and growing up and living life. But it's so worth it!

It's definitely not for you, however, if you want a life of nothing but comfort.

In the same way, if you're looking *only* for comfort and blessing, then don't seek God. Don't seek destiny. These endeavors always come with challenges and discomfort. Still, after the pain and the labor comes the blessing. God wants to birth some things in your life; are you ready for the labor pains?

Paul wrote, "If in this life only we have hope in Christ, we are of all men the most pitiable" (1 Corinthians 15:19). The man faced a lot of challenges and endured a lot of pain in his work as an apostle and evangelist. A lot of it wasn't fun. A lot of it wasn't comfortable. A lot of it didn't feel blessed. But still he carried on. Why? Because he knew the *real* blessing was to follow. He knew all his effort and pain was worth it.

The Christian life means living beyond self, doesn't it? I'm not living just to be happy; I'm living to obey God, serve God, and make a difference in people's lives for God. If I have some fun along the way, that's great—but that's not the goal. Wendy says it like this: "Earth life is short. Heaven life is long. And if we live only for the short term, we miss so much of what God really has for us in the long term."

If we live on purpose, we will be thoroughly challenged—but never defeated. Second Corinthians 4:7–9 says, "But we have this treasure in earthen vessels, that the excellence of the power may be of God and not of us. *We are* hard-pressed on every side, yet not crushed; *we are* perplexed, but not in despair; persecuted, but not forsaken; struck down, but not destroyed."

I think that's Paul's way of saying what David said long before in Psalm 30:5: "Weeping may endure for a night, / But joy *comes* in the morning."

In life, we're going to fall down sometimes. We have to face some challenges. We are going to encounter some difficulties. Even great men and women go through challenges, including spiritual giants like the apostle Paul.

When challenges come, it doesn't mean that you've slipped outside of God's will. It doesn't mean you've done something wrong or that the Lord has left you in some way. We simply live in a world that harbors a powerful enemy—and that enemy does not want you to fulfill God's will. He doesn't want you to be an example for Christ. He doesn't want you to give to the kingdom of God. He doesn't want you to prosper and make a difference in your world—and that's why a lot of the challenges come.

We *all* have battles we must face. We *all* have some negative circumstances to get through. We *all* have challenges to overcome. Yet God insists in His Word that when we feel our weakest, our lowest, and our worst, those are often the times when God does the absolute most in our lives.

So keep your faith up.

You are going to have some hard days—and even in the middle of them, you need to give God the glory. You need to hold your head up high. You need to say, "Oh, this is going to be nice... because when I'm weak, then I'm strong." You need to look at the devil and say, "You never should have backed me into this corner, devil, because when I'm weak, that's when I'm strong." You need to look at the circumstances of life and say, "Oh boy, you'd better take your best shot, because I'm about to turn this test into a testimony. I'm about to take this pain and make it my gain. I'm about to take this story and make some history. Make it good, devil, because it's only making my book better!"

Do you want to win and seize your destiny? Then you have to make that kind of spirit and attitude your own.

3

Where's Your Focus?

My friend, and spiritual father, Julius Young, at one time had cataracts. When his good eye got fogged over (his other eye was made of glass), he couldn't focus. He could still "see," but since he couldn't focus, he couldn't accomplish what he wanted to.

As we get older, many of us start losing the ability to focus on objects at certain distances away from us. That's why we buy glasses, to help us focus. We still have eyes; we still want to see; but if we can't focus, we can't do what we want to do.

In the same way, if you don't focus in your spiritual life, you won't be able to accomplish what you really want to. To achieve your most important goals, you must be able to focus.

So let me ask you: What are you looking at?

It's easy to get focused on all the wrong things. The world is fighting for your focus, and if you forget you are in a battle, it will be easy to get distracted. If you allow the world to grab and hold your attention, then you'll spend hours listening to and thinking about the world's messages—instead of God's—and as a result, you won't be able to do what you really want and need to do.

"Hey! You! Just look at the half-naked girl trying to sell you vodka!" The world is fighting for your focus.

"Pssst! Look at the guy and the girl on the beach trying to sell you a cigarette!" The world is fighting for your focus.

"Look at the news trying to tell you to watch all the trauma in the world! Look at the disease, disaster, pain, and problems." The world is fighting for your focus. It's trying to grab your attention.

Unfortunately, most of the time it's not that blatant. It can be very subtle. If you don't constantly remind yourself that just about everything the world wants you to look at is contrary to your vision and your destiny in God, soon you will be spending most of your time looking at the severe things, the desperate things, the negative things—and you won't even realize that you have lost your focus on God's will for your life.

So again, what are you looking at? Are you spending more time focusing on what the devil wants you looking at, rather than at what God wants you to focus on? Where's your focus?

Jesus says you will move toward whatever you look at. "The lamp of the body is the eye," said Jesus in Matthew 6:22–23. "If therefore your eye is good, your whole body will be full of light. But if your eye is bad, your whole body will be full of darkness."

In this passage Jesus is not talking about your physical body. He's talking about your life. He means that if your vision is good— if you are looking at the right things and if you remain focused on godly things—then your life will be lit up with blessing. Light in the Bible always signifies God, His presence and His blessing. Darkness is always the absence of God, the absence of God's presence, and the absence of His blessing. If you're focused on the right thing, there is light and blessing; but if you get focused on the wrong things, there's darkness. And when your life is full of light because you're focused on the right things, then you can see what's ahead with a lot more clarity.

One day I wanted to see the eagles out in my backyard. They have a big nest there, way up high in a tree. But they're so far above me that I can't see them clearly; I can make out their big white heads, but that's about it. To see them more clearly, I need my binoculars.

The first thing you have to do with binoculars is to get them focused. You have to adjust them so they're the right width for your eyes, and then adjust the lenses for the correct distance. Once I get them focused, I can zoom right in on those eagles. Not only can I see the eagles, but I can count the feathers on their white heads and check out the talons on their feet. I can look at their beaks and I can look in the nest and see the little eaglets poking out their heads.

In a similar way, when you get focused in the spiritual realm, you can see things in the distance much more clearly. You can see what God has ahead. You can see where God wants to take you!

The fact is, you can't go where God wants you to go if you don't stay focused on the things you need to keep looking at. James 1:8 says, "A double minded man is unstable in all his ways" (King James Version). One day you're serving God; the next day you're serving self. One day you have a vision; the next day you feel scared and nervous. What's the solution?

Get focused! You can't be double-minded and still get to where you want to be.

Don't lose your vision over bills, the condition of the world, or tragedy. Don't get caught up in other people's negative comments. If you do, pretty soon you'll lose your focus. Learn to aim your binoculars where God wants them to point.

LOOKING AT WHAT YOU CAN'T SEE

If focusing is so important to achieving your destiny, then what should you look at? Where should you fix your eyes as you pursue your vision?

Second Corinthians 4:18 gives us a big clue: "we do not look at the things which are seen, but at the things which are not seen. For the things which are seen *are* temporary, but the things which are not seen *are* eternal."

The word translated as "temporary" here means "subject to change." The things which are *seen* are subject to change. So what does that mean for you?

Sickness and disease are subject to change.

People who hate you are subject to change.

Financial challenges are subject to change.

The negative person in the office next to you is subject to change.

Your rebellious kids are subject to change.

Your problems are subject to change!

Remember, this life is not going to last forever. These challenges are but for a moment, and they're working for you, "a far more exceeding *and* eternal weight of glory" (2 Corinthians 4:17). Whatever comes against you is working for you...so long as you look at the things that are not seen—the eternal things—and don't allow yourself to get focused on the temporary things.

So again: What are you looking at, right now? What are you focused on? What's got your attention? Your problems? The pressures? Your challenges? The negatives? The things you don't like? The things you don't want? The things that make you sad? The things that make you mad? If you focus on those things, then you're going to miss the eternal weight of glory. You're going to miss the good thing that God is working out for you in the midst of whatever circumstances may currently be causing you grief.

Let's focus on God's Word, God's promises, and God's plan for our lives. Think about what it will be like to tell your story of victory when you get through this challenge. Focus your thoughts on God's love for you and that He is working to turn this around. Remember God is bigger than your adversary the devil. God is stronger than evil. Truth will overcome lies. At the end of the day you will be a winner in life.

The world can't see what God is doing. Unbelievers don't understand that the Lord is at work. If you and I aren't careful, we'll forget and become whiners, complainers, gripers, and moaners, as we focus on all the nasty stuff in this world. And there is some *stuff* in this world! Some of it will hit the fan in your own life...and it will get all over everything.

When that happens, you have a choice. What will you look at?

Paul says, "While we look, *not at the things which are seen*, but at the things which are not seen." And chief among those "unseen things" are the following three truths:

God Never Changes

One of the bedrock truths of Scripture is that God never changes. He said it like this to a faithful Old Testament prophet: "I the LORD do not change. So you, O descendants of Jacob, are not destroyed" (Malachi 3:6, NIV).

Can you imagine if God *did* change? One day He promises to help us; the next He decides we're on our own. One minute He wants to be our Savior; the next He decides to give us what our sins deserve. One moment He loves us; the next He hates us.

Who could live in a world like that? Fortunately, we don't have to, because God never changes. What He was in ancient times, He still is today. As He was faithful then, so He remains faithful today.

Hebrews 13:8 applies this encouraging truth about God the Father to Jesus when it says, "Jesus Christ is the same yesterday and today and forever" (NIV). That's important if you want to thrive when the challenges come! That's key if you want to grab your destiny, despite the problems you face!

If you want to keep running your race to destiny, then you have to keep your focus on Jesus, who never changes. That's why Hebrews 12:2–3 tells us, "looking unto Jesus, the author and finisher of *our* faith, who for the joy that was set before Him endured the cross, despising the shame, and has sat down at the right hand of the throne of God. For consider Him who endured such hostility from sinners against Himself, lest you become weary and discouraged in your souls."

When you lose your focus, it's easy to grow weary and lose heart. When you look at the stuff the world parades in front of your eyes, it's not hard to get discouraged, depressed, and even despondent. It all depends on your focus.

Do you want to win your race? Then fix your eyes on Jesus. Focus on *Him*!

That means that He's not a department of your life. He's not something you just think about on Sunday. He's not a segment you bring out when you find yourself facing disaster or an emergency. You're looking to Jesus, walking with Him, keeping focused on Him as you live your life. And when you keep focused on Jesus like that, you remember that "He Himself has said, *'I will never leave you nor forsake you'*" (Hebrews 13:5).

Have you ever heard someone pray, "Lord, don't leave me," or maybe they prayed, "Lord, be with me"? I know they're trying, but if you would read your Bible, you wouldn't have to pray those kinds of silly prayers. You see, God said, "I'll never leave you." He said He wouldn't forsake you. So don't pray, "Don't leave me." He already told you He wouldn't!

"But I just need to *feel* the Lord."

When you focus on Jesus, you rise above your feelings.

"But I just need to know for sure that He's here."

When you focus on Jesus, you know that He is with you, because He said He was and always will be.

When the problems come, God's with you.

When the challenge or disease comes, God is with you.

When the divorce lawyer comes, God's with you.

God will *never* leave you nor forsake you.

When you feel weak, that's when you know you're strong. So—will you glory in your weaknesses that the power of Christ might rest upon you? Do you believe it? Is it true for you?

Let's focus on Jesus.

God's Word Never Changes

No surprise here, but God's Word reflects God Himself. And since God never changes, His Word never changes.

Jesus once said, "Till heaven and earth pass away, [my Word] will by no means pass from the law till all is fulfilled" (Matthew 5:18). When the earthquake comes, stand on your Bible, because the Word can't be shaken. The foundations of this world can shudder and tremble, but the Word of God stands unshaken and unshakeable. Forever!

So again—what are you focused on? What are you standing on? What do you trust in? Jesus said the Word of God will never change.

"But the doctor said…" Well, *my* Doctor said He bore my sickness and He carried my disease, and with His stripes I was healed (1 Peter 2:24).

"But my banker said I'm going to have to file for bankruptcy." Well, *my* Banker said He blessed me and He'll prosper my life. I'm blessed in the city, blessed in the field, blessed coming in, and blessed going out. All that I set my hand to will prosper (Deuteronomy 28:3).

Whose report do you believe? You have to decide. Will you focus on the Word of God, or on something else?

God's Will Never Changes

The apostle Paul insisted, "For the gifts and calling of God are without repentance" (Romans 11:29, KJV). That means that God's purposes do not change simply because circumstances do. His plans for you do not change just because something bad happens in your life. He hasn't abandoned you or His will for you.

"Because God wanted to make *the unchanging nature of his purpose* very clear to the heirs of what was promised, he confirmed it with an oath," says Hebrews 6:17 (NIV, emphasis added). God doesn't have one plan for you one day and a completely different plan as soon as something goes wrong. " 'For I know the plans I have for you,' declares the LORD, 'plans to prosper you and not to harm you, plans to give you hope and a future' " (Jeremiah 29:11, NIV).

So even when the doctor says, "You have a physical problem," the Bible still says Jesus "healed *them* all" (Luke 6:19).

The lawsuit you were served may be dramatic. The attorneys may say there's no way you can win. The divorce may be a disaster. The problems of life are real—but *they* don't change God, God changes *them*. *They* don't move God, God moves *them*.

If, however, you begin to accept the problem as bigger and more powerful than the Lord, then you begin to lose...and then the problem starts to overwhelm you.

Remember, circumstances don't change God's will. When bad stuff happens, God hasn't changed His plans. Things change, but God's will doesn't. You and I may have to go through some fights, have some battles, and encounter some difficult times, but none of that changes God's will.

So get it straight: Circumstances don't change God, God's Word, or God's will. He changes them, they don't change Him.

HIGHEST LEVEL OF TRUTH

We have many truths in our world. You have to decide: what's the highest level of truth in *your* life?

How you feel about things is a truth. You may *feel* like doing this; you may *feel* like doing that. That's a truth. Are your feelings the highest truth in your life? If so, then you probably have lots of trouble, because if you're like me, feelings make you say and do things that later you wish you hadn't.

> When doctors diagnosed me with hepatitis C, some things did change in my life, but many things did not. I never said, "Oh, no! I will not be able to be the pastor of the church. Oh, no! I'll never be able to build that sanctuary! Oh, no! I'll never be able to fulfill God's will for me!" Why not? Because God's will doesn't change just because I have a battle to deal with. God is always God. Don't give up on your vision and dreams because you have a battle. Stay the course. God will help you through.

Professionals also have a truth—their diagnosis, their analysis, their experience, their education. Those are all truths. Is *that* your highest truth? Does their truth control your world? You have to decide, because it will make the difference between you getting strong and overcoming circumstances or staying weak and being defeated.

Mama also has a truth. In many homes, whatever Mama says, goes. Is Mama your highest level of truth? Or maybe it's Uncle George.

Who speaks the highest truth in your life?

"Well, the news media said…" That's a truth, for sure. But is it the highest?

"Well, everybody in the world thinks…" Again, that's another truth. But is the majority opinion, the most popular viewpoint, whatever everybody else says—is *that* the highest level of truth in your life?

Just what is the highest level of truth in your life?

The fifth chapter of Luke tells a great story about an incident in the life of Jesus that can help us to determine our highest level of truth.

So it was, as the multitude pressed about Him to hear the word of God, that He stood by the Lake of Gennesaret, and saw two boats standing by the lake; but the fishermen had gone from them and were washing *their* nets. Then He got into one of the boats, which was Simon's, and asked him to put out a little from the land. And He sat down and taught the multitudes from the boat.

When He had stopped speaking, He said to Simon, "Launch out into the deep and let down your nets for a catch."

But Simon answered and said to Him, "Master, we have toiled all night and caught nothing; nevertheless at Your word I will let down the net." And when they had done this, they caught a great number of fish, and their net was breaking. So they signaled to *their* partners in the other boat to come and help them. And they came and filled both the boats, so that they began to sink. (Luke 5:1–7)

Peter lent Jesus his boat so Jesus could finish His preaching. And then Jesus told Peter to let down his net for a catch. Why? He wanted to bless Peter. But like most of us, Peter immediately focused on how he felt and what he knew. And so he reacted predictably: "Lord, we've been fishing all night." On the Sea of Galilee, an experienced fisherman never worked in the day, only at night. Peter had grown up on this water, his father was a fisherman, so as a seasoned professional, he understood the ways things worked.

"I've been fishing all night," he said, "toiled for many hours and caught nothing! There isn't a fish to be had here right now. Besides that, Jesus, I'm tired. And forgive me, Jesus, but you just don't go fishing during the day on the Sea of Galilee! The fish see the net and swim the other way. The sun is shining into the water. You fish at nighttime; that's how you catch fish here. And really, Jesus, do I have to say it? You're, well, a *carpenter*. You see that tool belt around your waist? You know wood; I know fish."

Right? We've all been there!

"But the lawyer said it's a lost cause."

"But the doctor said it's incurable."

"But the banker said I have to file for bankruptcy."

"But my boss said it's over."

"But my husband said, 'I'm out of here.' "

"But…But…But…"

Peter got to the place where he shifted his thinking. And when he did, finally his own fatigue and his own professional opinion didn't matter anymore. Did you see what he said in verse five? "Nevertheless, at Your Word, I will…"

That's where we have to get!

"I feel like doing *this*; nevertheless, at Your Word, I'm going to trust You."

"The doctors said X; nevertheless, at Your Word, I know I'm healed."

"The banker said blah, blah, blah; nevertheless, at Your Word, I know all my needs are met and You will bless and prosper my life."

You have to get to the place where the highest level of truth in your life and in your world is what God said. What difference does it make what anyone else says? All of us just *have* to get there! We have to get to the place where we can say, "Nevertheless, at Your Word, I will..."

Yes, it's true, you may have a lot of troubles. Yes, it's true, things don't look very good. Yes, it's true, the diagnosis was bad.

But then you need to follow up that truth with a higher truth: "Nevertheless, at Your Word, I know that when I'm weak, that's when I'm strong. When I'm down, that's when I'm coming up."

When we have no answers in this world, then we find our answers in God. I'm usually my best when I feel my worst! It's true! And so I glory in my infirmities, because when I come to the end of myself, then God shows up and the greatest stuff of all happens—"good measure, pressed down, shaken together, and running over" (Luke 6:38).

THE BIG HOW

But *how* can you do that? How can you get to the place where you trust God and His Word as a higher truth above every other truth?

There is one simple answer, one simple way. You must have a *real* relationship with Jesus. It has to be more than church. It has to be true Christianity. It must be more than a Sunday morning event; it has to become a daily lifestyle. It has to be a sincere, alive, vibrant walk with God that includes prayer, Bible reading, Christian fellowship, service, and whatever else the Bible describes. That's what I mean by something that's real.

If you want that and know you need it, but are not sure how to get it, then what do you do? How do you develop a real relationship with Jesus?

It all starts with the choices you make concerning your faith and your relationship with God. Jesus said that if you want to see the kingdom of heaven, "You must be born again" (John 3:3, 7). And in Romans 10:9 Paul writes, "If you confess with your mouth that Jesus is Lord and believe in your heart that God raised him from the dead, you will be saved" (New Living Translation).

If you want to know God and walk with God, then it must start with being born of God—and when you believe in Him and confess Him as Lord, you're born of God.

But you don't want to stay a baby forever! You have to grow up to maturity. In order to do that, you have to know what God says and what God wants from you—and you can't get that from television or secular things. You can get that only from the Bible. So as you study and read the New Testament and listen to sound teaching from older, more mature Christians, you start understanding what God is saying to you, what God wants from you, what God has for you...and your relationship with Him grows.

As your relationship grows, your faith grows. That's what the Bible says: "faith *comes* by hearing, and hearing by the word of God" (Romans 10:17). As you hear and act on the Word of God, your spiritual confidence increases and you draw nearer to the heart of God. It's a simultaneous process of growing in your relationship with God and growing in your trust in God's Word.

It's a lot like a marriage relationship. As Wendy and I have grown in our relationship over the past thirty years, I know her better, I trust her more, and I understand more clearly (and quickly) what she says. Her words become more real and meaningful to me because our relationship has grown. I can't say, "I'm so close to Wendy—we've been together for thirty years, but I don't believe a word she says. And half the time, I don't know what she's talking about. But she sure is a great wife!" Our relationship and our communication have grown together simultaneously.

That's also true with God. Your relationship with Him starts by being born of God; it starts with putting your faith in God to save you. But then you have to spend time with Him, on your own, in His Word. Your relationship with Him grows as you get to know and understand what He says in the Bible. And then your faith and your knowledge and your understanding grow together and you get stronger in him. Soon, what He says becomes more "real" than what you feel or what you'd like to do or what you think. You have learned to trust His Word as your highest authority.

Of course, there are some days when I'd like to handle some financial matter or a parenting challenge or some other issue in a way other than how God says I should handle it. But then I say to myself, "You know what? God is smarter than I am, so I'd better stick with what He says rather than what I'm feeling right now."

Remember this: the Word is truer than your emotions or your thoughts, regardless of what challenges you may have to face. That means that:

- You can praise Him even when you face the messenger of Satan, sent to buffet you.

- You can praise Him when the news is bad.

- You can praise Him when you don't feel like it, even when the chemotherapy is making you sick.

- You can praise Him in the morning, praise Him at noontime, and praise Him at nighttime.

Why? Because you're not praising Him based on your circumstances; you're praising Him based on His promise—the highest level of truth in your life.

When you know the Lord, you have a *real* relationship with God. This isn't some philosophy or some weak religion. This isn't some man-made ideal. *You know Christ.* He strengthens you. He infuses your life with power. You have a real relationship with God—and that's how you're going to run your race to destiny.

I'm a guy who's always looking for the bottom line. I'm looking for the basics. What can I learn? What can I use? What will work every day?

Here's the bottom line: When you're facing challenges in life, do you know God or not? Do you have a real relationship with God, or are you just wearing a cross? Do you open that Bible, or do you just carry it around to make people think you care about the things of God? At the end of the day, do you know the Lord or not? What kind of relationship do you have with Him?

The apostle Paul declared in Philippians 4:13, "I can do all things through Christ who strengthens me." If you can't face the challenges and the difficulties and the hard days of life, then you have to ask yourself, "Do I know Christ?" If you know Christ, then you know you can get through these, for you can do *all* things through Christ who strengthens you.

This isn't some tricky thing. It's not some New Age thing. It's a *real* relationship with God. You must have it and develop it and learn to live with the daily mindset described by the old hymn: "And He walks with me, and He talks with me, and He tells me I am His own. And the joy we share as we tarry there, none other has ever known."[1]

CONTENT OR SATISFIED?

For a long period during his ministry, none of the churches that Paul helped to found gave him any material support. He noticed.

"I rejoiced in the Lord greatly that now at last your care for me has flourished again; though you surely did care, but you lacked opportunity," he wrote in Philippians 4:10. In other words, he was on his own and hungry for a long time—he didn't fast just because he wanted to. He found himself out on the mission field and struggling because he was on his own. All that time, he knew the church cared, but they had no opportunity to help him.

And then the apostle wrote a verse that confuses a lot of people. In verse 11 he wrote, "Not that I speak in regard to need, for I have learned in whatever state I am, to be content." Paul wrote this verse when he still had goals, dreams, and visions that hadn't yet happened for him.

A lot of people wonder, how could Paul be "content" but still want something more, something better? You might wonder the same thing. How can you be content with what you have and still strive for something more?

The answer, I think, is the difference between satisfaction and contentment.

[1] "In the Garden," words and music by C. Austin Miles.

I feel very content with my son in the twelfth grade, for example, doing his homework to get through high school. I feel content with his progress. But I'm *not* satisfied, because I want him to go on to college and then become an adult and a father and a minister or whatever God might call him to do. If he's still in high school ten years from now, we've got problems!

In other words, I'm content with the current situation, but I still have more dreams and desires and goals for him. I'm not going to get anxious about it; I'm not going to get frustrated; I'm not going to get angry that he's not there yet. He's just a teenager! But in the course of time, I want him to grow up and get out of the house.

There is no ultimate contradiction between being content with your current circumstances and wanting something different, something more. You can be content but still have dreams and desires, inspired by the Lord, that you want to accomplish.

Similarly, Hebrews 13:5 says, "*Let your* conduct *be* without covetousness [no greed, no selfishness]; *be* content with such things as you have." That doesn't mean, "Don't have vision." The verse just instructs you to remain content where you are, so long as you're there. Sure, ask God to expand your world. Make your plans as you walk close to Him. Shoot for something higher, richer, and deeper. Even as you remain content with how the Lord is dealing with you, stretch yourself a bit; don't allow yourself to get satisfied with the place you've already reached.

Since the apostle Paul knows, I think I ought to let him have the last word:

Not that I have already obtained all this, or have already been made perfect, but I press on to take hold of that for which Christ Jesus took hold of me. Brothers, I do not consider myself yet to have taken hold of it. But one thing I do: Forgetting what is behind and straining toward what is ahead, I press on toward the goal to win the prize for which God has called me heavenward in Christ Jesus.

All of us who are mature should take such a view of things. And if on some point you think differently, that too God will make clear to you. Only let us live up to what we have already attained. (Philippians 3:12–16, NIV)

Be content with what you have—live up to what you have already attained—but continue to strive for your destiny. That's God's way.

BRING IT ON

You have to get to the place where, in Jesus, you can handle whatever life brings your way. "Bring it on, devil; I've got my backup with me today. Make your attack good, because I want this testimony to be great! I know Jesus; He strengthens me."

In Philippians 4:12–13 Paul wrote, "I know how to be abased, and I know how to abound. Everywhere and in all things I have learned both to be full and to be hungry, both to abound and to suffer need. I can do all things through Christ who strengthens me."

There's the answer! How are you going to live this life? "I can do all things through Christ, who strengthens me." *That's* how I'm going to handle those hard days. *That's* how I'm going to stand on the Word of God when everything seems contrary to me. *That's* how I'm going to make it through those days when I feel weak and down, when I am abased, when I'm suffering and in need. The Amplified version of Philippians 4:13 says, "I have strength for all things in Christ Who empowers me [I am ready for anything and equal to anything through Him Who infuses inner strength into me; I am self-sufficient in Christ's sufficiency]."

Wow! I am ready for anything—and equal to anything—through Him Who infuses me with inner strength. That's good stuff!

Have you ever heard the coach say to his basketball or football team, "We have to match their intensity—someone has to make the play, so let's rise up and match their intensity"?

What does he mean? He means, "We're equal to whatever they bring to the floor or the field. So bring it on—we're equal to it. Bring it on—we'll send the ball right back to you. Bring it on—I am ready for and equal to whatever my opponent brings my way."

That's the same thing Paul said: "I'm ready for and equal to whatever the enemy brings. When I'm weak, that's my best day. That's when I'm strong, because Christ infuses me with inner strength."

So say it now, out loud: "I can do all things through Christ, who strengthens me. When I feel weak, regardless of the source, that's when He strengthens me."

So long as you're on your own, you don't need Him. But when you know you don't have what you need, then He's got your back. That's when that little grin crosses your face, because you know something that nobody else knows:

Right behind me is a big God. And because Christ infuses me with His power, I'm equal to and ready for anything.

Are *you*?

4

Getting Your Mind (and Life) Right

We've all been driving down the road when something to the side has caught our attention. All of a sudden we realize we are out of our lane and being honked at by drivers wondering what in the world we are doing. When you think on a certain thing, you subconsciously move toward it. We've all done it, many of us have been embarrassed by it, and some have found themselves in an accident because of it.

Call it the law of attraction, or "as a man thinks so is he," or "your vision is your future"; it is real in our lives every day. Maybe we should think of it as "your attitude controls your altitude." To go higher in God's will and plan for your life you must change things about your attitude that have held you down and held you back in the past.

Thoughts of pessimism, doubt, anger, and fear keep many talented people from realizing their potential. You have heard it before:

"If you believe you can't, you are right; if you believe you can, you are right." God says,

> My son, give attention to my words;
> Incline your ear to my sayings.
> Do not let them depart from your eyes;
> Keep them in the midst of your heart;
> For they *are* life to those who find them,
> And health to all their flesh.
> Keep your heart with all diligence,
> For out of it *spring* the issues of life.
> Put away from you a deceitful mouth,
> And put perverse lips far from you.

> (Proverbs 4:20–24)

But when we get God's thoughts (through his Word) in our lives, it produces good results. Everything from health to prosperity come with the right thoughts, beliefs, and attitudes.

I have a friend named Mwangi, who was raised in Uganda. He grew up poor and struggled under the poverty and corrupt government of his country. But Mwangi thought on better things. He wrote poetry and articles of a better life. He learned all that he could and refused to become negative and cynical in a world that tried to pull him down. As a young man, Mwangi began to be harassed because of some of his published writings. He was forced to leave his wife and four kids to flee for his life. But Mwangi's attitude controlled his altitude. Somehow he found his way to Christian Faith Center. He studied the Bible and worked his way onto the facilities staff. He was positive, faithful, and happy during these months of very difficult times. After four years, his wife and children finally made it to America. Today they are building their new lives in freedom and prosperity. He has several published poems and books. Their children are growing up in Christian Faith School and Mwangi is a blessed man.

He did not get bitter, he got better. His negative circumstances did not make him sour like old milk. He rose above them and overcame them.

Your attitude will take you up or take you down. That is exactly why God tells us to guard our hearts and take captive our thoughts. It's why He wants us to think on His ways. When we do that, we'll move toward what God has planned for our lives. He doesn't want us to lose our focus and end up where we don't want to be: "we do not look at the things which are seen, but at the things which are not seen. For the things which are seen *are* temporary, but the things which are not seen *are* eternal (2 Corinthians 4:18).

So the question is, what are you thinking about? And how are you thinking about that thing? The way you answer that question will go a long way in determining how—or even if—you run your race toward destiny.

KEEP IT POSITIVE

Sin did a lot of terrible things when it came into our world, and one of the terrible things it did is to make it more "natural" for us to think in the negative than it is to think in the positive. In other words, it's easier for us to think bad thoughts than good ones.

If you're a parent, you know that you don't have to teach your children how to dwell on the negative. You don't have to instruct them how to lie, cry, or complain (I know I didn't). They tend to do those things naturally.

On the contrary, we have to teach our children to always be honest and tell the truth. We have to instruct them that instead of grumbling and complaining, they should think and speak words of gratitude and appreciation. We train them to focus on what they do have instead of what they don't have.

Too often, I catch myself starting to think on and worry about the negative. When I come to church, I have to remind myself to only see the seats that have people in them, not the ones that remain empty. I must confess that my natural inclination is to look first at the empty seats and think about all the people who could and should be at church, but who for whatever reason aren't there.

I also have come to believe that it is not a good thing to "go negative"—to be so worried about what is wrong—when it comes to presenting the gospel of Jesus Christ. I don't believe I am to preach every Sunday about how the world is going to hell, how there are fornicators and adulterers in the church and in the world, how God will judge sinners, how we have so many problems. If I constantly put people's mind on the negative and don't talk about the abundance of God, the blessing of God, the healing of God, or the harvest we are to reap for Him, then I am leaving out the fullness of God's message, which is a positive message of love and forgiveness and blessing.

Since it's so easy for me to worry about the negative, I've had to learn to train and discipline my mind and do what Paul said: "[bring] every thought into captivity to the obedience of Christ" (2 Corinthians 10:5). When I do that, I think on the right things, the good things, the productive things, and ministry life goes that way.

But it's not easy to do that! It doesn't happen naturally, especially for those who have spent their lives dwelling on the negative. Negative is normal for the world. Every news channel, every talk show, every newspaper tells us what is going wrong in our world. Wars, rumors of wars, global warming, and famous people who have been arrested or some other problem—this is what consumes our media. It will take effort to think on godly things. It's difficult enough for all of us, because we live in a fallen world and in a body of flesh, both of which are influenced by and corrupted by sin.

Just because it's not easy, however, doesn't mean we can't do it. By training our minds to focus on the truth of God's Word, we can change our way of thinking and make our minds right. And when we do that, we can get on the road to destiny.

MIND GAMES

The human mind is a fascinating thing. One of the most interesting parts of it, I think, is that it will go out of its way and even fight in an effort to prove to itself that what it chooses to think is true and right.

For example, if an unemployed man becomes discouraged and starts believing and saying things like, "There are no good jobs out there," he will subconsciously make it true rather than go out and prove that his mind has lied to him. He may even go so far as to ignore a potentially good job, just to prove the truth of his assertion that there are no good jobs available. He would rather do that than humbly admit he was wrong—even though it's to his advantage to admit his error.

It is amazing how we can convince ourselves that certain things are true and be controlled by that thought whether it is true or not. A good percentage of people in our world believe they cannot change and so their lives are stuck in their current reality.

However, there is another group of people who believe and think on brighter days and new possibilities. They are on their way to higher lives relationally, financially, and in every way.

Negative thinking not only reinforces itself, it also reinforces bad behavior. If someone with a weight problem were to say, "I'll never be fit and healthy. I'll always be out of shape and always have a weight problem," then he or she will find a way to affirm a herd of rationalizations and excuses. And so you'll hear things like, "Well, I just have a slow metabolism," or "I have defective glands," or "Genetics makes it impossible for me to change." They will convince themselves there is nothing they can do about their situation. They may decide they are different from most people or that no one understands what they are going through.

When people think that way, their behavior will always stay as it is—and what they are saying will be affirmed. As much as they might say they want to lose weight and get in shape, they subconsciously go out of their way to make sure it doesn't happen by continuing to engage in unhealthy eating habits and remaining in a sedentary lifestyle.

Without a doubt, how you think can have a great influence on the quality of your life. For example, if you keep telling yourself that the amount of money you earn depends on the world around you—on the jobs you see as "available," on the government, on the IRS—then you will likely find yourself stuck in the rut of believing you can never make more.

Then, if for some reason you do begin making more, you'll probably fall back into your old ways of thinking and tell yourself, "This can't be happening. It just doesn't fit what I know to be true. I know *I* can't have more money!" And you will likely lose whatever you've gained. That way, you can get back to the thinking that makes you comfortable, the thinking that says you are limited by the world's circumstances and systems.

This principle has been demonstrated in studies of lottery winners, who have won millions of dollars. I have heard that more than 80 percent of lottery winners—eight in ten!—return to their former financial condition within a few years of winning the jackpot.

Why do you suppose that is? I believe it's because in the minds of most lottery winners, having that kind of money is too good to be true. They reason that if they have all that cash, then they've been believing a lie about their financial condition. So rather than adjust to their newfound wealth, they simply change their circumstances in order to get back to the thinking and the life to which they are accustomed.

It's not only negative thinking that will keep you from enjoying all God has for you and from effectively running your race to your destiny, "average" thinking can also limit you.

Most people start young with this kind of thinking. Many times in school, we're graded on what's known as a bell curve. In this grading system, teachers expect a small group of students to do very poorly, a small group to do very well, but the majority of students to perform somewhere in the middle. Most students are expected to be average. And eventually many students internalize the expectation. Average thinking—and average performance—is often reinforced throughout life. Excellence in anything is difficult. It takes hard work, perseverance, and dedication. Being average is a lot easier. And when you don't get rewarded for your hard work, then why bother? All those hours of overtime and you still didn't get the promotion. You finally got that big client, so why didn't you get that raise? You put a lot of time and effort and your heart into the relationship, so why did he still leave you? If average is all they expect and average is all you ever get, why try for anything more?

Average—which has been called the best of the worst and the worst of the best—became your goal in life. You do just enough to get by. So because of that kind of thinking and the approach to life that follows it, you have an *average* marriage, are raising *average* kids, have an *average* job, live in an *average* house, drive an *average* car, and serve God in an *average* way.

There may not be anything really wrong with your life, but everything is *just okay*. Average!

What has happened? Your thoughts have taken you with them to the world of "average." You thought of yourself as average, and that thought has controlled you and held you down. When you think that way, even when God blesses you with "more"—more of anything—you will have a difficult time sustaining the blessing, because you'll believe in your heart and in your mind that it's just too good to be true.

I once read about a study done with two groups of salesmen from a particular company. One group that had been selling huge amounts of product every month got moved into districts where the sales hadn't been as good—average, but nothing great. At the same time, the salesmen who had worked those "average" territories were moved to the locations where the more successful salesmen had worked.

You can probably guess what happened, can't you?

Within three months after the switch, the highly successful and productive group of salesmen had bumped up the sales in the previously average districts to the levels they had grown accustomed to in their previous territories. And the "average" salesmen? Their sales remained where they had been before, even though they were working supposedly more fertile ground.

As you might expect, the average salesmen found all kinds of excuses for their less-than-stellar sales, while the better salesmen immediately found new markets that before had been ignored.

What was going on here? One group of salesmen were used to being "above average." They expected to sell a large amount of product, even in sales districts that had never produced big numbers. But because these salesmen had set higher standards for themselves, they naturally "homed in" on the same kinds of sales they had always achieved. On the other hand, the salesmen who were used to being "average" allowed their old attitudes to take them where they truly expected to be—the land of the mediocre. Even though the new districts they were working seemed like fertile territory, they didn't produce the way the other group of salesmen had.

The point of this story is this: What you accomplish doesn't depend on where you are in the world around you, nearly as much as it depends on how you think—particularly what you focus on and what you believe about yourself.

You have to get away from the insanity of "average thinking," away from an approach to life where you do just enough to get by. That is not the abundant life Jesus wants for you! On the contrary, it's the kind of thinking that will keep you from moving beyond the "average." And ultimately it will keep you from enjoying the blessings God has for you. It's hard to reach for your destiny when you're content with "average"! In the book of Numbers we read how when the Israelites left Egypt they lived in the wilderness. It was a land of *just enough*: no homes, farms, or abundance, but they were free and *had enough*.

God never desired for them to stay there. They could have moved through there in weeks and possessed their promised land, a land of abundance, a land of *more than enough*.

What kept them in the wilderness—the land of *just enough*? Their unbelief, their fears, their negative thinking.

The adults all died in their *"just enough to get by"* condition, when God had wanted them to have more than enough.

To reach for your destiny you also need to guard against what I call "time-release beliefs." What are they? Basically, they're deeply held thoughts we carry with us, oftentimes throughout our lives.

I see at least two really scary things about time-release beliefs. First, they aren't even thoughts that you consciously harbor—indeed, you may not even know they are there. Second, they can just pop up on you at the worst possible times, causing some of the worst emotional responses and behavior imaginable.

Time-release beliefs get planted deep in your mind mostly through the examples of others (likely your parents or other family members) and through incidents you have observed.

Suppose you grew up in a home where your mother and/or father had a phobia about turning forty. Perhaps in the months leading up to her fortieth birthday, your mom verbalized her dread and fear at turning the big Four-O. But she did more than verbalize it; she acted on her fears and anxieties about aging, and her behavior and emotions became increasingly erratic. Now fast-forward twenty-five or thirty years. Your own fortieth birthday is approaching. You've never really thought about it before, and it really doesn't bother you. It's just a number, right? But you have been feeling a bit down lately; you notice you've been yelling at your kids more and your sister has accused you of having mood swings.

What's happening here? Very possibly, your mind has been infected with a time-release belief, specifically, the belief that turning forty is a negative event. You witnessed how difficult turning forty was for your mother, and as you're about to turn forty, you are having your own "midlife crisis." A negative belief that has been dormant all these years is now rearing its ugly head, causing you and your family grief. And you know the worst thing about this crisis? You're probably not even consciously aware of why you are acting the way you are.

Time-release beliefs can take you places you don't want to go, and for reasons you cannot begin to comprehend. If you want to reach your destiny, you have to strenuously guard against time-release beliefs.

But how exactly can you guard your heart against this and other kinds of wrong or unhealthy thinking? The Bible insists that it's a matter of war—a war fought in the battlefield located between your ears.

A WAR IN THE MIND

We hear a lot of references to war these days. There is the war on terror, the war on drugs, the war on poverty...the list goes on and on. In the Christian world, we often read and hear about spiritual warfare.

I believe in spiritual warfare, but I also believe that the greatest battle we fight isn't against the devil or against his minions. Our greatest battle is the one we fight in our own minds.

A lot of believers don't know this, but Satan already is defeated. Paul wrote of this defeat: "Having disarmed principalities and powers, He [Christ] made a public spectacle of them, triumphing over them in it" (Colossians 2:15). That means that Jesus stripped Satan and his demons of all authority and that He did it in an open show as He triumphed over them on the cross. That's why Paul could tell the believers in Rome, "And the God of peace will crush Satan under your feet shortly" (Romans 16:20). "You are of God, little children, and have overcome them, because He who is in you is greater than he who is in the world" (1 John 4:4).

The devil is completely and utterly defeated, and our job as believers is to go in and mop up and reinforce his defeat. We don't struggle with the devil; we just tread on serpents and scorpions and all his power (Luke 10:19). We don't wrestle with demons; we cast out demons (Mark 16:17). We don't fight against Satan; we just celebrate his eternal defeat.

But there is still warfare and there still is a struggle, which Paul describes this way: "For though we walk in the flesh, we do not war according to the flesh. For the weapons of our warfare *are* not carnal but mighty in God for pulling down strongholds, casting down arguments and every high thing that exalts itself against the knowledge of God, *bringing every thought into captivity to the obedience of Christ*" (2 Corinthians 10:3–5, emphasis added).

In other words, our battle isn't in the physical realm but in the mental realm. The warfare we fight comes primarily in our way of thinking. *That's* where we have to fight for the thoughts of God, where we have to repel the lies we've fed ourselves and been fed by others throughout our lives. That's where we have to fight to make sure we are living and thinking the will of God in every way.

Sadly, however, most believers today are losing the war. Why? Because they don't take the thoughts of God with them into the world after they leave church on Sunday. They leave church and get caught up in the world. For example, thinking about the brand-new car the next-door neighbor just purchased and how they could never afford to get anything that nice, or about losing out on that promotion. Or they begin worrying about the rising costs of gasoline and health insurance and how the last measly raise they got doesn't even cover their cost of living. Their minds are full with thoughts of the world not the thoughts and the ways of God.

So they believe what the world says about the economy, not what the Word says. They believe what the world says about their jobs and career, not what the Word says. They believe what the world says about finances, not what the Word says. And because they believe what the world says and not what the Word says, they miss out on God's will for them as individuals. Add to this the negative and average thoughts they've inherited or picked up during their lifetime, and it's no wonder they're losing the war.

Don't follow their example! Win the battle for your mind! Think

God's thoughts instead of those of the devil, the world, or your own flesh!

Friend, there's a battle to be fought, and it's a daily battle to pull down what Paul called "strongholds" in your mind. Now, a stronghold is just that—something that has a strong hold on your thinking. It's more than just a passing thought or something you briefly contemplated this morning; it's a stubborn way of thinking that you can't shake on your own, a corrupt way of thinking that takes you emotionally, spiritually, and physically where you won't want to go—and where God doesn't want you to go.

How can your thinking lead to strongholds? Maybe you don't like the way you look, and you believe you can never change. Maybe you believe that your finances will never get better. Maybe you have strongholds of anger, bitterness, resentment, sarcasm, or other negative attitudes. Maybe you see yourself as inferior, as not being "good enough." You have to go to war against all those kinds of thoughts. You have to capture them and bring them into subjection to the Word of God, the only source of spiritual truth your mind should dwell on. Focus those thoughts on what God says about you.

Let me be completely honest here: We all need to fight this war, but it's not easy. We can't fight this war sitting in church or Bible study. We can certainly receive ammunition to fight the war during times of fellowship and worship, but you fight the real war as you live the truth of God's Word away from the relative safety and security of the church sanctuary.

You fight the battle in your mind as you're at work Monday through Friday, as you're dealing with your spouse and children, as you're facing financial or other needs, as you're facing a decision you're going to have to live with.

God calls you to capture every thought and bring them all into the obedience of Christ. He instructs you to subject your every thought to the truth of God's Word. He counsels you to think the way God thinks about every part of your life. And while it's not easy, when you do it, some miraculous things start happening.

As you claim victories over the strongholds in your mind, you start to lose your focus on low living or average living or on time-release beliefs. And as you lose your focus on those worthless things, you enter into the high life God has for you. You start leaving behind barriers and limitations and you start rising to a higher level of life—on all levels—than you ever thought was possible.

As in so many arenas of life, you are faced with a choice in this area. You can continue to believe that thinking the thoughts of God won't work for you—"I've tried it before and it didn't work. God somehow has blessed millions of others but has missed me"—or you can choose to go to war in your mind, make your thoughts obedient to Christ, and get out there and begin running your race to your destiny.

THE VALUE OF A SOUND MIND

I want to leave this discussion with the words of Paul ringing in your ears:

> For God has not given us a spirit of fear, but of power and of love and of a sound mind. (2 Timothy 1:7)

When you read this verse, doesn't it at first seem strange that Paul would mention a sound mind? He'd been talking about spiritual things such as fear and power and love—so why would he throw in "a sound mind"?

In fact, the reference to a sound mind fits perfectly when you realize that the power of God cannot work through you and in you if your mind isn't right. Other translations of this verse use the phrase "a disciplined mind," which tells me that if we want to have a life of power and love and destiny, we have to focus our mind on God's thinking. If we want to overcome our fears, our timidity, and the other things that hold us back, we need to focus our minds on what God thinks.

And how do we do that? We do that by focusing our thoughts on the Word of God, the Scripture. Over the past thirty years, I have read some verses and passages of the Bible literally thousands of times. I've posted them in my car, on my computer, in my day planner. In doing that, I have learned how to better capture my own thoughts and make them obedient to the Word of God.

Whatever growth and success I've had is because God has helped me to the point where I have been able to commit myself to habitually thinking the thoughts of God. I've learned that I can't be so arrogant that I choose to think my own thoughts; instead, I must have the humility to look at the Word of God and say, "God, you are right!"

And when *you* begin to think that way, you will be on your way to destiny.

5

A New Family Heritage

It has become all the rage for people to do everything they can to uncover their roots—to learn about their recent family history as well as their more distant heritage. People want to know not only who their parents are, but also who previous generations of their ancestors were and what they did.

Television talk show hosts like to do special shows that attempt to reunite people with their long-lost friends or lovers or biological fathers and mothers. Other folks go to great pains to look up their "family trees," so that they can find out where they came from and how they got here. Still others go out of their way to demonstrate their pride in their ethnic heritage—European, African, Middle Eastern, Asian, and so on.

I suppose it's natural and normal for us to have some degree of interest in our earthly heritage. And while I don't want to diminish the importance of such things, I do want to point out that those of us who know Jesus Christ as our personal Savior have a family heritage that goes much deeper and will last much longer than any earthly or natural one.

As children of the living God, we are members of a new family, complete with new family roots, a new destiny, and a new family heritage. And if we want to be all that God has called us to be—if we want to successfully run our race toward our personal destinies—we need to understand what being a member of God's eternal family is all about.

FAMILY BENEFITS

Personally, I've not spent five minutes studying my family name or researching my family background and heritage. So far as I'm concerned, I'm a Treat—just like my father before me and his father before him—and that's all I need to know. I don't care which of my ancestors came over on the *Mayflower*, and I don't care which of my forefathers served in what capacity in the military or in the government.

While there's nothing wrong with wanting to know those things, I don't concern myself about them, simply because I know who I am. I know to which family I belong and what my heritage is—in a biblical, spiritual, and eternal sense.

I am convinced that there is an inverse relationship between what you desire to know about your earthly heritage and what you desire to know about your eternal heritage. In other words, the less you know about your heritage in Christ, the more you tend to worry about your earthly heritage. Conversely, the more you know about your heritage with your heavenly Father, the less you concern yourself with your genealogical family tree.

Of course, this doesn't mean that we aren't to honor our earthly mothers and fathers or love and respect our relatives. To disrespect or ignore them would be in direct disobedience to the Word of God. And it also doesn't mean that we can't take a certain amount of pride in our ethnicity and family background (unless, of course, you approach your ethnic and family heritage as something that makes you "better" than someone of a different ethnicity or family; I'll get into that more in-depth later in this chapter).

What it really means is that you make your new family heritage—the eternal, God-given one—preeminent in your life and in your thinking. It means that you know and love your Father in heaven and that you walk in the joy and security of knowing that He has a Book of Life up in heaven and that your name is in it. It means knowing you became part of a family tree that includes all of those who have, through Jesus Christ, received God's Holy Spirit when He adopted you—an experience that allows you to call him "Abba [Daddy], Father" (see Romans 8:15).

I love my earthly family and I enjoy it when we can get together for family reunions and other gatherings. But as much as I love and enjoy the people God has given me for an earthly family, I can't wait for the biggest family reunion of all eternity—the one where all of us who know Jesus Christ will gather around the throne of God and unite in singing and shouting our praises to Him.

But the benefits of being a part of God's eternal family don't start in eternity. On the contrary, God has promised those who put their trust in Jesus Christ for their salvation a multitude of benefits in *this* life.

Some time ago, I heard someone say that there's only one thing worse than not being able to read, and that's being able to read but not reading, anyway. I think I would add to that, being able to read but not reading and grasping for ourselves the truths and promises of the written Word of God, the Bible.

The Word of God is many things to the believer, including an avenue for change. But too many believers don't change—at least not in all the ways God wants them to—simply because they don't understand what God's Word says about them personally as children of God. The Bible contains a long list of promises for the believer, but too many Christians simply don't know how to claim those promises for themselves.

The Bible is filled from cover to cover with God's promises for those who put their faith and trust in Him, for those who have become a part of His eternal family by placing their faith in Jesus Christ. And while there isn't enough room in this book to talk about all of those promises, I'd like to focus here on a short passage of Scripture that gives us some solid basics when it comes to the benefits of being in this "new" family.

The apostle Paul, writing to the church in the Greek city of Corinth, wrote the following about what it means to become a part of God's eternal family:

> Therefore, if anyone is in Christ, he is a new creation; the old has gone, the new has come! All this is from God, who reconciled us to himself through Christ and gave us the ministry of reconciliation: that God was reconciling the world to himself in Christ, not counting men's sins against them. And he has committed to us the message of reconciliation. We are therefore Christ's ambassadors, as though God were making his appeal through us. We implore you on Christ's behalf: Be reconciled to God. (2 Corinthians 5:17–20, NIV)

God wants us to understand that we have a new family and a new heritage. We are new creations for whom the old has passed away and the new has come. Indeed, when we make Jesus Christ Lord of our lives, we are reconciled *with* God and reunited to our family roots *in* God, all because our heavenly Father, from whom we were hopelessly lost, sent Jesus to rescue us and bring us back to Himself. Jesus came specifically "to seek and to save what was lost" (Luke 19:10, NIV). It is this reconciliation—one God Himself initiated when He sent Jesus Christ to earth to die for us—and not our earthly heritage or anything else about us that brings us into His eternal family.

But it does more than that, as great as that is! It also empowers us to be everything He said we could be and to do everything He said we could do. In fact, you have the destiny you have been given because you are part of this new family of God.

HAVE CONFIDENCE IN GOD, NOT YOUR PEDIGREE

In our day we hear a lot of teaching about the effects of family heritage and background—both the negatives and the positives—on our lives as individuals. And although our families of origin can certainly have an effect on our present lives, we know from carefully reading and studying the Word of God that our position as members of God's eternal family is infinitely more important than our natural family heritage.

Some of us look at our earthly heritage—at all the great things our ancestors did and all the notoriety they earned—and choose to feel a sense of pride. Others of us look at our family history—including very recent history—with a sense of shame and dread, convinced that we are doomed to failure or to mediocrity because of that flawed background.

Yet God calls each of us to look at our family histories and say, "It really doesn't matter what kind of background I come from, because

I belong to the family of God. I am in Christ today, so everything else about my family background is basically meaningless!"

That was Paul's point when he wrote to the Philippians, "If anyone else thinks he has reasons to put confidence in the flesh, I have more: circumcised on the eighth day, of the people of Israel, of the tribe of Benjamin, a Hebrew of Hebrews; in regard to the law, a Pharisee; as for zeal, persecuting the church; as for legalistic righteousness, fault-less" (Philippians 3:4–6, NIV).

Paul wanted the Philippian Christians to understand that they couldn't have found someone with a higher religious pedigree than himself. But more importantly, he wanted them to understand that his background didn't mean *anything* when it came to his faith and his calling to serve Jesus Christ. What really mattered, he wanted them to know, is the fact that he had become a part of God's eternal family through faith in Christ, and that nothing else about him or his pedigree mattered any longer.

> But whatever was to my profit I now consider loss for the sake of Christ. What is more, I consider everything a loss compared to the surpassing greatness of knowing Christ Jesus my Lord, for whose sake I have lost all things. I consider them rubbish, that I may gain Christ and be found in him, not having a righteousness of my own that comes from the law, but that which is through faith in Christ— the righteousness that comes from God and is by faith. (Philippians 3:7–9, NIV)

There can be no doubt that Paul had a right—at least, in the human sense—to feel proud of his heritage. It was easy to trace his ethnic, family, and religious heritage back to God's own plan to bring salvation to the world. His race, the Jews, was fathered by Abraham and used by God to establish and fulfill the covenant that brought salvation to all humankind, Jew and Gentile alike.

Yet what was Paul's approach to his stellar ethnic, family, and religious heritage? In his own words: "I consider them rubbish." He went on to write, "Brothers, I do not consider myself yet to have taken hold of it. But one thing I do: Forgetting what is behind and straining toward what is ahead, I press on toward the goal to win the prize for which God has called me heavenward in Christ Jesus" (Philippians 3:13–14, NIV).

That is exactly the way we modern-day believers should think when it comes to our own families and pedigrees, the positive and negative alike. We are to "forget what is behind" in our backgrounds—no matter what they may look like, no matter how noble or poor they may appear—and focus instead on our new family heritage. That means putting our ethnic, family, and religious heritage in their proper place and moving forward in Christ, just as Paul did. It means not living according to the flesh or thinking in terms of our own pedigree, but instead living, thinking, and moving by the Spirit of God.

And, finally, it means seeing ourselves as members of a new heavenly family, a new race of people that God created through the work of His Son, Jesus Christ. And what a new race it is!

ALL IN THE FAMILY

I remember well the day I was to be ordained at the Crenshaw Christian Center—twenty-six years ago, as of this writing. I remember telling a man of God who had had a big influence on my life and plans for ministry that Frederick K. C. Price, the founder and pastor of Crenshaw, would be ordaining me. His response was, "But he's *black*."

I remember feeling a little taken aback that someone would point out the color of this godly man's skin. And, to be honest, I hadn't even thought of Dr. Price in terms of his race. I walked away shaking my head, wondering what I was to think of such a comment. In Christ, race and nationality are not an issue. In God's family there is neither Jew nor Gentile, black nor white, African nor European (Colossians 3:11).

Since that time, I have made reconciliation—racial and otherwise—a regular part of my preaching and ministry. That's because I have recognized from Scripture that when you make Jesus Christ Lord of your life, you join a new "race" of people, one that is united in Christ without regard to race, family background, social standing, or denominational background. That is what the apostle Peter meant when he wrote, "But you are a chosen people, a royal priesthood, a holy nation, a people belonging to God, that you may declare the praises of him who called you out of darkness into his wonderful light" (1 Peter 2:9, NIV).

I believe that we are to reject anything that divides the Body of Christ or that makes false distinctions between us. We need to make sure that the world around us knows that it's not our way to make an issue of our differences, and that it is our way to focus on the truth that we are united under Jesus Christ in the eternal family of the one, true living God.

And as Paul tells us, that is the *only* heritage that really matters: "You are all sons of God through faith in Christ Jesus, for all of you who were baptized into Christ have clothed yourselves with Christ. There is neither Jew nor Greek, slave nor free, male nor female, for you are all one in Christ Jesus. If you belong to Christ, then you are Abraham's seed, and heirs according to the promise" (Galatians 3:26–29, NIV).

In the eternal family of God, there are no Jewish believers, no

Gentile believers, no white believers, and no black believers. There are no Methodist believers, no Presbyterian believers, no Baptist believers, and no Charismatic believers. And there are no rich believers and no poor believers. That is because, as God insists, we are all united into one body through Jesus Christ.

I absolutely refuse to draw lines of distinction between believers on the basis of race, family background, denomination, or any other barrier that some believers, sadly enough, tend to focus on. There are several reasons for that, the most important of which is that I know that if I were to hold on to those kinds of delineations and separations, it would keep me from being everything God wants me to be. In short, prejudice, no matter what it's based on, will limit me. I believe the same is true for all believers—and if that sounds strange to you, then bear with me.

I have learned that we can't—absolutely *cannot*—believe in ourselves or see ourselves as God sees us when we mentally put people into different categories. That's because we will either think more highly of ourselves than we should (thinking we are "better" than another) or we will see ourselves as more lowly than God wants us to ("worse" than another, or inferior to another). So Paul writes, "For by the grace given me I say to every one of you: Do not think of yourself more highly than you ought, but rather think of yourself with sober judgment, in accordance with the measure of faith God has given you" (Romans 12:3, NIV).

Prejudice will pick out and exclude and discriminate against any one person or group of people it wants to. You can categorize, criticize, and look down your nose at any person that you in your fleshly, ungodly thinking, see as beneath you. But I can guarantee you this: doing so will hurt you worse than it will hurt the object of your disdain. And I can guarantee you that you will never be all God created you to be until you stop thinking like the world and start thinking like a Christian—the same way Jesus Himself thought.

Under the New Covenant, in God's eyes, there are only two races: those who are born again and those who are not. As believers, that is the only difference we are to know. That's all we are to see and all we are to believe about ourselves. We are children of the King, part of this great family of God.

And God has called us to invite others into His family, the church.

When you come to faith in Jesus Christ, you have begun a reconciliation that will last into all of eternity—a reconciliation between yourself and a loving, gracious heavenly Father. But it doesn't stop there!

In addition to reconciling us to Himself, God has given those of us who have put our faith in Christ a ministry of reconciliation. That means we should be out there saying to the lost and lonely and hurting and sick and dying, "I want to take you to meet your Dad. You've been a long-lost orphan, and you need to come home to your Father."

God saved us and reconciled us to Himself, but He didn't do it just so we could sit back and enjoy our fellowship with Him, all by ourselves. No, He wants us to go out and, in the words of Jesus Himself, "make disciples." We are to be inviting others into the family of God. Don't neglect this part of your new family heritage, because it's wrapped up in how you run your race to destiny.

Paul put it this way: "For we are God's workmanship, created in Christ Jesus to do good works, which God prepared in advance for us to do" (Ephesians 2:10, NIV).

How many of us know that we now have the word of reconciliation? How many of us understand that we're not here to go out and tell people how ugly they are? We're not here to go out and demand that people stop smoking and drinking, get their hair cut, or change their sexual behavior. We may believe that people need to do those things, but that's not what we're about. That's not the message we are to take to the world around us.

We have a message of reconciliation—reconciliation between a loving and holy God and a lost and needy world. This is a message of love, a message of healing and blessing. It's a message of a God who wants to do something *good* in people's lives, if only they would put their trust in Him.

Remember what Paul wrote: "And he has committed to us the message of reconciliation. We are therefore Christ's ambassadors, as though God were making his appeal through us. We implore you on Christ's behalf: Be reconciled to God" (2 Corinthians 5:19–20, NIV).

When we put our faith in Jesus Christ and make Him the Lord of our lives, we become part of God's family, a family that He sees as righteous and a family that in unity is to do everything it can to reconcile others to God, to invite and welcome them in. We have a new name, a new family, and a message of reconciliation that the world desperately needs to hear and to see.

It's part of your destiny.

CHILDREN OF THE KING

We must never forget that we believers possess the right to be called God's children and that this is a right we have received directly from the hand of God Himself. "Yet to all who received him," the apostle John wrote, "to those who believed in his name, he gave the right to become children of God—children born not of natural descent, nor of human decision or a husband's will, but born of God" (John 1:12–13, NIV).

But we must also never forget that there is much more to our faith than one day being welcomed into eternity in God's presence. You see, God not only miraculously brings us into His eternal family, but He also equips us to live victorious, overcoming lives on this earth and in this age.

In his first epistle, John gave us a wonderful definition of what it means to truly be a member of God's eternal family:

Everyone who believes that Jesus is the Christ is born of God, and everyone who loves the father loves his child as well. This is how we know that we love the children of God: by loving God and carrying out his commands. This is love for God: to obey his commands. And his commands are not burdensome, for everyone born of God overcomes the world. This is the victory that has overcome the world, even our faith. Who is it that overcomes the world? Only he who believes that Jesus is the Son of God. (1 John 5:1–5, NIV)

Before anything else, we need to understand that we're not Christians until we're born again. And what does that mean? Simply put, it means that we put our faith in Jesus Christ and believe that He is the Anointed One, the Messiah, the Savior.

Second, we need to understand that we prove we are born into God's family by loving Him and joyfully carrying out His commands. Contrary to what many think, those commands aren't a burden or a bother. Why not? Because if we've been born again, we will overcome the world. As John wrote, "This is love for God: to obey his commands. And his commands are not burdensome, for everyone born of God overcomes the world. This is the victory that has overcome the world, even our faith. Who is it that overcomes the world? Only he who believes that Jesus is the Son of God" (1 John 5:3–5, NIV).

It can't be much more direct than that, can it?

It is God's plan for every person in His family, everyone who is "born again," to be an overcomer. It is His plan for you to meet and beat every challenge, to approach and overcome every obstacle, and to go out and make a real difference in your own corner of the world.

Every son and every daughter of God is meant—*called*—to overcome negativity, overcome doubt, overcome hatred, and overcome fear. As the apostle Paul wrote to the first-century church in Rome, "in all these things we are *more than conquerors* through Him who loved us" (Romans 8:37, emphasis added).

This may surprise you, but God intends that the church—meaning the family of God as a whole—be the most positive, most excited, most successful group of people on planet Earth. He intends for us to be the happiest people on the globe because, first and foremost, we are born of God; and second, because no matter what happens to us, we overcome, we win, we succeed, and we conquer.

And while I'm not sure exactly what it means to be "*more* than conquerors" (after all, if something is conquered, isn't it conquered?), I do know that it's what we are called to be over this world's systems. So let's see and believe with all our hearts that in Jesus, we're more than conquerors. Let's incorporate that into the job. Let's incorporate that into the challenges we face in our families. Let's put that into the vision of our new ministries, our new companies, and our new churches.

When we make that our focus and our way of thinking, we'll do great things and be great people for God. Whether you're Swedish or Norwegian, English or Irish, African or Middle Eastern, Native

American or Latin, your earthly ethnic background is nothing in comparison to the new family heritage you were "reborn" into when your heavenly Father wrote your name down in His Book of Life.

You are a member of a great family—the family of God! There are no limits to your future and potential.

6

Love Yourself
and Your Neighbor

One day, in the basement of the second-phase house of the Washington Drug Rehabilitation Center, I sat in prayer. As a twenty-year-old Bible school student preparing for a full-time ministry—as well as a young man dealing with other problems, some of which involved my former addictions—I talked to God and asked Him to help me deal with everything that was going on in my life.

As I talked to God about the problems I'd been facing, I clearly heard Him speak to me. He told me very directly, "Your biggest problem is that you love your neighbor as yourself."

And I thought, *Huh?*

My mind immediately went to the passage in the Gospel of Matthew, where Jesus fielded a question by a Pharisee about what was the greatest of all the commandments. Jesus told him, " 'Love the Lord your God with all your heart and with all your soul and with all your mind.' This is the first and greatest commandment. And the second is like it: 'Love your neighbor as yourself'" (Matthew 22:37–39, NIV). Jesus finished this all-important teaching by saying, "All the Law and the Prophets hang on these two commandments" (v. 40).

I felt perplexed and taken aback at what I was sure was a personal message from the Lord. All I could do in that moment of confusion was continue praying. "So-o-o-o…I love my neighbor as myself…uh, isn't that what I'm *supposed* to do?" I asked.

"Yes, it is," came the answer, "but the problem is, you don't love yourself as you should. In fact, you hate yourself, and you treat everyone around you the way you treat yourself. Because you feel so bad about yourself, you feel bad about others, and it shows in the way you treat them."

I knew right away that if I was ever going to be the kind of minister I wanted to be—and, more importantly, the kind of person God wanted me to be—then I was going to have to first learn what it meant to love myself. When I learned to love myself I would also learn to love those around me.

WHY LOVE OURSELVES?

We Christians don't have much of a problem with the commandment of loving God with all our hearts, souls, and minds. Most of us also understand that we're to love our neighbors. These two commandments are inseparable, and that means that if we love God with all our hearts, souls, and minds, an outgrowth of that love for God will be love for our neighbors.

We run into problems, however, with the idea of loving ourselves. We seem to catch what Jesus said about loving our neighbors, while skipping over the "ourselves" part. To many Christians, the idea of loving yourself runs counter to everything they've been taught about humility, about the command to "deny themselves."

This may shock some people—especially those from "religious" backgrounds—but if we want to love our neighbors the way God wants us to love them, we must learn to love ourselves. If we are going to give to others as God has given to us, sacrificially and without concern for ourselves, we have to love who we are and what we are in Christ.

I know that when I consider my life blessed, I want to see others blessed—in fact, I want to bless them myself. When I feel good and happy, I want other people around me to feel the same way. In a way, I want them to share in the same positive feelings I have.

On the other hand, when I am not feeling good and happy—when I feel miserable, sad, or depressed—it's very difficult for me to do anything to make others feel blessed. In fact, it's a great temptation to try to drag others into my own pit of misery and self-pity.

I believe that many of the ills and problems we have in our society—crime, the breakdown of the family, illegitimacy, hatred, bigotry, isolation, loneliness, and anything else you care to add to the list—stem from the fact that we don't love ourselves. Those of us who have learned how to love ourselves in a healthy, biblical way, however, tend to be the happiest, most joyful people, the kinds of men and women who regularly bless others around them.

This is otherwise known as "loving your neighbors."

Think of the tragic story of a boy who grows up without his father. A man leaves his son when the boy is little, and the child is raised by a poor, frustrated, and angry mother. That is a boy who statistics say will grow up to be a criminal, an abuser, and an absentee father himself. Such a little boy isn't going to grow up to love himself, or anyone else. He'll feel worthless, unloved, unlovable, and angry at the world around him and at everyone who crosses his path.

Now think of the boy who grows up in a home with a father and a mother who regularly give him positive reinforcement. "God loves you," they tell him, "and your mommy and daddy love you, too." This is a boy who will grow up to be a mighty man of valor, a man who loves those around him, including his own wife and children, and including everyone God puts in his sphere of influence.

The problem with most people—and that includes a lot of Bible-believing Christians—is that we not only don't love ourselves, we despise and even hate ourselves. And we do so because we somehow equate "denying ourselves" with self-loathing. We're told to put God's will ahead of our own will, and the needs of others ahead of our own needs, but we pervert this to mean our will shouldn't matter at all and our needs shouldn't be met. And when we believe this, we see ourselves as less than what God created us and saved us to be.

People can't trust other people because they can't trust themselves. If they see themselves as being untrustworthy, they'll look at others with the same suspicion. And people can't put their confidence in others if they feel no confidence in themselves. If they see themselves as people who are likely to let others down, they will see everyone else in that way also. Likewise, we can't love other people when we loathe ourselves. If we can't see ourselves as lovable, then how are we going to see anyone else as lovable?

The apostle John wrote of the importance of loving one another: "If someone says, 'I love God,' and hates his brother, he is a liar; for he who does not love his brother whom he has seen, how can he love God whom he has not seen?" (1 John 4:20). John is telling us here that loving God and loving others go hand in hand.

But just as loving God and loving others go hand in hand, so does loving *ourselves* and loving others. John also tells us, "We love Him because He first loved us" (1 John 4:19). One comes before the other. Do you see the progression? God loved us first, so that we could love

Him in return. And because He loves us and we love Him, we are then able to love ourselves in a biblical, godly way. Giving and receiving love is the way of Christianity. We cannot receive love if we feel guilty, unworthy, or angry at ourselves. If we can't receive love we can't give it. Loving yourself and loving your neighbor are part of the giving and receiving of God's loving lifestyle. And finally, because we're able to love ourselves, we are able to love others.

Only when you can see yourself through God's eyes will you be able to remove the limitations that keep you from being fully blessed. Only when you learn to love yourself because He has declared you lovable will you be able to become a blessing to those around you.

Here's the bottom line: you can't love your neighbor unless you love yourself. So you have to begin to believe that you are who God says you are. You have to begin to think that what God thinks about you is true. And when you learn to think that way and feel that way, then you begin to live God's will for your life and so start traveling your road to destiny.

Unfortunately, most of us base how we feel about ourselves on what others—our parents, our teachers, our government, our religious leaders, and so forth—say about us and do for us, and not on what God says about us and has done for us. And while some of those people may have had your very best at heart, none of them loved you perfectly the way God does.

We have to break those chains of unloving thoughts and words that others may have exposed us to. We need to say to ourselves, "Anything that anyone said to me that doesn't agree with what God says about how much He loves me, is wrong." Even when someone said something meant to motivate you to something better, but said it in a less than loving way, then it was absolutely wrong. Don't receive words that will add to inferiority in your life.

I grew up with a fairly positive, loving family. I have known people, however, who grew up in homes where abuse—verbal and physical alike—was the order of the day. Some grew up being told that they were worthless, stupid, and without value, and it has been a struggle for them to find a way to love themselves so that they can love their neighbors.

I'm happy to tell you that you can overcome such negative thoughts and replace them with something much more positive, true, and honoring to God. And that happens as you see in God's Word the indisputable, written proof that God Himself has declared you both lovable and worthy. You are His child, you are loved, and you are valuable.

A GOD WHO LOVES YOU— AND *LIKES* YOU, TOO!

I recently saw a bumper sticker that read: "Jesus is coming back soon, and boy is He mad!" Obviously, such an attempt at humor came from the minds of people who don't know the real Jesus and who don't understand the true nature of God. They have no way of understanding that God is a God of love, that He is excited about people, that He wants to do good in our lives, and that He thinks thoughts of peace toward us, not thoughts of evil.

When you were growing up, did you live in the security and confidence of a home where you felt liked and appreciated? I'm not talking about "loved," because most parents love their children, even if they don't know how to demonstrate it properly. Did your parents seem to feel good about you and want you to be around them?

This may be a generalization, but I don't believe that most people, if they were to honestly answer those questions, really believed that their parents liked them just the way they were. Most of us probably felt our parents were angry at us or disapproved of us because of our "strange" clothes or hairstyle, or because of the music we listened to or the way we talked. Some of us may have even believed that we were a source of embarrassment for them. Many were raised feeling they could never do enough or were never good enough.

I wish it weren't so, but those kinds of negative feelings often linger well into adulthood—and they can be a problem in how we see our relationship with God and how He feels about us. I believe that is why so many people have such a difficult time loving themselves and resting in the love of God. They are just *sure* that He is angry at them, disappointed in them, and ready to give up on them. In short, they just can't believe that God loves them—let alone likes them. And if someone can't be sure that their *Creator* loves and likes them, there is no way they can love or like themselves.

One reason the Jewish religious establishment of Jesus' time didn't like Him, and even hated Him, is that He loved, liked, and often hung out with what they considered the "wrong" people. Jesus didn't spend a lot of His time with those who thought of themselves as righteous or "good enough" for God. He spent His time with tax collectors, prostitutes, swindlers, and others who desperately needed Him.

Jesus spent time with people from the wrong side of the tracks for the same reason we spend our time with people we know: He liked them. He had dinner with them, talked to them, healed them, blessed them, forgave them, and prospered them.

Jesus' consistent love for those whom the religious leaders found unlovable angered those in power because they weren't as interested in genuinely loving God as they were in carrying on their man-made traditions. They weren't as interested in seeing people come to true repentance and a real relationship with God as they were in making sure people followed, to the letter, their self-imposed rules.

So Jesus had some uncomfortable things to say to them, such as, "Woe to you Pharisees, because you give God a tenth of your mint, rue and all other kinds of garden herbs, but you neglect justice and the love of God" (Luke 11:42, NIV), and, "I know you. I know that you do not have the love of God in your hearts" (John 5:42, NIV).

Unlike these religious leaders, Jesus loved God with His whole heart and therefore cared deeply about people. He loved them as individuals—and He *liked* them, too. What a great contrast between religion and the Person of the true and living God! While religion is concerned primarily with appearances, God is concerned above all else with the heart. While religion seems angry and often rejects people, God is a God of love who accepts us as we are and changes us from the inside out into something beautiful, holy, and good.

That is the picture of God we should stay focused on as we learn to love ourselves.

When people feel bad about themselves—when they don't love themselves—they tend to engage in bad behavior. People who don't love themselves tend to abuse drugs and alcohol; they tend to engage in frequent sexual immorality; and they tend to gravitate toward unhealthy or sinful things. I believe that is partly why poverty tends

Adversity—loss, illness, financial hardship—pulls you down, but God pulls you up. Which one will you respond to? When I was going through treatment, chemotherapy brought depression and a sense of despair, but I fought it every day. I tried to keep my mind and emotions focused on the goodness of God and the good things of my family, friends, and church. It's hard to get healed in your body when you're depressed and down. Stay up and look up to God to get you through.

to hang on people who don't love themselves as they should. They stay poor because subconsciously they believe that "bad people" deserve to remain poor.

I wonder: do you believe you can love yourself, and at the same time mistreat or put yourself down, or see yourself as less than what God created you to be? Can you love yourself and allow yourself to stay in poverty? I would say you can no more love yourself and do those things than you can truly care about your physical health and at the same time abuse your body by smoking cigarettes, drinking too much, or eating too much.

I'm not trying create new problems for anyone here! I'm just trying to bring awareness and shed some light on some common misperceptions of God so that you can be set free to enjoy His love. He really does love you—even likes you—just because He does. In fact, that was the very reason He gave to the Israelites so many centuries ago for setting His love on them: "The LORD did not set his affection on you and choose you because you were more numerous than other peoples, for you were the fewest of all peoples. But it was because the LORD loved you" (Deuteronomy 7:7–8a, NIV).

We've been taught a lot of things about God over the centuries, but one thing we've not heard much about is how our God actually likes us and enjoys us. As God Himself said, speaking through the prophet, "The LORD your God in your midst, / The Mighty One, will save; / He will rejoice over you with gladness, / He will quiet *you* with His love, / He will rejoice over you with singing" (Zephaniah 3:17).

The Lord spoke even more profound words of personal love, concern, and goodwill toward us through His prophet Jeremiah, who recorded these words:

For I know the thoughts that I think toward you, says the LORD, thoughts of peace and not of evil, to give you a future and a hope. Then you will call upon Me and go and pray to Me, and I will listen to you. And you will seek Me and find *Me,* when you search for Me with all your heart. I will be found by you, says the LORD. (Jeremiah 29:11–14)

There are a few Scripture passages that I encourage everyone to read, to underline, to circle, to highlight—whatever it takes to set off these key passages in their Bibles. This is one of them. This well-known and often-quoted passage is a blessing to anyone at any time, but it is especially comforting and assuring to those who have a difficult time loving themselves because they have a difficult time believing or perceiving the love of their Creator.

There's something you need to know if you're going to learn to love yourself in the proper way, and it's this: God isn't sitting up in heaven, angry and thinking thoughts of vengeance toward you. He's thinking good thoughts. He's thinking of how He can bless you and give you a hopeful and bright future. And He's thinking not just about how much He loves you, but about how much He likes you and enjoys you as a unique creation.

Stop thinking of God as an impossible-to-please Creator who stomps around heaven slamming doors! He's not an angry dictator who won't speak to you because you aren't "good enough." He is not, never has been, and never will be frustrated, bitter, or resentful at you. He thinks higher thoughts of you, thoughts of love, thoughts of mercy, and thoughts of grace and peace. As soon as you can grasp the reality of who God is and how He feels about you *right now,* you'll be able to love yourself as He would have you do. And when that happens, you will find yourself conquering yet another leg on your race to your own personal destiny.

PART 2

Following Your Course

7

The Heart: Birthplace of Your Future

I was born in Spanaway, Washington, a little suburb of Tacoma. Spanaway is a nice little community. There was no industry there, no real businesses to speak of, just the Little Park Café.

I lived on one street in Spanaway for almost twenty years. When I was twelve, we moved a little farther back into the woods on the same street because my folks thought it was getting too busy up front.

For nineteen years, I called Spanaway "home." I went to the same school and had the same friends all the way from kindergarten through high school.

A big deal to us was driving to town. One time I thought we might drive to downtown Seattle. My mom said, "Nah, I wouldn't do that. There are a lot of one-way streets down there." I remember listening to neighbors who actually did brave the drive to downtown Seattle tell us about their experience afterward: "Whew! There is a *lot* of traffic. And the one-way streets will confuse you. You'll be lost before you know it! You'll never get out of there."

That was our world.

One time, my brother and I got on an airplane to visit our grandparents in Arizona. That was a *big* deal. It was the first time we'd ever done *anything* like that. We just grew up in our little town and never ventured far from it. Our world was very small.

When I was nineteen years old, I got arrested several times—if I remember right, five times over the course of a few months, all for drug-related issues: DUI, car wrecks, a couple of drug busts.

So I landed on probation. A little while later I was loaded again, and when my parents saw it, they called my probation officer.

"You know what?" he said to me. "If the judge knows you're still using drugs, he's going to sentence you to prison. He'll revoke the deferred sentences and you'll be doing prison time. You have one option—you can go to a live-in drug program."

So I went to Washington Drug Rehabilitation Center in Seattle; I was supposed to be there a minimum of two years, but I thought, *I'm a smart kid; I'll get out of here in a couple of months.*

But after the first two weeks, I turned in all the drugs I'd smuggled in. It kind of shocked me that I was giving up drugs. And I started to realize, *Sheesh, maybe there really is a different way of life that I've never known.*

Looking back, I think that I considered drugs my way of finding something meaningful. I was searching for something I could feel, something I could control, something I could do with my life. When I looked at my parents, just trying to make a living and working at jobs that weren't that great, I thought, *There has to be something else.* They weren't happy and eventually their unhappiness led them to get a divorce. I don't blame them for that; I think they were doing the best they knew how. But as I looked at their lives—a typical American experience in many ways, a couple who went to work and just tried to find a way to exist—I thought, *I don't want that. I'd rather stay loaded than become that.* I was scared of getting stuck in that kind of life, so drugs became my way out. I saw drugs as something that could make me different, a way to be rich. Today I know that's just stupid, but as a teenaged kid living in an unhappy home, it made a certain amount of sense to me.

In this drug program I met Julius Young, who at that time was sixty years old. He was a black man from Washington, D.C., who had done twenty-four years in prison as a heroin addict and gangster. He had even killed people. But when he was fifty-something, God got hold of his life and he got saved. At age fifty-eight he got out of prison and started the Washington Drug Rehabilitation Center. He had prayed to God, "If you'll get me out, I'll spend the rest of my life helping kids who are on the road I was on."

I was one of those kids.

A CHANGE OF DIRECTION

Julius may have been a short little welterweight boxer, but man, was he *big* on the inside! And he accepted me and loved me. He called me "Big Red."

So I found myself living in a house with him and twenty other drug addicts, half of whom were trying to escape, have sex, get high, and who knows what else. But as I watched Julius, I decided, *I want this!*

Within a few weeks, I said, "I'm going for it." I doubted that I could do it, but I gave up the drugs and dedicated my life to Christ. I didn't know anything about it at the time, since we never went to church as kids, and I wasn't sure I could make it, but I wanted to try.

God used Julius's example to show me another way. What I saw in him was a real relationship with God that was very spiritual but not at all religious. He had something real and something tangible, and I wanted that "something" for myself.

So at age nineteen, God opened up a whole new way of thinking to me. And although I had no way of knowing it at the time, immediately my world began to radically expand.

After I'd been with Julius for over a year, going to church with him regularly and watching the reality of his faith outside of church, I said, "Julius, I think I want to be in ministry. I think I want to go to Bible school."

"Okay," he said. "You need to go to Philadelphia Church Bible School." That was the school our church sponsored, so that's where I went.

My first day of Bible school—I was twenty years old at the time—I met Wendy. I saw her and thought, *She's cool.* Julius had tried to get me to date a few of the girls in the drug program, but I had insisted, "Not the drug addicts! Let's go find me a good Christian girl." And then I met Wendy.

At school I was totally committed. I was *so* serious that I probably offended a lot of people who didn't appreciate my stern attitude and hyperdisciplined approach. But I came by those characteristics honestly. The Washington Drug Center was a lot like the military—extremely disciplined, extremely stringent, and very structured. Julius based most of his treatment on reality attack therapy from William Glasser—a very bottom-line, make a decision, get in touch with reality kind of approach. This wasn't a touchy-feely, get in touch with your emotions, and feel the love kind of program. It was a no-nonsense approach and it worked for me. That's what God used to get me saved, keep me straight, and prevent me from becoming just another casualty of life.

Despite my abrasive approach, every year of Bible school I was elected president of my class—and every year I got mad about it. I'd get up and give these fiery speeches: "I'm a drug addict! I live in a drug program! You kids have been raised in church—and you want *me* to be president of your class? What's the matter with you?" I was just ticked off, and as I said, probably very offensive.

Wendy had a very different background from mine. Her dad was a Methodist pastor and every two to four years the denomination would move her family to another city. She never left the Northwest, but she was used to making new friends, living in different homes, having new people in her life, and serving in new churches. But like me, she, too, was very serious about her faith and deeply dedicated to her Lord. We both often said, "We're not playing games here. We're serving God."

In high school I always did the bare minimum, just enough to scrape by and get my diploma. But after four years of Bible school, I graduated in December of 1979 as valedictorian.

I learned how to preach the same way I learned most of the nuts and bolts of ministry: by getting my hands dirty. Before graduating from Bible school, I started a daily fifteen-minute radio program. I also began visiting prisons and local nursing homes every week.

Wendy and I had gotten married in my second year of school and we started Christian Faith Center two weeks after graduating. I was twenty-four and she was twenty-two. We began with about thirty people who had attended a Monday night Bible study; most of them were residents or graduates of Washington Drug Center. We had nothing. We rented a little school gymnasium and called it Christian Faith Center. We scrounged together some speakers, made a little PA system of them, and proclaimed, "We're having church!"

It didn't seem like much at the time, but we had a vision. Within a few months, we were in Los Angeles, being ordained by Dr. Fred

Price, pastor of Crenshaw Christian Center. Soon we were teaching all over America, making many new friends and experiencing new opportunities.

Within a couple years I was preaching in South Africa. Soon after that I was speaking at the largest church in the world, Yoido Christian Center in Seoul, Korea, for Dr. David Yonggi Cho. We traveled around Europe, then down to Australia and around Asia.

Within five short years after I got saved at age nineteen, the whole world opened up to me. God had enlarged my borders in a way I never could have imagined—but one thing had to happen first. My heart had to change and enlarge. I had to expand my heart from Spanaway to the world.

And would you like to know the truth? If you want to run to your own destiny, something very similar will have to happen for you.

LET YOUR HEART OPEN UP

Some men and women leave their hometown but continue to carry it in their heart. They don't let their heart open up. They confine it to one corner of God's creation and say, "That's it. That's all. That's everything."

But if you don't open your heart your world will stay small. You'll stay in Spanaway when God may be calling you to some new adventure in Tahiti or Uzbekistan or Madagascar or who knows where.

Get God and His Word in your heart! Let His Word plant a sense of calling and purpose deep in the innermost part of your being. Start running your race to destiny instead of just hanging around, talking about what you *can't* do. Let your heart open up.

Remember this: *The heart is the birthplace of your future.*

If your heart has no ambitions beyond Spanaway, then Spanaway is where you'll stay. And that's not a bad thing, so long as God has called you there and that's where your destiny lies. But if He has bigger things in mind for you, things that enlarge your borders and challenge your mind and increase your faith and improve your effectiveness for Him, then why on earth would you want to stay confined to one little corner of the globe? Why fence yourself into a tiny lot if God offers you the world?

If you want a future bigger than what you're experiencing now, then you have to enlarge your heart. You really have no other choice.

Sadly, some of us are just happy to be on the team. I remember exactly what that felt like, because until my junior year, I was the smallest kid in high school. In my senior year I grew to be the tallest kid in school, but by then I was addicted to drugs and smoked out on pot and wasn't much good for sports.

But as the smallest kid in school, I was picked last, every time. In fact, I wouldn't have been picked at all if they didn't *have* to pick me. So when my name got called (finally), I was just glad to be on the team.

When I played basketball and baseball, I felt happy just to get a jersey. I never thought about being a starter or playing on a winning team or becoming a champion. I just didn't think that way.

Are you anything like that? Are you just happy to be on the team?

What if God has something *more* in mind for you?

I believe God says to you, "I don't want you to feel happy just to be on the team. You are not limited by your physical abilities. You are not limited by how you were raised or how you were born. You're *My* child now. You are *My* son now, or *My* daughter. I don't want you to be happy just because you've made the team. I want you to *run to win*."

The apostle Paul certainly had this winning attitude. That is why he wrote,

Do you not know that in a race all the runners run, but only one gets the prize? Run in such a way as to get the prize.

Everyone who competes in the games goes into strict training. They do it to get a crown that will not last; but we do it to get a crown that will last forever. Therefore I do not run like a man running aimlessly; I do not fight like a man beating the air. No, I beat my body and make it my slave. (1 Corinthians 9:24–27, NIV)

Paul ran to win and he encouraged others to do the same. And really, it's the only way to live the Christian life. Live out your days with the attitude "I'm going to live for destiny! I'm going to live with purpose. I'm not here just to pay the bills. I'm not here just surviving. I'm not barely hanging on until Jesus comes. No, I'm going to live my life to fulfill my destiny. I'm going to run to win!"

If that sounds like a path you want to pursue, then there's only one thing to do: enlarge your heart.

How do you do that? How do you develop the heart of a winner? In its basic form, the heart of a winner is a heart after God.

In Matthew 12:35, Jesus told us, "A good man out of the good treasure of his heart brings forth good things, and an evil man out of the evil treasure brings forth evil things." We could say it like this: the successful man, out of the success of his heart, brings forth a successful life; but the failing man, out of the failure of his heart, brings forth failure in his life.

In Proverbs 4:23 God tells us to "guard your heart" (NIV). Defend it. Keep it. Protect it with all diligence. Why? Because "out of it, spring the issues of life." The word "issue" literally means "borders." The Hebrew dictionary explains the word "issues" as having to do with borders, as in property borders. God is showing us that we define how large or how small our lives are by the attitude of our hearts. If we see opportunity, possibility, and the greatness of God in our lives we will live larger, fulfilled lives. If we see limitations, excuses, and negativity we live small, prejudiced, and unfilled lives. Out of your heart come the borders of your life. If you want to live a large life, you have to get it in your heart. If you are going to stay in that little tiny life, then just keep your heart small. Your heart establishes the borders of your life.

Some Christians are like Aladdin's genie. Remember the genie? He was mighty powerful; he could grant wishes, but he lived in that tiny lamp. You have the power of God within you, but when you accept the devil's lies of barely getting by and just going through the motions, you become like the genie: great big mighty power, tiny little living space. You fit your life into the bottle instead of bringing forth a large, successful life out of your heart.

Right now, your heart is birthing your future. For some, that thought is exciting. They can hardly wait! But for others, it's boring. Their heart is stuck in Spanaway and its stunted condition is defining their tomorrows.

If you want to increase your finances, you have to change your heart.

If you want more relationships and more friendships, you have to change your heart.

If you want more opportunities to partner with God in expanding His kingdom, then you have to change your heart, for out of your heart come the borders of your life.

Both the enemy and this world are trying to contaminate your heart. And when your heart gets contaminated, you lose heart. The enemy gets in there, bringing discouragement, despair, anger, and bitterness. And when you lose heart, you walk off the field a loser.

THE DANGER OF LOSING HEART

We all know people who, when they were young, had visions and dreams. They were going to start a company and become million-aires. They were going to overcome their family limitations and do great things. But then the divorce came, the disease appeared, the accident happened. And now they are working a job they don't like, doing things they don't enjoy. They have given up on their dreams. Why?

Because they didn't have the heart to get through all the "stuff" that happens in life. They lost heart and just couldn't keep on with all they said they wanted to do.

I was watching a college football game recently when the announcer said, "That team has lost its heart." He didn't mean that someone's physical heart was lying out on the fifty-yard line. He meant that it had lost its drive, its competitive spirit. It had lost its vision to win this football game. Maybe they were running out of time, or maybe the score was too big of an obstacle. But for whatever reason, the players had lost their heart. You could see it in how they walked; you could see it in how they ran plays. You could see it in how they executed life at that moment.

People with heart will win. People who have lost heart usually lose.

The heart of a winner is also a heart of hope. And what is hope? Hope is an optimistic vision of the future. Hope sees good stuff ahead.

Hebrews 11:1 tells us that "faith is the substance of things hoped for." That means you have to have hope for your faith to work.

Hope sees the new home. Hope sees a happy family. Hope sees a prosperous company. Hope sees that new career. Hope sees a college diploma.

What hope sees, faith goes to work to get. It brings substance to what you hope for. Faith says, "I believe I have the money, so I am going to college." Faith says, "I believe I'm healed, so I'm getting up out of bed and going to work." Faith is the substance of what you hope for. Faith and hope working together will make things happen in your life. However, if you have no hope, then you have nothing for your faith to produce.

Some people say, "Well, I'm just not that kind of person. I'm just not an optimistic person. I wasn't born that way; it's not my personality." But Scripture insists that hope is not a personality, but a choice.

No doubt some personalities really are naturally optimistic and others are more naturally pessimistic. But suppose I am given to hitting people in the nose; that doesn't mean I have the right to do it. I need to change, to renew my mind and stop hitting people in the nose. In the same way, if you are given to pessimism, that doesn't give you an excuse to stay that way. You need to renew your funky self and get some hope in your life.

A basic aspect of Christianity is hope. Hope sparks a positive outlook, a bright view of the future. As a Christian, I have hope. I have hope that eternally I'll be with God and enjoy a heavenly existence, but I also hope that while I'm still on here on earth, God is helping me. You always see this positive attitude around "real" Christians. They're upbeat, happy, and joyful.

I think Jesus was a very happy guy. I don't think he was long-faced and depressed. Certainly He carried an awareness of the sins and the evils of the world—more than any of us could ever understand—and yet He continually expressed His hope in God and in His destiny. That's why He could say things like, "Peace I leave with you" (John 14:27) and "I have told you this so that my joy may be in you and that your joy may be complete" (John 15:11, NIV). Jesus was a man of unquenchable hope.

God calls us to be optimistic, positive, encouraged, and enthusiastic about life. After all, we believe that the One who died for us also rose again—and that's an optimistic, positive faith. We believe that we, too, will rise from the dead. We believe that God never leaves us. We believe Satan is already defeated. We believe we can charge hell with a squirt gun—*and win!*

That is the way God meant Christians to be—positive, optimistic, enthusiastic. That's the kind of people we are.

But if you adopt a pessimistic, "nothing ever works, I'll never get out of debt, I can't overcome, I can't win for losing" kind of attitude, then you will reject hope and you'll miss God's will for your life.

Why do you hear so many Christians find it so hard to overcome negative habits or addictions? Why do some true believers—who love the Lord, believe the Bible, and come to church regularly—nonetheless struggle with pornography, alcoholism, drug abuse, or other persistent problems? Why is life so hard for them?

I think it's because they have no hope.

First John 3:3 declares, "everyone who has this hope in Him purifies himself, just as He is pure." We struggle with negative things whenever we lose hope. When you lose hope, the sense of giving up and giving in takes over. Hopelessness produces helplessness.

Why do you keep going back to the pot? Why do you need that joint to find some peace? You have no hope. So you go to the joint to suck down some peace and try to medicate your pain. Or you have to do a line of coke—why? Because you don't have hope. If you had hope, you'd be enthusiastic about life. You'd be encouraged and empowered. But when you lose hope, you want a line of coke to pick you up a little.

Hopelessness produces helplessness, and so you go to the drugs, you go to the alcohol, you go to the pornography, you go to the sex, you go to the addiction, because of how awful you feel. Lift the level of hope and you won't want the drugs anymore; you won't want the drink; you won't want the world. "He that has this hope purifies himself."

The next time you start thinking about going back to the world and returning to your old ways, go back to your hope instead. Say, "All right, come on, God. Come on, Holy Spirit—I want to focus on my hope, my dream, on an optimistic view."

Romans 8:24–26 helps you to do just that. Paul writes,

> For we were saved in this hope, but hope that is seen is not hope; for why does one still hope for what he sees? But if we hope for what we do not see, we eagerly wait for *it* with perseverance.
>
> Likewise the Spirit also helps in our weaknesses.

You can't see how it's going to happen. You can't see how you're *ever* going to get out of debt. You can't see how your marriage could ever get better. You can't see how to overcome this health problem. You just can't see how it's going to work out.

But hope enables you to believe what you can't see. If you could see it, then you wouldn't need hope! So when you can't see it, just smile and say, "All right, my hope is working. I can't see it, but I'm hoping. I'm believing. God is going to make a way."

Hope keeps you dreaming. It keeps you looking for answers. It keeps you trying. It gives you a reason to exercise, talk to your spouse, discipline your kids, and go to church. You can do all the things God asks you to do *only* because you have hope in your heart for improvement, for a positive future. A heart of hope is a heart set on winning.

PREPARE FOR YOUR VICTORY

Have you ever heard of an actor or musician who practiced accepting his first Oscar or her first Grammy long before he or she ever actually won? What they are doing is getting ready for their future and preparing for their victory.

When an actor or a musician stands in front of the mirror at home and says, "I'd like to thank my agent and all the little people that made this happen," that person is putting himself or herself in that place of success.

Why can't you do something similar? You can sit and think how bad your life is and how hard it is and how negative your circumstances are, or you can practice your testimony of success and healing and victory, and start moving toward it.

Of course, as you work toward any goal, you're going to face challenges. If you set the goal of earning a college degree, then you are going to face homework, studies, schedules, and so forth. Some people balk at this and so don't go for it. They stay stuck in Spanaway.

If you have a goal of building a company, then you have to deal with budgets, business plans, and competitive and corporate politics. All good goals will create challenges, problems, and pains for you— but that is part of reaching the goal and accomplishing the dream.

With every good goal and desire comes an obstacle. Running a marathon, climbing a mountain, building a house, or starting a church are all exciting goals. But they will bring many challenges and problems.

Your heart decides how you will deal with the challenges of life. Your heart decides how you will face them. Your heart decides whether you win or lose, whether you overcome or give up, whether you go on and get better or fall down and get bitter.

The only real question is: *What do you choose?*

8

What's Your Vision?

According to Proverbs 29:18, "Where there is no vision, the people perish" (KJV). When you lack a vision for your life—when you see no specific purpose in your existence—life has a way of passing you by. Vision is crucial to your life, because you come into this world believing that God wants you to become someone and something great and your vision is your roadmap to greatness.

It is God's will that you live with a vision and a purpose. That's how all of us are born. We see things, desire things, and dream for them. It's natural for every child to want to be someone great or successful or powerful. It's built-in that kids have a vision of a great future. That's normal in the heart of every human being; we are made in the image and likeness of God.

But what happens once we grow up and go through some challenges? Many of us tend to lose our vision. We give up on the dream. We drop out of the race. That's why God says to us, "Hey, guys— when you lose your vision, you perish."

What does He mean?

When you don't have a positive vision for your life, you lose the discipline it takes to live life successfully. The New King James Version translates Proverbs 29:18 like this: "Where *there is* no revelation, the people cast off restraint." When you lose sight of the destiny God has in mind for you, you let discipline fall away—and with it goes a successful life.

RACING TAKES DISCIPLINE

When I was young, I raced bicycles. I always had more discipline to train when I had a race coming up. I consistently put more miles on the bike in preparation for a race than I did in the off-season when I had no specific reason to train. I would still work in the off-season, but nothing like when the race season hit and I had to get ready for that 150-mile road race. At that point I got *very* disciplined! I trained hard and prepared well.

Recently, I decided to climb Mount Rainier for the third time. As I was getting ready for the climb, my trainer told me I had to climb stairs; then he put forty pounds on my back. That took *work*! I needed discipline to train to climb Mount Rainier. It took discipline to run those stairs, carry that pack, work those legs lifts, and do everything necessary to get ready. But I did it. Why? Because I love discipline so much? No way! I did it because I had a vision, and with vision comes discipline and motivation to do whatever it takes.

If you have a vision to get your college degree, you get up early, get to your class, and do your homework. But students with no vision don't go to class. Where there is no vision, you hear excuses like, "The dog ate my homework."

When you lose your vision, you start maintaining and nothing more. You do just enough to get by. You kind of hang in there, punch the clock, and go through the routine, but discipline has evaporated from your life. Why? Because there is no vision.

Maybe you shy away from discipline because someone in your past tried to force discipline on you, either through religious legalism or by demanding and commanding. That never works. You can't make a person be disciplined just for the sake of being disciplined. Oh, a lot of people try it: "You are *going* to get up, young man, and you are *going* to clean your room. And if you don't, I'm going to spank you!" But in the long run, it never works.

If, however, there is a vision...if you have a purpose...well, *now* we're talking! Where there is no vision, people sleep in. Where there is great vision, people get excited, motivated, and moving. Where there is great vision, there's great discipline. Vision motivates you, it pulls you, and it keeps you going.

God wants you to live on vision. God wants you to look at each day and say, "Here's where I'm going and here's what I'm doing—and here's what I believe God has for me," and then get so excited about it that your vision gets you up early and keeps you up late. Your vision is your future, your future starts now.

"That sounds great," someone says, "but I don't have a vision for my life, and I don't know how to get one. I want to live in God's will, but how am I supposed to know what God has in mind for me? How am I supposed to discover my destiny? I'm just an average person. How am I supposed to figure all of that out?"

Do you want to know the truth? Actually, it's not hard to know God's will and have a vision of what God has for your destiny. I really mean that! It's not hard at all. And do you know why? It's because your relationship with God is a real relationship. Here's what I mean.

My relationship with God is just as real as my relationship with my kids. I don't know what my kids are doing every minute of every day, but I do know they are in my will. You say, "Pastor, how can you know they are in your will, even when you don't know what they're doing?" I know it because they love their parents and I know they desire to be Christian young people. So they're doing homework, getting through school, and growing up as godly young men and women. They're in my will.

Do I want to control every minute of every day in their lives? No, I have no desire to get into all that. They're kids! They need to figure it out on their own. Sure, they need to get discipline. They also need to make mistakes. They need to fall down and learn how to get up—but they're in my will the whole time.

Some people think God is going to control every little part of their life and tell them every little thing. Sorry, but He isn't.

"Does the Lord want me to live in this house or live in that house?" I'm pretty sure He doesn't much care; *He's* not going to live there, after all. He lives in you, so live where you want to live.

"Does the Lord want me to buy this car or that car?" Buy the one you like; *He's* not going to be driving it. When He wants to go somewhere, He takes a fiery chariot, not your car.

Please understand this: God does not—and doesn't *want* to—control every little thing in your life. He certainly is concerned about every detail of your life, but He has no interest in making all of your decisions for you. You are His child, not His puppet.

One of my sons went off to college thousands of miles away, in Australia. He went there to study and intern in a church. I didn't know everything he was doing while he was there. (I did wonder if he would meet some cute Australian girl—but so long as she wanted to live in Seattle, that was cool with me.) Still, he was in my will, so long as he was seeking God and growing up as a Christian man, studying and moving forward in his life. I didn't need to know, nor did I *want* to know, every little thing.

Did he make some mistakes? Probably. Did he have some bad days? Probably. Did I want that to happen? No, but it didn't mean his life had moved outside of my will.

Your heavenly Father's will is a lot like that. Unless you're rebelling against His Word and rejecting something He told you to do, you're in His will. So relax! Just say, "Where are we going now, Father?" Get rid of the doubts and the questions that will keep you from your future and from your destiny.

When you carry an attitude of "I'm not sure I am doing the job God wants me to do. I don't know if I am where God wants me to be," you are greatly hindered in moving toward your destiny. If you live that way for five years, ten years, twenty years, or thirty years— always questioning, wondering, doubting, and never being sure— where do you suppose you'll end up? What do you suppose happens?

You won't live as a person of destiny, that's for sure.

This kind of continual hand-wringing and second-guessing does not always have to be at the forefront of your mind. Even when such doubt exists as little question marks in the back of your mind, it can trip you up. Do you realize that a permanently unsure subconscious can keep you from reaching your destiny?

That's why our gracious God says to you and me, "Get in My will, trust it—and then go for it!" Follow His Word and His Spirit, trust what's in your heart, and your steps will be ordered by the Lord (Psalm 37:23).

GOD-GIVEN DESIRES

Have you ever pondered Psalm 37:3, where God says, "Trust in the LORD, and do good"? He means that you are to place your trust in God by keeping your walk with Him strong, and then do good.

Don't openly rebel. Don't violate His Word. Don't go off in areas you know aren't right. Stay close. "Feed on His faithfulness"—and then watch what happens:

"Delight yourself also in the LORD, / And He shall give you the desires of your heart" (v. 4).

But I already hear the questions! "But how do I know if it's God's will?" Well, are you close to God? Do you love God? Are you delighted to be a Christian? Are you doing good things? If so, then what do *you* want to do? God said He'd give you the desires of your heart. So, what do you want to do? Whatever it is, get going—no more doubts, no more questions, no more wondering. Get moving toward the desire of your heart. God gives you desires that are unique to you because it's His will for you.

What's so confusing about that? It's something you already want to do and, quite probably, something you're already good at. So stop questioning God and yourself. Delight yourself in the Lord, stay excited in your relationship with Him, remain close to God, feed on His faithfulness—and He will give you the desires of your heart.

You want to start that new business? Then do it.

You want to get your degree? Then go get it.

You want to be a teacher? So become one.

What do *you* want to do? So long as you're questioning and wondering, you'll never take the next step. Get to the place where you say, "I'm doing good. I'm living for the Lord. I'm not rebelling. So here's God's will for me. This is what God has for me." And never question it again.

And it gets even better! Look what God says next:

Commit your way to the LORD,
    Trust also in Him,

And He shall bring *it* to pass.

He shall bring forth your righteousness as the light,

And your justice as the noonday.

Rest in the LORD.

(vv. 5–7a)

You don't have to stress about this. You don't have to wonder, doubt, or continually feel unsure about it. Rest in the Lord. Wait patiently. And even when you see something out of the corner of your eye that really bothers you, "Do not fret because of him who prospers in his way" (v. 7).

That's God's Word to us—but what often happens with us? We lose our vision. We see our neighbor win the big job and make the big dollars, and we get envious. We get into negative emotions when other people get blessed.

Anytime you find yourself upset or maybe jealous when someone else prospers, it's because you're planning *not* to prosper yourself. Now this may not be a conscious thought. Maybe you harbor this belief unconsciously because you got the idea from your family, the way you were brought up; somehow you got it in your mind that *you* will not prosper. When you get upset because someone else gets blessed, it's because you're *not* blessed and you don't see yourself being blessed in that same way. This stems from not understanding the personality of God and His Word.

When I see others getting blessed, I get excited, because that means I can get blessed, too. When someone else starts to grow a great church, I say, "Great! Go for it, dude! That just proves that I can do it, too! So go ahead, blaze the trail, make the way—and show me how to do it."

Get excited when other people are blessed! And then follow their example. There's no need for competition; there's plenty of room for you.

"Cease from anger, and forsake wrath; / Do not fret—*it* only *causes* harm," verse 8 says. All the negative emotions—anger, fear, worry, unforgiveness, and frustration—cause harm, nothing else.

And anyway, if we believe what God says, there is no reason to fret. Why not? "The steps of a *good* man [and a good woman] are ordered by the LORD, / And He delights in his way. / Though he fall, he shall not be utterly cast down; / For the LORD upholds *him with* His hand. / I have been young, and [someday I'll be] old; / Yet I have not seen the righteous forsaken, / Nor his descendants begging bread. / *He is* ever merciful, and lends; / And His descendants *are* blessed" (vv. 23–26).

So don't worry about it. Don't stress about it. Don't fret about it. Trust in the Lord and God will order your steps. He'll show you the way. He'll open the door. He has promised!

I'm not bragging, but I *know* I am exactly where God wants me to be. How can I be so sure? Well, I'm not rebelling. I'm not in sin. I'm not doing something He doesn't want me to do, so I know He's ordered my steps to this point. That doesn't mean I haven't fallen a few times! Just because you are in God's will doesn't mean every day is going to be rosy. Every once in a while, you are going to get a thorn. You will fall once in a while; you will stumble or have a bad day. You may get fired, go through a challenge, and have to pick yourself up—you still live in a world with an adversary, but God will hold you through the fall.

He's merciful; He doesn't expect you to be perfect. He doesn't expect you to get everything right. He doesn't expect you to be brilliant. He knows what He's dealing with; He knows who you are, that you are but dust (Psalm 103:14). And He promises to lend you a hand. He'll provide for you. He'll help make a way.

Stop questioning God's will. Stop worrying. When you're right with God, He gives you the desires of your heart.

You know what that means, then, don't you? It's time for you to make up your mind and *go for it!* No doubts, no questions, no holding back, no negative emotions.

Run to your destiny!

OWN THE VISION

Some of us have a problem in running to our destiny because we take the visions of others, add them to our own, and try to do both in our lifetime. The problem is, such a strategy distracts and dilutes your energy from your true vision and ultimately brings dissatisfaction to your life.

For instance, let's say you have a friend who is involved with a council at school. That friend says to you, "Hey, you really need to come and be a part of our council to help the kids." Although it's really not something you are interested in, you want to be nice. So you schedule a meeting and invest time, energy, and money into it because it is a good cause.

Then somebody else comes along and says, "We're having a special meeting to help with the homeless." That's a good thing, too; so now you have another meeting on your calendar that takes attention and a little money.

Pretty soon all of these little commitments to someone else's vision add up. They take a lot of your time and energy and money. You find your life energy being sapped by the visions and dreams of other people—and your own dream starts fading away. Your vision is still there, but you feel spent because you poured out a little here and a little there for others' dreams, leaving you nothing for your own. And while you are being nice, you sacrifice your destiny.

This is a tough one for me, because as pastor, I'm supposed to be nice to *everybody*. It's my job. Every week I get letters, sometimes many, that say, "The Lord said that you should do this." "The Lord told us that you should come to our conference." "The Lord said that you should speak to our church." "The Lord said that you should help this mission...support this ministry...give money to this cause." And you know what? It would be impossible to do it all.

Once I was reading over some letters, and if I had done everything that the Lord supposedly told others I should do, I would have to have been on three continents at one time. According to the letters, the Lord said I should speak in Europe; the Lord said I should be in Asia; and the Lord said I should speak in Africa—all at the same time in the same week.

The Lord seemed to be very confused! Maybe the Lord should have checked His calendar; or better yet, He should have checked *my* calendar before He volunteered me.

I'm making light of this, but you understand my point: if you start doing what everybody else thinks you should do, you'll soon be weighted down. And it's *so* easy to start trying to please people instead of pleasing the Lord! It reminds me of the story in 1 Kings 13:7–31, about the prophet who prophesied doom against Israel. God told him not to stop on his way back home, but another prophet sought him out and said, basically, "God changed his mind. Now he wants you to come home with me." So the first prophet did so and was mauled and killed by a lion. I guess the moral of the story is, you'd better listen to what God tells you, and not depend on what other people say God is telling you!

Proverbs 29:25 says, "The fear of man brings a snare." The fear of what Dad might think, or what Mom might think, or what our pastor might think, can sometimes keep us from the fear of God. The real question is always: What does *God* think?

You have to be careful not to pick up other people's visions. You can start living for their dream and not for what God has put on your own heart. One man said to me years ago, "At a certain point in your life, your success will be dictated not by what you say *yes* to, but by what you have the strength to say *no* to."

Lay aside the guilt that so easily besets you and make sure that you are not spending too much time, energy, and money on fulfilling others' visions and dreams, only to find that you have nothing left for your own.

CAPTURE YOUR VISION

In running your race to destiny with God, I think the Old Testament prophet Habakkuk can give you some help. He wrote in chapter 2 of his little book, "Then the LORD answered me and said: / 'Write the vision / And make *it* plain on tablets, / That he may run who reads it' " (v. 2).

Have *you* ever written down your vision of God's will for your future? I think you should. In fact, I want to challenge you to write down your vision, right now. Get it on paper. Sometimes, just seeing something in black and white makes it real. The vision is no longer just in your heart, or just in your head. Seeing the words, holding the paper they are written on, somehow gives substance to your vision. And when your vision is real you'll become committed to it.

So clearly write down your vision. In your own words, plainly describe your destiny. God told Habakkuk, "make it plain," which literally means "simple and concise." You do the same thing.

And don't think you need to write a book! Some people bring me pages and pages. That's not a vision; that's a novel. The vision is a simple statement: "Here's where I'm going with my family, my career, my health. Here's where I'm going financially." Write down the vision in simple, clear, concise language.

And then run with it!

But some people may resist writing down their vision for their life. Why? I think two things may account for this.

One is that they don't know what they want, or what they believe God's will is for their future. They've never settled it. They've never developed a clear picture, never gotten focused, never gotten on course. They stay unfocused and uncommitted to life.

The other reason people don't write down their vision is that they're afraid they're wrong, afraid they're going to make a mistake. They say things like, "Maybe this isn't God's will, after all. What if I'm wrong?"

I have only one thing to say to that: write down the vision to the best of your ability, anyway. Commit your way unto the Lord. And if it's not exactly what God wants, then He has promised to direct your steps. He'll bring you to where He wants you to go. He does not promise to direct you while you remain sitting, but He does guarantee that He'll direct your steps. So get moving and commit your way to Him!

Most of us make commitments every day. When you go to lunch, you commit to pay by giving the waiter your charge card. You commit to pay by signing the receipt. You might tell a salesman you want to buy a car, but until you sign the loan papers, you are not really committed. If you don't sign it, you don't get the car. Why not? Because if you don't write it down, you're not committed.

Or maybe you fall in love and you want to get married. You *really* love her. I hear it all the time: "I really love her, Pastor."

"Uh-huh."

"The Lord brought that girl to me. The Lord gave me that girl right there, Pastor."

"All right, then. I want you to sign this marriage certificate. I want you to write it down."

"Hey—I ain't ready for marriage!"

"Then don't talk to me about love. You don't know the difference between love and lust. When you're ready to commit and sign this marriage certificate, then come on back to me. Because if you won't write it down, then you're not committed."

"Well, what is that marriage certificate? It's just a piece of paper."

"I know, it is nothing; so go ahead and sign it."

"That piece of paper does not mean anything in my heart."

"I know; so go ahead and sign it, then."

See? He doesn't want to write it down, because he knows it *does* mean something.

Recognize that there's a big difference between what you're committed to and what you're just checking out. Commit your way unto the Lord! Paul counsels us to keep our eyes on the prize (1 Corinthians 9:24, 27; Philippians 3:14)—but how can you keep it before your eyes, if you never write it down?

LIVE FOR DESTINY

Toward the very end of his life, the apostle Paul wrote, "I have fought the good fight, I have finished the race, I have kept the faith" (2 Timothy 4:7).

How do you suppose he knew that his fight had ended? How do you think he knew that he had finished his race? There's really only one way that I can think of: he knew what his destiny was, and he knew he had fulfilled it. God had enabled him to pursue his vision and complete his dream, and therefore he knew that "the time of my departure is at hand" (v. 6). Paul died a satisfied man because he had a clear vision for his life, which he pursued with everything he had. He finished his race strong because he lived as a man of destiny.

You can finish your own race, too. You can run your race and fulfill God's will, plan, and purpose for your life. You can do it because you, too, are a person of destiny. And by now, you should know exactly what that destiny is.

9

Believing You Can…
Because God Says You Can

It promised to be a glorious day. The people of Israel stood on the very brink of greatness, on the cusp of personally claiming what God had promised them so many years before. This was the very same group of people that, not long before, God had miraculously delivered out of bondage and slavery to the Egyptians.

Encamped in the wilderness in a place called Kadesh-Barnea, not far from the land God had promised them, the people awaited the reports of twelve spies Moses had sent to explore Canaan.

The people could almost *see* the land from where they were, and I can't help but think that the people were breathless with anticipation as they awaited the spies' reports. *Is the land as beautiful as we've heard?* They must have wondered. *What are the fruit and vegetables like? Is the land good for farming? What obstacles might we have to face when it comes time to take the land?*

The twelve spies, one from each tribe of Israel, went into Canaan and explored it thoroughly. They walked on the ground, touched its natural features, tasted its fruit, looked at its beauty, and observed what kind of people lived there. Oh, what a beautiful place it was! Truly, it was a place flowing with milk and honey, a place of abundance—just as God had promised. The spies even brought back some samples of the produce that grew there, including a bunch of sweet, delicious grapes so big it took two strong men to carry it.

"We went to the land where you sent us," the spies told Moses, Aaron, and the rest upon their return. "It truly flows with milk and honey, and this *is* its fruit" (Numbers 13:27). At that point in the story, it looked as if these people, the ones who had personally suffered under the oppression and slavery of the Egyptians, would move quickly into this land of plenty, where they would live out the rest of their lives in the security of their very own God-given homeland.

But there was a problem. One really *big* problem.

You would think that the people of Israel would be confidently chomping at the bit to go in and take the land. After all, just a few days before, God had nearly destroyed the nation of Egypt on their behalf with ten miraculous plagues, plagues that were obviously from the hand of the Lord. They had seen the whole Egyptian army buried in the depths of the Red Sea—the same Red Sea they had walked through on dry ground. And they had enjoyed the miraculous provision of God in meeting their needs for food and water.

After all that, you would think they'd be feeling bold, strong, excited, and completely ready to go *right now* and possess what God had already given them.

But that wasn't the case. Instead of focusing on the part of the report that told them the land was everything God had said it would be, they focused on the reports from ten of the spies who told them of the giants who lived there:

> "Nevertheless the people who dwell in the land *are* strong; the cities *are* fortified *and* very large; moreover we saw the descendants of Anak there. The Amalekites dwell in the land of the South; the Hittites, the Jebusites, and the Amorites dwell in the mountains; and the Canaanites dwell by the sea and along the banks of the Jordan." (Numbers 13:28–29)

Nevertheless…So began that tragic transition from a bright focus on the beauty and blessing of Canaan to a much darker focus on the giants. The ten spies with the negative reports couldn't argue the fact that Canaan was a wonderful place that would make a perfect home for their people. They just couldn't get over the giants. The Egyptians were one thing—but these *giants*? Well, that was a whole different ball game.

In the midst of their flood of negative words, one solitary voice spoke a very different message that day. The Bible tells us, "Then Caleb quieted the people before Moses, and said, 'Let us go up at once and take possession, for we are well able to overcome it'" (Numbers 13:30). Yet while Caleb spoke with absolute certainty about the nation's ability to take possession of that which God had already given them, the other spies continued to speak words of fear, doubt, and inferiority:

> But the men who had gone up with him said, "We are not able to go up against the people, for they *are* stronger than we." And they gave the children of Israel a bad report of the land which they had spied out, saying, "The land through which we have gone as spies *is* a land that devours its inhabitants, and all the people whom we saw in it

are men of *great* stature. There we saw the giants (the descendants of Anak came from the giants); and we were like grasshoppers in our own sight, and so we were in their sight." (Numbers 13:31–33)

Notice that nowhere in this passage did any of those spies say, "God can't do it!" or "The giants are bigger than our God!" or "There's no way we can win because God is too small!" They never once said, "The Lord could never overcome this people!" No! They didn't voice even a single doubt about God. In fact, they never mentioned God at all. They remained stubbornly focused on their doubts about themselves: "*We* are not able..."

No one could argue with the facts contained in the reports of the spies. The men in Canaan were indeed strong. But were they stronger than Egypt, the kingdom God had just defeated for them? These people were indeed big. But were they bigger than the Lord, the One who had delivered them from what was at the time the greatest nation in the world? Bigger than the God who directly and explicitly promised them that they would take this land?

Why didn't they remember the power of God?

One of the many great spiritual lessons of this passage is that when we forget about what God has told us, promised us, said about us, and already done for us, we begin to doubt ourselves. And when we begin to doubt ourselves, we forget about God.

Those spies stood on the brink of greatness that day at Kadesh-Barnea. They stood at the very edge of leading their people in claiming what God had centuries before promised them. But they allowed their doubts to consume them. Their reservations about what *they* could do reduced them to speaking only about the size and strength of the giants who stood in their way. "Yes, again and again they tempted God, / And limited the Holy One of Israel. / They did not remember His power" (Psalm 78:41–42a).

When I started treatment for hep C, the doctors said there was only a very small chance I would clear the virus. I was on a new experimental program and they were very pessimistic about my progress. But I held on to their words that there was a chance—however small—of recovery, and believed that as long as there was a possibility of me getting better, I was going to be okay.

Even though the odds against me were overwhelming, I didn't focus on the negative. I tightly grasped on to faith and hope and confidently believed I would overcome this disease.

CHOOSING VICTORY

Now the people of Israel had a choice to make, a choice between being "we are well able" thinkers or "we are grasshoppers" thinkers. Tragically for them, they chose the "grasshopper" route, the route that appeared easiest and safest. They chose the route straight back to the bondage and slavery of Egypt:

And all the children of Israel complained against Moses and Aaron, and the whole congregation said to them, "If only we had died in the land of Egypt! Or if only we had died in this wilderness! Why has the LORD brought us to this land to fall by the sword, that our wives and children should become victims? Would it not be better for us to return to Egypt?" So they said to one another, "Let us select a leader and return to Egypt." (Numbers 14:2–4)

What we believe about ourselves will go a long way toward deciding what we'll do with our lives. The vast majority of the Israelites encamped at Kadesh-Barnea believed what the ten faithless, cowardly spies said about them—namely, that they looked like grasshoppers, mere insects, to the giants in the land.

So what happened to those who chose to listen to the advice of those ten faithless spies? They died in that wilderness, never having seen or lived in the Promised Land. They never ran in its fields, never bathed in its streams, never took a bracing lungful of air in a land they should have called their own. As for the spies, ten of them died on the spot, while only two—Caleb and Joshua, the only two who continued to believe in God and in themselves—eventually entered Canaan and possessed it.

This story presents to us an all-important question: Do we want to be victors, those who claim everything God has promised them, those who believe they can just because God says so? Or do we want to be grasshoppers? Do we want to claim our destiny, or give it up?

There's an old proverb about what those who say they can and those who say they can't have in common: they're *both* right!

I don't want this to come off sounding like New Age teaching or a worldly motivational talk that is 100 percent focused on "you," but there is a direct relationship between how successfully and effectively you run your race to the destiny God has put before you and how you perceive your ability to run that race.

To take that even a step further, how you see yourself is exactly the same way others will see you. What is in your mind and in your heart will find a way to show itself outwardly—and people will perceive you by what you exude. In general, it's true that:

- If you want others to believe you can, then *you* have to believe you can.

- If you want others to respect you, then you have to respect *yourself.*

- If you want others to treat you with dignity, then you have to see *yourself* as worthy of dignity.

- If you don't like being "walked on" by others, then you have to have the attitude that you won't be a doormat.

- If you believe that all things are possible for you, then others will say, "I think this guy can do anything he decides to do."

But this truth, like so many others, cuts both ways. If you see yourself as unworthy and unable to fulfill what God has for you, then others will see you that same way. If you see yourself as unable to get the job you want, as unable to have the happy marriage you want, as unable to minister to a certain person or group, as unable to do anything God has put in front of you, then I have news for you: you'll end up being right! That's because your mind—which is set in a "can't-do" mode rather than "can-do" mode—will set you up for failure (see chapter 4).

That is exactly what happened in the hearts and minds, and eventually the lives, of those ten spies who felt so frightened by the spectacle of the giants. "We were like grasshoppers in our own sight," they wailed, "and so we were in their sight." So how could *they* help lead the people into the Promised Land?

I don't know a lot about entomology (the study of insects), but I can tell you that grasshoppers don't live especially interesting lives. They hatch from the eggs their mothers laid, grow into adulthood at an inch or two long, hop around and eat grass all day, mate, and then die. All of that in the space of a month or two! Grasshoppers don't inherit anything; they don't receive promises from anyone; they never claim or receive anything; and, so far as I know, no grasshopper has ever conquered anything (we'll talk about the locusts described by the prophet Joel some other time).

It shouldn't be too difficult, then, to decide that you don't want to be a grasshopper! Or be controlled by a grasshopper mentality.

In the case of the Israelites, it was the grasshopper mentality that caused them to rebel against the Lord. They had heard the promises of God concerning the Promised Land, had seen the miracles He had performed in taking them out of Egypt and through the wilderness, and had heard the reports of the spies who described the land flowing with milk and honey. And yet, somehow, that wasn't a big enough vision for them. They let grasshopper thinking take over their thoughts, and before you know it, they hopped their way right out of the Promised Land.

A DIFFERENT KIND OF SPIRIT

While ten of the spies who spied out Canaan and those who listened to them had spirits of fear, insecurity, and inferiority, Caleb and Joshua had a very different kind of spirit. They had the kind of faith and the kind of inner assurance and confidence that gave them the courage to want to take on what the majority feared to do.

That is what moved Joshua to say to the people of Israel, "The land we passed through to spy out *is* an exceedingly good land. If the LORD delights in us, then He will bring us into this land and give it to us, 'a land which flows with milk and honey.' Only do not rebel against the LORD, nor fear the people of the land, for they *are* our bread; their protection has departed from them, and the LORD *is* with us. Do not fear them" (Numbers 14:7–9). Did you notice how Joshua's message contrasted with that of the ten cowardly spies?

The ten said, "They are stronger than we are." Joshua said, "Their protection has departed from them."

The ten said, "The land…devours its inhabitants." Joshua called it a "land which flows with milk and honey."

The ten said, "The giants are too big." Joshua said, "They are our bread."

The ten said, "We were like grasshoppers." Joshua said, "The LORD is with us."

So many of us have been taught to be low-minded, to think that it's godly and spiritual to deny our ability to do the things God calls us to do. We have learned to think of ourselves as inferior, and somehow to imagine that such a thought pleases God. But by engaging in low-minded, small-minded, and falsely humble patterns of thinking, you don't help God and you don't prove that you are spiritual. Quite the contrary! You're actually hindering or denying the work of the Lord in your life.

This sad episode in the history of Israel demonstrates that when we limit ourselves mentally or verbally, we actually limit what God can do through us. And far from being godly when we put ourselves down, we are disobeying the command of almighty God.

God was angry at the inferiority talk of the Israelites and at the disobedience that their inferiority talk caused. He was angry that they couldn't believe they could possess the Promised Land, which He Himself had given them—so angry, in fact, that He was about to strike them dead right on the spot. God spared the people only because of the earnest intercession of Moses. But that didn't mean they would avoid serious consequences for their unbelief:

Then the LORD said [to Moses]: "I have pardoned, according to your word; but truly, as I live, all the earth shall be filled with the glory of the LORD—because all these men who have seen My glory and the signs which I did in Egypt and in the wilderness, and have put Me to the test now these ten times, and have not heeded My voice, they certainly shall not see the land of which I swore to their fathers, nor shall any of those who rejected Me see it. (Numbers 14:20–23)

That false humility, that religious inferiority, that feeling down and feeling bad about yourself, isn't spiritual at all. In fact, it's from the world and from the devil, and it's meant to keep you from enjoying all that God has for you and being all He wants you to be. It doesn't help you to reach your destiny; it keeps you from it.

Caleb and Joshua had that "we can" spirit, and because of that, they would one day physically possess and dwell in the Promised Land. The other spies, as well as every person in Israel aged twenty years and older, saw themselves as mere grasshoppers who couldn't do anything against those Canaanite giants. As a result, they all died in the wilderness, without claiming for themselves what God had promised His chosen people.

All of us have a crucial question to answer: What is it going to be for us? Are we going to believe that we can claim the promises of God and do the things He's called us to do? Will we possess what He's already given us? Or will we see ourselves as weak and unable and end up dying in our own personal wilderness?

God wants you to claim and possess the promised land He's already given you. He wants you to claim your particular promised land as you believe what He says about you. He calls you to believe in yourself and in the abilities He's given you, so that you can move forward and run your race toward your destiny.

HE SAYS SO, THAT'S WHY

Earlier I talked about the importance of believing that you are who God says you are, for it's absolutely necessary to think that way if you are to walk in and receive His promises. Now, I want to take that a step further and declare the importance of believing you are completely able to do the things God has called you to do, simply because He says so.

When you believe you are who God says you are, and then believe you can do the things He calls you to do, simply because He says you can, then you'll put yourself in position to possess your very own promised land, whatever that may be. But you will never—*never*—be able to claim your own promised land, prosper, conquer the giants in front of you, or claim your destiny, if you see yourself as weak and unable.

You must be able to say from your heart, as did Caleb, "I am well able to possess it!" When you do that, nothing—even that which seems extremely unlikely or even impossible—will be too difficult for you.

I've befriended a group of bikers who live nearby. It's fun to share the Christian life with them. They're basically good guys and I actually like them, but they're also Heathens with a capital *H*. I'm talking about foul-language-using, beer-drinking, cigarette-smoking, wild-partying, fornicating guys—guys who, like so many in our world, need Jesus.

It's funny to me to think about how I've been able to build a relationship with these guys. I've never compromised what I believe with them in any way, but at the same time, I've never condemned them or tried to tell them how to live. I don't try to come across as Mr. Holy and Righteous, and I don't take with me an attitude that I'm better than they are because I'm a believer. I don't tell them not to cuss, not to smoke, not to chase women. I just try to be their friend, try to do a little "lifting" for them, and always speak words of encouragement when that's what's needed.

To me, this is my own personal mission field. As a pastor, I don't get to hang out with a lot of dyed-in-the-wool sinners. I'm usually in church with my congregation. And to be honest, I see it as a privilege to hang out with these guys, and I even enjoy being with them.

In more worldly terms, you might say these guys all have a long way to go—but I'm believing God for their salvation! In fact, I can see that, little by little, they're coming around to receiving the message of God's love.

But I know this little personal mission field of mine never would have opened up to me if I'd approached these men with an attitude, even an unspoken one, that I was a scared and weak religious nut. I haven't tried to be something I'm not with these guys, and I haven't tried to hide some insecurity or lack of confidence as I approach them. I haven't had to. All I've done is approach them with a God-given confidence. Not only has God given me the opportunity to reach out to these guys, but He's also declared me *able* to do it.

It doesn't matter where you are or who you're around, if you carry yourself as the man of God or the woman of God you are—even if people don't like you or the message you carry—in a very real way they'll respect you. But what happens if you don't respect yourself and you see yourself as a grasshopper? Well, then, they'll see you that way, too.

Do you want to overcome your giants? Do you want to be thought of and seen as a conqueror and not a grasshopper? Do you want to be able to do the things God calls you to do? If so, then you have to believe in your heart and mind that you are able, simply because God says you are.

The devil wants you to remain stuck in your "I can't" thinking. He wants you to believe that you're not good enough, not blessed enough, not called enough, not talented enough, not smart enough, not connected enough, not wise enough, and not capable enough to run the race to your God-ordained destiny. In short, he wants you to doubt yourself and consequently doubt your God.

That's why it's so vitally important that you endorse and adopt God's own thinking about your ability to do what's He's set before you. When you feel those thoughts of negativity and inferiority creeping in, capture them and overrule them with the eternal truth of the written Word of God.

When your mind tells you, "I can't do it!" capture that thought and replace it with, "I can do all things through Christ who strengthens me" (Philippians 4:13).

When your mind tells you, "There are too many obstacles and too many giants!" capture that thought and replace it with, "I have overcome the world" (John 16:33).

When your mind tells you, "I'm just not good enough!" capture that thought and replace it with, "He who is in you is greater than he who is in the world" (1 John 4:4).

When your mind tells you, "Maybe I should turn back!" capture that thought and replace it with "He who has begun a good work in you will complete *it* until the day of Jesus Christ" (Philippians 1:6).

God wants you to overcome the giants that stand in the way of you claiming and possessing what He's already given you. There is simply no place in your life as a believer for thinking that you can't overcome whatever comes your way, or that you can't possess what is already yours.

God has declared you able and made you worthy. He has empowered you with everything you need to possess all that He has for you. He has allowed you to say with absolute certainty, "I can do *all* things through Christ who strengthens me."

So where is there any place in your life for arguing with God and telling him, "I can't"?

It's up to you to cast down every argument and make the Word of God paramount in your thinking. When you do that, you'll be able to honestly say to yourself, "I can, and I will, because God says so!"

10

Overcoming Your Fears, Limitations, and Insecurities

When you want to do something great in life, it often helps to look to some of the great heroes of the Bible for inspiration and example. Many of us do that because we believe they had something special going on, something maybe we don't have today. It's also hard for us to believe that they had any of the same weaknesses that hold us back today.

But if you read carefully and look deeply into the lives of most of the biblical heroes, you will see that many of them came from or lived in worse conditions than most of us. You will also see that many of them faced the very same fears and inadequacies that dog us today. Some of them didn't think they were good enough to do the things God called them to do. Others seemed deathly afraid of the obstacles they would have to overcome on their way to finishing the race God had laid out for them.

Yet today we call them "heroes"! Why? They earned their honored place in the pages of Scripture because they received what God said about them, believed what He said more than they believed their negative circumstances (no matter how daunting and frightening they may have seemed), and so rose to greatness in the kingdom of God.

Many of these men and women still stand as wonderful examples of what it means to run the race toward destiny—and one in particular stands out as an encouraging example of overcoming some very real inadequacies.

BELIEVE THE PROMISE

On the surface, it looks as though Moses should never have had to worry about limitations and insecurities. Though his mother gave him up early, sending him down a river in a basket for his own protection, he was quickly found and adopted by the daughter of Pharaoh and raised to be an important figure in Egyptian society.

But as Moses began to look around, he started to see that something wasn't quite right in his adopted nation—or in his own life. He began to question his own place in the world, as well as the place of the Jewish slaves who were such a common sight around Egypt. One day, he saw an injustice he just couldn't stand: an Egyptian physically abusing one of the Hebrews, his very own kin. In anger, Moses killed the Egyptian and hid the body. When his crime eventually came to light, he fled to a barren place called Midian, where he married a shepherd's daughter and took up sheepherding himself.

At first, it looked as though Moses had fallen as far as he could. He went from being a well-educated adopted son of the king's daughter, probably living in the courts of Pharaoh, training to be a great military leader, to being a simple shepherd. It appeared that Moses had completely blown his chance for greatness.

But God had another plan, one that would make Moses one of the greatest leaders in history.

One day as Moses tended his father-in-law's sheep, he heard God Himself speak to him from a burning bush. God gave him a simple message (which I'm paraphrasing): "I have seen and heard what is going on with My people in Egypt. I know how badly they have been treated, and now the time has come for me to bring them out of captivity and take them to the Promised Land" (see Exodus 3:7–8).

Then came the payoff, the call of God on the life of Moses. God expected him to become something more than he could ever have imagined. "Come now, therefore, and I will send you to Pharaoh that you may bring My people, the children of Israel, out of Egypt" (Exodus 3:10).

Now, if Moses had been that mythical biblical hero with whom we started out this chapter, he no doubt would have jumped at this call. We can imagine him responding in any number of expected ways:

"Glory to God! It's about *time* I get out of this desert!"

"Hallelujah! I knew there was a greater purpose for my life!"

"*Finally*, I can enter into my destiny. Thank You, Lord! But what took You so long?"

Moses apparently didn't read the script, however. After he had spent many long years in the desert, tending sheep, how did he *actually* respond when God showed up and told him that he'd been chosen to lead the Israelites out of captivity and slavery? "Who *am* I that I should go to Pharaoh, and that I should bring the children of Israel out of Egypt?" he demanded (Exodus 3:11).

Moses immediately responded to God's call with a declaration of his own inadequacy. When he said, "Who am I?" he was really telling God, "Lord, I'm a nobody. I don't have the qualifications to lead millions of people out of slavery. And another thing, Lord: these people are slaves, and Pharaoh isn't going to just smile and tell all of us to be on our way. Lord, you've got the wrong guy."

But God was ready for Moses's objections. "I will certainly be with you," the Lord told Moses. "And this *shall be* a sign to you that I have sent you: When you have brought the people out of Egypt, you shall serve God on this mountain" (v. 12).

Still, Moses wasn't ready to say yes just yet. Instead of offering his joyful obedience, he offered God another objection: "Indeed, when I come to the children of Israel and say to them, 'The God of your fathers has sent me to you,' and they say to me, 'What is His name?' what shall I say to them?"

Again, God was ready:

And God said to Moses, "I AM WHO I AM." And He said, "Thus you shall say to the children of Israel, 'I AM has sent me to you.'" Moreover God said to Moses, "Thus you shall say to the children of Israel: 'The LORD God of your fathers, the God of Abraham, the God of Isaac, and the God of Jacob, has sent me to you. This *is* My name forever, and this *is* My memorial to all generations.'" (Exodus 3:14–15)

God then gave Moses some very specific instructions about what he was to do next. He even assured him, "I will stretch out My hand and strike Egypt with all My wonders which I will do in its midst; and after that he will let you go. And I will give this people favor in the sight of the Egyptians; and it shall be, when you go, that you shall not go empty-handed" (Exodus 3:20–21).

Still, Moses didn't feel eager to go. He didn't feel convinced. He thought God still had the wrong man. And so despite God's assurance to Moses that He would be with him; despite telling him who was sending him and what to say when people asked for His name;

despite giving him specific instructions for success; and despite telling him very specifically how this amazing story would end, God still didn't have Moses's full confidence. In fact, God got only another question: "But suppose they will not believe me or listen to my voice; suppose they say, 'The LORD has not appeared to you'" (Exodus 4:1).

Now it was time for God to pull out the heavy artillery. He'd already given Moses His word. He'd already given him verbal instructions, promises, and assurances. Now it was time for a display of power.

"What's that in your hand?" God asked Moses.

"A rod," answered Moses.

"Cast it on the ground," God commanded. And when Moses obeyed, the rod turned into a snake, right before his very eyes. He must have jumped! I would have.

"Reach out your hand and take it by the tail," God said. I'm sure Moses must have looked at God a little sideways, but he did as he was told anyway—and immediately the snake became a rod again.

And if that weren't enough, God then told Moses to put his hand in his cloak. The old shepherd did so, and when Moses pulled his hand out again, it was "white as snow." Next God told Moses to put his hand back inside the cloak, and then pull it out once more. When he did so, his hand was restored.

> "Then it will be," [God told Moses] "if they do not believe you, nor heed the message of the first sign, that they may believe the message of the latter sign. And it shall be, if they do not believe even these two signs, or listen to your voice, that you shall take water from the river and pour *it* on the dry *land*. The water which you take from the river will become blood on the dry *land*." (Exodus 4:8–9)

Wow! I can't even imagine what Moses thought of all this. Certainly he had never seen anything like it. So now he'd be more than ready to take up God's challenge, right?

You'd expect him to be fired up and ready to go. After all, he'd heard the voice of God Himself. He'd been given assurances that he wouldn't be alone. He'd seen miracles, signs, and wonders.

But none of that was enough for him, because all he could focus on was his own shortcomings. "O my Lord," he objected, "I *am* not eloquent, neither before nor since You have spoken to Your servant; but I *am* slow of speech and slow of tongue" (Exodus 4:10).

Do you see what happened in this scene? Moses was arguing with God, giving reason after reason, excuse after excuse, why he couldn't do what God was telling him to do. Like the Hebrew spies he would get so angry with in a few months, Moses never once said, "God, You can't do it." But over and over he insisted, "God, *I* can't do it."

Moses had the same problem that so many people throughout history have had: he didn't believe he was qualified to do what God asked him to do. He was so focused on his own limitations that he failed to remember that God will *never* call someone to do something He doesn't also equip that person to do.

But as long as you don't think you can, God can't work in your life. You can't stop God from fulfilling His will but you can stop Him from working in your life.

The way God has set things up, we are His hands, His feet, and His voice. And if we don't go when He tells us to, He doesn't go. Until we as God's people stop focusing on our shortcomings—no matter how real they may be—and begin believing that we are who and what God says we are, He can't and won't do what He wants to do with us on this earth.

Moses didn't believe he could do what God had called him to do.

Why not? He had completely focused on what he saw as his own limitations. Finally, he got down to saying what he'd probably been thinking all along: "O Lord, please send someone else to do it" (Exodus 4:13, NIV).

Up to this point in the story, God had been very patient in telling Moses what was about to happen, and even showing him the kind of power he would be representing as he led the people of Israel out of Egypt. But something about Moses's request to send someone else really angered the Lord and Moses came dangerously close to missing out on God's call to greatness. The Bible says in verses 14–16,

> So the anger of the LORD was kindled against Moses, and He said: "Is not Aaron the Levite your brother? I know that he can speak well. And look, he is also coming out to meet you. When he sees you, he will be glad in his heart. Now you shall speak to him and put the words in his mouth. And I will be with your mouth and with his mouth, and I will teach you what you shall do. So he shall be your spokesman to the people. And he himself shall be as a mouth for you, and you shall be to him as God.

God allowed Moses's brother Aaron to become Moses's "mouthpiece." (However, it was Aaron who led the people to build a golden calf and sin against God.) With all that settled, Moses finally headed back to Egypt to begin the process of bringing his people out of captivity.

And you know what? Somewhere between God's first conversation with Moses and Moses's first confrontation with Pharaoh, a huge change occurred inside Moses in how he saw himself and in how he carried himself. At some point Moses made the decision to trust in God and the power of His might, rather than trusting what he saw in himself. No longer did he seem concerned about his own limitations, which at first seemed so crippling to him. After spending some time alone with God, his mind began to be renewed and he started to focus not on his own shortcomings, but on who God was and who God said *he* was. Anyone who does great things needs to come to that same point. When Moses made that transformation he was on his way to becoming the greatest leader Israel would ever know.

A short while after his experience at the burning bush, Moses spoke plagues upon a stubborn Egypt, stretched out his staff and parted the Red Sea—and with the same rod that God turned into a snake, he directed the waters that drowned an entire Egyptian army. Today we still remember and celebrate the life of Moses because he became a man of such strength and boldness that he led two million people out of Egypt and to the very edge of the Promised Land.

Not bad for a man who could at first do nothing but talk about his own limitations! Not bad for a man who, only a short while before, could do nothing but talk about how he was a nobody, how no one would listen to him, and how he couldn't even speak without stuttering!

Moses's rise to greatness provides all of us with a key lesson. He shows us that we can be transformed as he was, when we begin to believe what God says about us—when what He says is more important and more trustworthy than what we know about ourselves and our own weaknesses and limitations—then there is no limit to what He will help you, use you, and call you to do in your lifetime. We can transform ourselves like Moses was transformed by renewing our minds to God's way of thinking instead of relying on our own, often negative, thinking about ourselves. To accomplish this, we study God's Word and, according to Romans 12:2, "not be conformed to this world, but be transformed by the renewing of your mind, that you may prove what *is* that good and acceptable and perfect will of God."

I've often sat and daydreamed about what would happen if I had a whole congregation of people who believed in themselves the way Moses learned to. I have wondered, *What would happen if every family in our church hosted and led a home meeting? What would happen if every person reached out and touched the lives of everybody on his or her block and everybody in his or her office? What would happen if every person in our congregation went out and laid hands on and prayed for sick people? What would happen if every person brought in tithes and offerings every week?*

But why stop there? Why not dream about what would happen if we had churches all over our nation and all over the world that were full of people who believed in themselves, who saw beyond their own limitations, and who focused on who and what God says they are? I think Jesus would come back very quickly, because in no time at all the gospel would get preached in every nation (see Matthew 24:14).

You see, when we believe we really are who and what God says we are, we begin to fulfill the ministries He has called us to—and make no mistake, He calls each of us who knows Him to some sort of ministry. Instead of thinking, *I'd better not say anything about Jesus because I don't speak very well, so they might not like me*, we begin thinking, *Who cares if people don't like me? What about heaven? What about eternity? Isn't that more important than whether they like me or not?*

In other words, we start thinking the thoughts of God!

GOD WON'T GIVE UP ON YOU

Moses started out doubting himself, questioning his own abilities, and worrying about his personal deficiencies. He didn't want the position God had called him to and had no interest in answering the call. But after some encouragement, instruction, and direction from the mouth of God Himself, Moses said what he should have said in the first place: "Yes, Lord!"

God didn't give up on Moses, although Moses himself gave the Lord every reason to do so. The Lord didn't say, "All right, I'm tired of talking. If you don't want to do it, then feel free to die in the desert as a nobody. I'll go find someone else to do it. By the way, I hope you enjoy tending those scrawny sheep." No, God kept working with this man, talking him through his own insecurities and easing his mind about his own limitations until He brought him to a place where he could believe in himself and believe that he could do the things God had called him to do.

Don't think for a minute that this is merely a story about Moses! God didn't put the story about Moses in the Bible merely so we could salute another hero. God recounts His experience with Moses in order to tell us, "If I could use a man like Moses, and if I worked through him and in him, despite his limitations—then certainly I can work through *you*."

God has a special race and a special destiny for each of us. He has one for me and He has one for you. And He's not about to give up on you just because you have a few little limitations—whether they are real or ones you just think you have. No, He's going to work through those limitations and He's going to assure you and reassure you that He'll be with you through every challenge, every pothole, and every trial you face on your way to your personal destiny.

God will never let you get away from His calling or that sense of purpose. He'll keep challenging you, pushing you, and moving you to believe you are who He says you are. And He'll move you toward believing that He has that special destiny just for you, and that none of your personal limitations or weaknesses can keep you from it.

Maybe you've spent time arguing with God, telling Him about

the limitations you believe should keep you from doing the things He has called you to do. But there is something I want you to understand, something an older pastor told me he learned after forty years in the ministry and during his personal study of the Word of God. Are you ready? Here it is:

God is smarter than we are!

A lot of Christians would do well to learn that lesson (they would do even better not to take forty years to learn it!). You see, God is infinitely smarter than even the most brilliant, wise human. And if He says we can do something, then we can do it, no matter what kind of personal limitations we have.

Furthermore, if God says He wants you to do something, He wants *you*—not your neighbor, or the guy sitting in the pew in front of you, or anyone else.

Finally, if God says that you can be successful, that you can be great, that you can be prosperous, and that you can make a difference, *then believe Him*! Believe Him no matter what your mind or your circumstances may say about what limits you.

Believe Him, and you'll no longer be held back by your own limitations, your own insecurities, and your own fears. Believe Him, and your destiny is within reach.

LIMITED BY FEAR

The world loves the spirit of fear. That is one reason there are so many television shows and movies that feed on a spirit of fear and why so many people flock to see these scream fests. These things feed on the fear of all kinds of things—diseases, disasters, apocalypses, monsters, murderers, and various other purveyors of mayhem. Part of the appeal of these things is that feeling that what is happening on the screen *could* happen to you.

I think it's sad how the world seems so attracted to that spirit of fear; but what's tragic is that the church, the Body of Christ herself, also buys into that spirit of fear. It is one thing to know that the movie or television show is evil and feeds on fear and that we should avoid it. But how do we deal with the fear generated within the church?

Fear is a very powerful force, almost as powerful as faith (only in reverse). The writer of Hebrews tells us that faith is "the substance of things hoped for, the evidence of things not seen" (Hebrews 11:1). On the other side of the ledger, fear is what brings substance to the things you hope to avoid, the things you dread.

One of the clichés so many people use, including those in church, is "I was afraid that was going to happen!" But in a very real way, that is more than just a figure of speech, more than a simple cliché so often spoken without thought. Why do I say that? Because I believe that fear makes things happen, just as faith makes things happen.

It should be obvious that there are some things we should be afraid of, things that it's normal to fear (or at least feel leery of). But there are fears that God doesn't want us to have, and those are the ones we need to address if we are going to be what He's called us to be and do what He's called us to do. Throughout Scripture we are commanded to "Fear not."

Polls and research done in the 1950s showed that death was the population's number one fear. For reasons I won't go into here, people back then were afraid to die. But as sad and debilitating as the fear of dying can be, what's even worse is that so many people today are afraid to live. Contemporary people fear a downturn in the economy; they fear not having a job; they fear losing their income; they fear the national debt; they fear rejection; they fear getting sick. You'd have to write a book (or create a library of books) just to catalog the many fears people struggle with today.

We know that one of the biggest fears people have is that of speaking in front of a crowd. But why do you think that seems so scary? I think it's partly because people feel inadequate when it comes to communicating what they want to say, and they are afraid of sounding foolish. That's probably part of what Moses was feeling when he told God, "O my Lord, I *am* not eloquent, neither before nor since You have spoken to Your servant; but I *am* slow of speech and slow of tongue" (Exodus 4:10).

Fear feeds on our limitations and insecurities, keeping us from being and doing all that God has called us to. It begins a vicious cycle that continues feeding on itself until our fears paralyze us and make us all but useless—to ourselves, to others, and to God.

Fear is a powerful force indeed, but God has given us a powerful weapon that can overcome all fear. He tells us about it in one of Paul's letters to Timothy: "For God has not given us a spirit of fear, but of power and of love and of a sound mind" (2 Timothy 1:7).

Stop and think about that verse for a minute. Meditate on what it is saying. It's telling us that fear is not from God—and that means those feelings of inadequacy and dread, those thoughts that you can't do something He wants you to do, are not from Him. So if they're not from Him, that must mean they're from someplace else, right? What *is* from God, Paul is telling us, is the spirit of power and love and a sound mind—the very things that chase fear away.

One of the main themes in this book has been how focusing on the right things will take you a long way in your race toward the personal destiny God has put in front of you. That applies to dealing with your fears, too. If you believe in yourself—if you believe what God says about you and how He feels about you, and believe in your heart that God has called you to be something—then you will drive out of your heart and mind every element of fear and invite in that spirit of power and love and a sound mind.

That sounds like a great trade-off, doesn't it?

When we are afraid, we can't flow in power, in love, and in a sound mind. Fear holds us back and keeps us from doing the things God wants us to do. It keeps people who may be gifted as teachers and ministers from doing what God has gifted them and called them to do. It keeps those with an entrepreneurial spirit from starting organizations and birthing great companies and becoming excellent leaders.

Proverbs tells us, "The wicked flee when no one pursues, / But the righteous are bold as a lion" (v. 28:1). Are you like the wicked, afraid of what might go wrong, afraid you might fail, afraid that there might be difficult times ahead, afraid of what you've heard could happen soon, afraid because you feel limited and insecure? Or are you like the lion, the king of the jungle, who roars and makes everyone shudder?

God calls us to cast aside our timidity and our thoughts of personal limitations and insecurities. He calls us to move forward, to be bold as lions, and live with freedom and boldness.

AN AMAZING TRANSFORMATION

Moses almost missed his destiny because he kept saying, "I can't." Some of us are very much like Moses. We are very creative in finding reasons why something won't work. We're really good at uncovering reasons to say, "I can't."

Enough of that! Instead, we need to use our God-given creative abilities to find ways to pursue whatever God has called us to do. That is what it takes to successfully run your race toward your destiny.

Moses eventually figured that out. He figured it out so well, in fact, that when he came to the end of his life—this man who once gave every reason in the book why he could not lead God's people—he stood before the people and charged Joshua, his replacement, with words very unlike those he spoke at the burning bush. Listen to what a man sounds like who has come to know God so well that he's come to see his limitations and insecurities as irrelevant:

> Then Moses summoned Joshua and said to him in the presence of all Israel, "Be strong and courageous, for you must go with this people into the land that the LORD swore to their forefathers to give them, and you must divide it among them as their inheritance. The LORD himself goes before you and will be with you; he will never leave you nor forsake you. Do not be afraid; do not be discouraged." (Deuteronomy 31:7–8, NIV)

That's quite a change, isn't it? A startling change! Well, maybe not so startling when you realize what triggered it. Moses was transformed from fearful to bold, from insecure to confident, by one thing only. As the writer of Hebrews tells us, Moses left Egypt by faith, "not fearing the king's anger; he persevered *because he saw him who is invisible*" (11:27, NIV, emphasis added).

Do you genuinely want to pursue your destiny? Do you want to leave your insecurities and your fears and your limitations far behind and grasp the tremendous future God places before you? If so, then do what Moses did: fix your eyes on Him who is invisible—and soon you'll have a lot more in common with the strong and bold Moses than with the guy who thought stuttering was too big an obstacle for God to overcome.

PART 3

Staying on Course

11

Growing Your Faith

As humans we often find it more comfortable to avoid situations that make us uneasy. We like to play it safe. Although this approach is easier to deal with, it doesn't get us anywhere. We can't grow if we start out in our little box and don't step out at all. Some of us are so cautious and careful—we keep our life so self-contained—that we don't need God. If God stayed in bed one day, we wouldn't care, because we have it all under control. We live our lives in such a way that we don't really need God every day. A pastor once said to me, "If the Lord didn't show up in our service, we wouldn't know it. We have it so planned out, so 'humanized,' so religious. We typed it out and wrote it down. We have a program and a structure. We don't even need the Holy Ghost. If He doesn't show up, we wouldn't know."

What if God wasn't helping *you*? Would you know it? Do you have such a self-contained life—are you so careful and controlled—that you never step out or trust Him?

We need to get to the place where our Christianity is more than Sunday morning, where our faith in God is more than a song or a poem. We need to come to the place where we truly know Him and truly trust Him.

When we regularly find ourselves in places where we don't know what to say, don't have the wisdom to deal with some problem, and are not sure how we're going to get through the circumstance—it's all right! It's all right because that's when we know that God is going to show up.

When I come to the end of myself, I find *Him*. When I'm weak, that's when I'm strong. When I don't know what to do, that's when I find out what *He* wants to do.

How many Christians live in such a way that they don't need God? They do not believe Him for anything. They don't have a vision for anything that anyone without God couldn't do just as well.

Let's consider the man with a wife and children, who lives in a small house, with a small mortgage, an economy car, and an uninspiring job. They bump along. They meet their expenses, and life is safe but boring. His greatest joy is working in his garage making the wood furniture that furnishes his entire house. The thought of turning his hobby into a business has never even crossed his mind, when in reality he has a God-given talent that would enable him to more than provide for his family and bring him joy at the same time.

How many of us live a life that is comfortable, easy, in which we have it figured out, we have it budgeted, we've got the job done? We're not reaching for *anything* that we need God to do.

Unfortunately, I think that's the majority. And if I'm right, this tells me that most people settle for less than destiny.

Do you realize that God will never call you to a life that you can live without exercising faith in Him? He'll never call you to do something that you can do without Him. He will never say to you, "Find a comfort zone and stay right there. I'll come back when it's time for you to go to heaven."

But how many of us have exactly that attitude? "I don't need God until I see the Pearly Gates." People often live their lives so much lower than what God planned. They rarely consider what God would have to say about their plans or behavior. They do not aspire to greatness. They do not serve or give, and they rarely attend church. They do everything on their own and do not fully benefit from their relationship with God the Father because they really do not know Him. They think, "I'm a Christian, so I'm going to heaven when I die." They don't consider there may be more to being a Christian that they are not taking advantage of. The Word says, "My people are destroyed for lack of knowledge" (Hosea 4:6a).

We must not organize our lives so that we don't need God at all. If we live by our budget, calendar, BlackBerry, and spreadsheet we have probably taken God out of the equation and are trying to live a safe life that takes no faith. Having children, starting new careers, reaching for our dreams, all take God's help. If I'm where God wants me, then there's always this X factor, this God factor, where frankly *I don't know how it's all going to work*. I have no idea how I can be that or do that—but I believe God will help me, because that's what He calls me to.

LIVE BY FAITH

Jesus constantly reminded His followers that although many things are impossible with man, all things are possible with God. In fact, that's a common theme throughout God's Word:

- "Is anything too hard for the LORD?" (Genesis 18:14)

- "I am the LORD, the God of all mankind. Is anything too hard for me?" (Jeremiah 32:27, NIV)

- "The LORD does whatever pleases him, / in the heavens and on the earth, / in the seas and all their depths." (Psalm 135:6, NIV)

- "For nothing is impossible with God." (Luke 1:37, NIV)

- "But Jesus looked at them and said, 'With men *it is* impossible, but not with God; for with God all things are possible.'" (Mark 10:27)

So I think we're getting the picture that *with God, all things are possible.* You have to get your thinking to go beyond what is naturally possible for you, what you can stretch yourself to understand and achieve on your own, and get to the place that is impossible for you, but is possible through God, which is where vision, faith, and dreams take over.

For a recent fund-raising campaign for our new sanctuary, we chose the title "Start with the Impossible." We knew a lot of people would approach the campaign like this: "All right, we looked at our budget, and we decided we could give a tithe plus another two percent to the building program." Or they'd say, "I could double my tithe. I could give twenty percent to the church building program."

That's great... but what's the impossible part? What if God spoke to you and said, "Here's what I want you to do. It's not in your budget, but if you'll trust Me, I'll bring you the increase. I'll bring you a new contract. I'll bring you a raise on the job. I'll do things that you can't budget and you can't control." Could you trust Him, could you believe Him for *that*? And that was our challenge to the congregation: "Let's get beyond what we can pencil out and let's see what God will do with our lives."

I think that's genuine Christianity. Anybody in the world who doesn't believe in God can put together a plan and a budget—but we have God. So let's believe Him for beyond what we can see in the natural!

But that brings up a question, doesn't it? A very personal question: What are *you* willing to believe God for? What are *you* willing to trust Him for that's outside the merely natural? What are *you* willing to have faith in Him for?

You cannot get to your destiny without exercising your faith. It just can't happen. Hebrews 11:6 declares that "without faith it is impossible to please God" (NIV), and it's just as impossible to pursue your vision or reach your destiny without exercising faith.

What kind of faith?

In Matthew 8, a Roman soldier, a centurion, approached the Lord to tell Him that his servant was suffering some dreadful torment. And he wanted to know if Jesus would heal him.

"I will come," Jesus said. But then the centurion unexpectedly replied, "You don't need to come to my house. I know you are a man under authority, even as I am. Just speak the word, and my servant will be healed."

Jesus clearly did not expect the man's response. He openly marveled at the centurion and declared his faith to be the greatest He had seen in all of Israel. Isn't that an amazing thing? In all of Israel, it was a Roman centurion, a pagan soldier, who had greater faith than all the religious people in a very religious nation (and that included all His own disciples)!

Then in verse 13 Jesus said, "Go your way. As you have believed, so let it be done for you." And at that very hour, the man's servant was healed.

Frankly, this account should make a few questions pop up in your mind. Did the Lord know this centurion? *No.* Did He know about the servant who was dreadfully tormented? *No.* Did He get a word from heaven? *No.* Did he see a sign? *No.* Did He get a message from the Holy Spirit? *No.* He could have left town and the guy would have remained sick—but when the centurion exercised his faith, Jesus told him, "As you have believed, so let it be done."

So again, let me ask: What do you believe God for? What are you asking and trusting God for? What are you having faith for? If all you're doing is trusting God for "whatever the Lord wills," then I can tell you right now that not much is going to happen in your life. I don't mean to pop your bubble or make you feel bad, but I do want to make you aware of the truth.

God created you in His likeness and image. He gave you a will and desires. When you pray, Jesus said, believe that you have received it and you shall have it. That's using faith. God isn't going to instigate *everything* in your life. You're not a robot waiting for God to push a button. Use your faith!

So I ask again: What do you believe God for?

When you received salvation, you used your faith. God wanted you to get saved long before it happened, but you didn't get saved when God wanted you to; you got saved when you used your faith. Romans 10:9 says, "if you confess with your mouth the Lord Jesus and believe in your heart that God has raised Him from the dead, you will be saved." Did God want you to get saved sooner than you did? Sure, He did; but it happened when you believed.

When did you get filled with the Holy Ghost? When you believed and received. The Bible says ask, believe, and you will receive.

The Lord is not going to push anything on you. The Lord wants you to tithe, but is He going to make you? No. If the Lord wants you to love your wife, is He going to make you send roses to her? No. *You* love your wife. *You* obey the Bible. *You* ask and *you* receive.

"[W]hatever things you ask when you pray," Jesus told us, "believe that you receive *them*, and you will have *them*" (Mark 11:24). You have to believe. It all happens according to your faith—and it doesn't matter who you are.

In Matthew 15, Jesus encountered a pagan woman from the region of Tyre and Sidon—an area of the country that in ancient times was controlled by the Philistines. This Canaanite woman had a demon-possessed daughter whom she wanted Jesus to cure. At first, Jesus refused even to speak to her. When He finally did talk to her, He told her, "It is not good to take the children's bread and throw *it* to the little dogs" (v. 26). Let me ask you something—what would an answer like *that* do to your own faith?

Apparently, it didn't faze the woman at all. She had heard of this Jewish holy man and healer, and she was determined to get His help. So she persisted. At last Jesus said to her, "O woman, great *is* your faith! Let it be to you as you desire" (v. 28). And at that moment her daughter was made whole.

Do you know that in all of the Gospels, Jesus calls someone's faith "great" only twice? He used the word to describe the faith of the Roman centurion we just met, and he used it again to describe the faith of this Canaanite woman. Only two people in all four of the Gospels have "great" faith, according to Jesus—and both of them are from pagan countries!

You don't have to be a superstar to gain the help you need to reach your destiny. You don't have to be born into a family with a rich spiritual heritage. You don't have to have your name in the papers or be on anyone's "who's who" list.

You just have to exercise your faith.

So what do you want? What do *you* believe for? What are *you* asking of God—and not just asking, but believing God for? You don't need God just to survive and get through another day. But you *do* need Him if you want to do and be something great, as He desires for you.

HOW MUCH FAITH DO YOU NEED?

In Matthew 17, the disciples wondered why they could not cast out a demon. Jesus named their unbelief as the cause. Or, as the New International Version says, "Because you have so little faith. I tell you the truth, if you have faith as small as a mustard seed, you can say to this mountain, 'Move from here to there' and it will move. Nothing will be impossible for you" (v. 20).

Jesus compared faith to a mustard seed. And what's a seed? It is a living and growing thing. The Amplified Bible translates this verse, "If you have faith that's growing like a seed." So how do things grow? They get active, energized. The seed germinates and now it's moving and growing. Seeds don't grow in the package, they must be planted.

It's like that with your faith. It has to move and grow, and it does that when you get involved with it. You have to get your faith *working*. When you start believing God for things, you get your faith activated and living like a seed. And then it will grow.

And how do things grow? How can you grow that seed of faith?

It all comes back to my definition of a real relationship with God, where you walk with Him every day, experiencing life with Jesus. It's praying for your kids and then doing the things Scripture teaches you to do in order to be a good parent—and then adding your faith to the mix, believing that God's going to help your kids even beyond what you can imagine. It's managing your money and giving your tithe and being diligent with your finances, but then believing that God can do a miracle and bring you finances for other things beyond what you can ask or think. It's trying to be a good husband, communicating with your wife, dwelling with her with understanding, as 1 Peter 3:7 says, but also trusting God to bless your marriage in ways you can't even picture.

A living faith is practical. It's committed to obeying whatever God says and also expects God to go *beyond* and do extraordinary things in your life (see Ephesians 3:20). In a way, I guess, it's a bit mystical, a bit Pentecostal. It's this attitude that says, "Okay, if I have a relationship with Jesus, than life is more than following religious principles. It's something real in my spirit and in my relationship with God. It's something that causes good things, even amazing things, to happen in my family life and financial life and every part of my life. It goes beyond what can be explained in the natural."

I think it comes down to what Paul said in 1 Corinthians 4:20: "For the kingdom of God is not a matter of talk but of power" (NIV).

If we don't act on that truth, do we really have God? Or are we just playing religious games? But if our God is real, then we can expect real, supernatural things to happen in response to our exercise of faith.

When you live your faith, amazing things can happen. As you live your faith, like a seed it grows.

Once, just getting out of debt was all you could believe for; then, pretty soon, you could believe for the ability to earn one million dollars; then it grows to become giving away a million dollars to bless other people.

From faith to faith, your faith is living and growing like a seed. That's how you fulfill your destiny.

Of course, you're not just waiting around for God to send the million-dollar check in the mail! But every day, you take another step. Trust, believe, and know that God is going to make a way. Try to do more than you know you can do in the natural, because that is what it means to live by faith.

That is the kind of faith that God responds to. Jesus said it would work if it was just like a mustard seed, and that's pretty small. It does have to be genuine, though, and it does have to be growing. But if you can exercise *that* kind of faith, then you have what you need to run your race to destiny and so fulfill the vision that God puts in your heart.

God is your source of power and wisdom, and God says that whatever you desire, *if you'll have faith*, you'll move the mountain or build the business or erase the debt or influence the king or whatever the challenge might be.

Start with what you have. Practice with what you have. When you use your faith, it grows. Let me give you an example of how to do this.

Many times through the years a young couple has come to me and said, "Pastor, we're praying for our first home. We don't want to go in debt, so we're going to believe for the money to buy the house. Would you pray for us?"

"First," I usually say, "let's stop before we pray." I learned that little technique from Jesus; He often did that with people. He'd usually say, "What are we praying about here? What do you really want?" So I ask the couple what they want me to pray for.

"Well," they say, "we want this house, and it's going to cost $300,000"—which is not an expensive house in today's world. We're not talking a mansion here.

"Tell me, how much do you make?" I ask.

"Well, we make $50,000 a year."

"And how much can you save?"

"We can do a thousand a month." That's a good savings account for some people who are trying to raise a family. It amounts to $12,000 a year—but $300,000 is still a long way away. It would take a pretty good miracle to get the cash to buy *this* house!

So I say, "Could you believe for $30,000, a ten percent down payment? And then you'd have a payment of this much a month at this percent interest. I'll bet if you start there, your faith will grow and probably, before too many years, you'll own that house debt-free. But if you plan to wait to get $300,000 before you buy anything, then probably by the time you get the money, the house is going to cost $400,000—and you're going to struggle."

So start where you are. As you use your faith, it will grow—and with each step of faith, you'll be that much closer to your destiny.

Also, if you want to run to your destiny and seize it, then you have to stop talking about what you can't do, about what you can't afford, and about what you don't feel like. You can't have faith in God and talk negative. You can't exercise faith in an almighty God and still talk lack and shortage and poverty. You just can't have faith in God and talk all that trash. Trash talking just won't work with God.

The Bible says, "Death and life *are* in the power of the tongue" (Proverbs 18:21), and the words are meant literally.

When a top official of the ancient king of Israel heard Elisha the prophet say that the Lord was about to lift a terrible siege on Samaria, and that the next day there would be plenty to eat in the starving city, he replied, "Look, even if the LORD should open the floodgates of the heavens, could this happen?" Now, that's trash talking. That's telling God that He can't possibly do what He says He's going to do. That's looking at things only in the natural and not counting on God to do something in the supernatural.

Elisha did not appreciate the man's response. So he said, "You will see it with your own eyes, but you will not eat any of it!"

And do you know what happened? The next day, God did a miracle, just as He had promised. The news of God's provision spread so fast throughout the city that Samaria's starving inhabitants charged out the gates to gather as much food as possible. Remember the man who just the day before had trash talked Elisha's prophecy? He was standing in one of those gates when a hungry crowd rushed outside the city walls—and according to God's Word, "the people trampled him in the

I was on chemotherapy for eleven months, and almost every day, somebody—usually those who were not real close to me—would say, "How do you feel?"

My friends knew me well enough to see how I felt and so they rarely asked. One day someone asked that question and I just exploded. "Look at me. Why ask? Just *look*. I feel terrible. I'm losing weight, my hair is falling out—and you have to ask how I *feel?*"

I did regret my outburst and I quickly developed a faith-based answer: "It doesn't matter how I feel. I'm going to serve God, I'm going to fulfill God's will, I'm pressing on with destiny, and I refuse to stop. No matter how I feel." Feelings are not facts; they change regularly and they don't have to control us.

Second Corinthians 5:7 says that we walk by faith, not by sight. We walk by faith, not by our feelings. We walk by faith, not by our emotions. When someone asks, "How do you feel?" and you feel terrible, tell them, "It doesn't matter." Our feelings go up and down, but that doesn't change our faith.

Walk by faith!

gate, and he died." And so, just as Elisha had said, "You shall see it with your eyes, but you shall not eat any of it" (2 Kings 7:1–20).

I would not suggest that you make a habit of trash talking God's promises. Believe it, speak it, and receive it.

PUT GOD AT THE CENTER

If you set your life course by exercising your faith, then you don't need to be concerned about being in God's will. You are and you will be blessed. But if you can set your life course *without* faith, then that's a very different story; in that case, you're condemned. The Bible says that whatever does not come from faith is sin (Romans 14:23). Anything not of faith is self-centered, self-sufficient, and selfish—and that's the core of sin.

So you build your marriage with faith and you raise your kids with faith. Why? Because by trusting God to help you, you are putting God at the core. You are remembering that it's not about you, it's about Him.

If you get your plan and budget and schedule all mapped out, and God isn't in it, then I'm telling you right now, it's outside of God's will. You are missing God's best, because whatever didn't take faith doesn't need God—and that's sin.

You need faith to fulfill your destiny; you don't need faith just to be average.

You need faith to run your race and then stand before God in heaven and hear Him say, "Well done, good and faithful servant." You don't need to have any faith at all for the Lord to say, "Well, looks like *you're* done." Getting to heaven isn't the goal; it's fulfilling His plan for our lives.

To fulfill vision and be purpose driven, you must live by faith. Faith is the substance of what you're hoping for. Faith is the substance of your vision and your dreams. Without faith it is impossible to please Him (Hebrews 11:1–6).

And faith is the only force that will get you to destiny.

12

Using Your Spiritual Force

Have you ever watched as some destructive weather event around the world—whether a huge mudslide or rising floodwaters or a monster avalanche—took houses right off their foundations or moved whole chunks of a mountain right down the slope and into a valley? Isn't it amazing how the force of momentum can wash away an entire city? When things really get moving, there's no telling what kind of wallop they can produce.

Do you know that, in the spiritual realm, a similar kind of force is required? To fulfill your visions and realize your dreams and accomplish your purpose, you must apply force. I'm talking here about the force of action, the force of movement, the force of momentum.

Sometimes in our Christian lives we have faith in God that He will help us in our marriage, our business, and our future. We're focused on it. We set our course—but somehow, we never apply force. We never take a step of action. We never get moving—and it is crucial to recognize that without the force of movement, nothing much is going to happen for you.

So where does this force come from? Who supplies it? You do.

Many people think God is going to make them successful. But you know something? He's not. Read Joshua 1:8 carefully:

This Book of the Law [the Word of God] shall not depart from your mouth, but you shall meditate in it day and night, that you may observe to do according to all that is written in it. For then you will make your way prosperous, and then you will have good success.

In this famous passage, God is instructing Joshua, the successor of Moses, on how to conduct his affairs as he leads the nation of Israel into the Promised Land. Take a good look at it, and then ponder some key questions. Ready?

Q: Who makes his way prosperous?
A: Joshua.
Q: Who achieves good success?
A: Joshua.
Q: How does he achieve this success?
A: By meditating on and doing the will of God.

When you read the passage carefully, you see that while God supplies the instructions and the power, Joshua supplies the elbow grease. God expects Joshua to take an active role in the drama that's about to unfold. He expects the young general to partner with Him in the coming conquest, not merely to sit on the sidelines as a spectator.

Do you really want to run to your destiny? If so, then you need to speak God's Word, think His Word, and do His Word. When you do that, God will provide the tools, the principles, the opportunities, and the relationships. And then do you know what happens? Then *you* will make your way prosperous and *you* will have good success.

DOES GOD HAVE THE
MONEY YOU NEED?

I suppose every young Christian at one time or another prays God would just provide him or her with money. And it seems the answer is always no.

God doesn't have money; He lives in a spirit world and He doesn't carry cash. God doesn't have a wallet or a purse. He just doesn't work that way.

But if you'll get moving—if you'll take a step of faith, if you'll apply some force to your faith—then He'll bring your finances in order, He'll bring you a relationship, He'll bring you a job opportunity, He'll bring you an open door, He'll give you an idea, He'll show you some wisdom. *You* start the process in your life, and then God will bless you and prosper your work. In that way you will follow in the footsteps of Joshua: *you* will make your way prosperous and *you* will have good success.

In the last chapter we recalled an incident from 2 Kings 7 in which the ancient Syrian army had attacked Israel. They had surrounded the capital city of Samaria, where the king and the prophet Elisha were. The Syrians were starving them out: no food and no water went into the city. The invaders were just waiting for the Israelites to die.

You already know how that story ends, but here I'd like to focus on what happened just before the end. You see, there were four lepers in the city who were dying, along with everyone else. In those days, people suffering from leprosy were the most hopeless members of society you could find. Their loathsome disease made them outcasts; healthy people both despised and feared them. Having leprosy meant deep despair and utter discouragement, for those who had it were totally isolated and separated from the general community.

They were poor because no one would give them work. The man or woman with leprosy was in the most hopeless of circumstances. With that background, listen to the story of these four lepers:

> Now there were four leprous men at the entrance of the gate; and they said to one another, "Why are we sitting here until we die? If we say, 'We will enter the city,' the famine *is* in the city, and we shall die there. And if we sit here, we die also. Now therefore, come, let us surrender to the army of the Syrians. If they keep us alive, we shall live; and if they kill us, we shall only die." (2 Kings 7:3–4)

You see what they were doing? They were weighing their options. And their logic is flawless. They knew if they managed to sneak into the city, they'd die there, because no one in it had any food—and even if they did, they certainly weren't about to give it to some dirty lepers. On the other hand, if they continued to sit where they were, they would also die, because they had no more food or water than did the people in the city. As they looked around, gnawing on their tongues, they saw only one group with both food and water: the besieging Syrians. These invaders represented the lepers' only hope. Of course, the Syrians might kill them if they dared to make contact; but how would that make their circumstances any worse? The first two options led without question to death, and while the third option might also lead to death, it also might lead to life. So really, they had nothing to lose by taking a step.

> And they rose at twilight to go to the camp of the Syrians; and when they had come to the outskirts of the Syrian camp, to their surprise no one *was* there. For the Lord had caused the army of the Syrians to hear the noise of chariots and the noise of horses—the noise of a great army; so they said to one another, "Look, the king of Israel has

hired against us the kings of the Hittites and the kings of the Egyptians to attack us!" Therefore they arose and fled at twilight, and left the camp intact—their tents, their horses, and their donkeys—and they fled for their lives. And when these lepers came to the outskirts of the camp, they went into one tent and ate and drank, and carried from it silver and gold and clothing, and went and hid *them*; then they came back and entered another tent, and carried *some* from there *also*, and went and hid *it*. (vv. 5–8)

Doesn't that illustrate the force of movement? "If we sit here, we're going to die; so let's do *something*." So they started walking.

And you know what God said? "*Finally!* Now, there's something I can work with. Finally, there's something I can do, because they're moving."

These men tapped into the force of momentum. They did what they could, and then God did what only God can do. When you step out in faith, God will make miraculous things happen.

Those four downcast lepers had been struggling along, in pain, discouraged, in despair, at the bottom of the pit. Suddenly the Syrians thought they heard warhorses and chariots and a mighty army coming after them—and the Syrians ran. So by the time the lepers

Since having hep C, I've met many people with various diseases who are not dealing with it. Take a step, get out of your boat, do something to move forward. Don't let bad things hang around your spirit, soul, or body. It will never get easier to face the problem.

Move toward healing and health in whatever ways you can. Don't sit back and let the negative grow and overtake you. When you begin to move forward, God's healing can start to flow in you.

came into town, they looked around at piles of unguarded food and drink and said, "Woo-hoo, we found the mother lode!"

What would have happened had the lepers not walked into the abandoned Syrian camp? What would have taken place had they not put some shoe leather to their faith? Where would they have been if one of them had said, "Hey, I know what to do! Let's just sit here and wait for God to shower manna down on us, like He did with Moses in the good old days"?

I doubt very much they would have gotten their fill. Eventually the famished people in the city would have noticed that the invaders had left—and I highly doubt they would have made it a priority to feed four starving lepers.

You see the connection between those lepers and us, don't you? So often we focus on our limitations and never take any steps to move beyond our current circumstances.

How many people say they can't get a job? They don't know what to do, so they just get discouraged and depressed and then just start sitting around the house. Well, there are no jobs in your house—other than the ones your wife gives you, and she *ain't* paying that much!

The problem is we face an obstacle, some kind of roadblock, and instead of figuring out a way around it we get discouraged and feel paralyzed and so we just sit in our anxiety and stew in our worry.

Take a step! Apply some force! Get a little movement going!

As the leader of our church, I remember the day when I couldn't find anybody who would help us with our first building. *Nobody* would participate in the building program—so I just started taking some steps. I met with people; I knocked on every door. I got out there, taking some small steps for God, just waiting for *somebody* to hear the noise.

And you know what? Somebody did. Somebody heard that a

young church was trying some good things. They learned that God was doing something interesting down there, and so they decided they wanted to be a part of it.

It's no different for you. You have to take that step. You have to get in gear and *do* something. Start somewhere! Go get a book from the library and start studying. Do something, anything! Apply some force. Do what you can do, and then watch God do what only He can do.

MAKE A CALL

The Bible tells us that faith without action is dead (James 2:17). That's another way of saying that you need to apply some force to your faith. And what does that mean, in practical terms?

Send the letter. Make the call. Get a new contact. Try a new sales approach. Find a new business partner. Do whatever you need to do. Do *something* every day to take a step toward your destiny, toward God's plan for your life.

And make sure you don't forget what Psalm 37:5 tells you: "Commit your way to the LORD, / Trust also in Him, / And He shall bring *it* to pass."

Commit to your vision, to your purpose and to your destiny. To "commit" to something means to give 100 percent. It means you're not just trying it; you're going for it, without reservation.

Because we're sincere Christians, we want to do our best to find and do God's will. We want to walk with God and follow God, so we pray and talk with mature Christian friends. We get good counsel and we start to sense what the Holy Spirit is saying in our heart. Then we say, "Here is the career that I believe God is leading me to. Here's the way I believe God is calling me to go. Here's the marriage, the family, the life, the ministry, the business God has for me." In that way we do our best to ascertain God's will and God's plan for our life.

But what happens then, so many times? We don't commit to it. We keep wondering and questioning ourselves. We spend our whole life asking, "Am I really in God's will?" Especially when problems come up and challenges hit us, we begin to question what we've done. When things get hard, if we're not genuinely committed, often we start looking for a way out.

But that's not God's way to success in life. "Commit your way to the LORD." You stick to it, no matter what. You make the commitment and don't back down.

If you are in school, commit to it. Focus and do the very best you can do. If you're sitting in class thinking, *I wish I was out at the park. I wish I was home. I wish I was anywhere but here,* then you are not going to learn. You are not going to get what God could give you there—and then at some later point you're going to say, "Well, I went there, and they didn't help me much." Well, of course they didn't. You were never committed to being there! You might have been trying it, testing it, wondering about it—but you certainly didn't commit your way unto the Lord.

When things get hard in marriage, if you start saying, "Well, maybe it wasn't God's will for me to marry this person; maybe I should have married that other person," then you're going to miss God's destiny for you. You may never know what kind of patience you could have had, what kind of strength you possess, to make that marriage work and so become better than anything you ever dreamed. You never will find out any of that, for one simple reason: You're not committed.

In sports, you have to go up against a tough opponent to find out how good you really are. You have to be tested to your max. Only then will you find out what you really have on the inside. And the only way you are going to win against a tough opponent is if you're totally committed. If you commit your way to the Lord, then you'll find out how good you are. Then you'll find out what really lives on the inside of you.

So don't be at work, wishing you were on vacation.

Don't be on vacation, wishing it could last longer because you don't want to go back to work.

Don't be at home, thinking you should be working more.

Don't be at work, feeling guilty because you haven't spent much time with the kids at home (especially since you've been home enough, but the TV got your attention).

Commit your way unto the Lord! Commit your way, give 100 percent, no options, no back door—and God will bless you. Say, "All right, here I go. If there's something else, Lord, then You're going to have to show me. If there's another plan You have for me, then direct my steps, because I'm committing this to You. I'm going one hundred percent. If You don't want me to do it, then talk to me *now*!"

You know what God will say? "Go, boy, go!" "Get on with it, girl. Go ahead!" He'll redirect you if you get a little off course. As I've said, none of us is perfect, but God isn't looking for perfection; He's looking for character.

And what happens when you commit your way to the Lord? The Word of God answers, "And He shall bring it to pass."

How exciting! When you apply the force God expects of you, He applies the force you desire of Him.

YOU ARE A GOOD PERSON

Are you a good person? That's not a trick question; I really want an answer. Are you a good person?

Before you reply, I'd like to remind you of the amazing promise of Psalm 37:23. In that verse the Word of God says, "The steps of a *good* man are ordered by the LORD, / And He [the LORD] delights in his way."

So, back to the question. Are you a good person?

Let me answer it for you: "Yes, you are!" I didn't say a *perfect* person, but you're a *good* person. If you are reading this book in a sincere effort to seek God; if you're praying, praising, and serving; if you're trying to make your family work and trying to be a positive influence in your community—then yes, you really are a good person.

Many people question that conclusion. They just aren't clear on where they stand with God—and so they forget that God is not asking for perfection, but for a genuine commitment to His will, His Word, and His way.

Do you remember Barnabas, the friend and coworker of the apostle Paul? He was not a perfect man. He made mistakes, just like all of us. In fact, at one point he and Paul got into such a heated argument that they just couldn't work together anymore, at least for some time (Acts 15:39). He didn't have a spotless record! And yet the Word of God calls him "a good man, full of the Holy Spirit and of faith" (Acts 11:24).

If you genuinely desire to do good, if you take practical steps to bring good to others, and if you desire more than anything to honor God and serve Him faithfully, then in the eyes of Scripture, you are a good person—and that entitles you to some precious real estate in God's kingdom. For the Bible tells good men and good women, "Your steps are ordered by the LORD" and "He delights [not just tolerates!] in your way."

So stop wondering. Stop worrying. As a good man or woman, you are right where God wants you to be.

God acts on behalf of those who step out in faith. He doesn't do it the same way every time, of course, nor does He publish a schedule of when and how He will respond. But when you step out in faith—when you apply some force, no matter how little—He steps in and does what only He can do.

In Elisha's day there were four lepers who learned this lesson. In Jesus' day, the number swelled to ten. Luke tells us:

> Then as He entered a certain village, there met Him ten men who were lepers, who stood afar off. And they lifted *their* voices and said, "Jesus, Master, have mercy on us!"
>
> So when He saw *them*, He said to them, "Go, show yourselves to the priests." And so it was that as they went, they were cleansed. (Luke 17:12–14)

Here were ten sick men, discouraged, in despair, rejected, lonely, hurting, and poor. They had their faith, they had their focus, and they knew what they wanted. They approached Jesus and boldly asked for it. But did you catch when they received what they asked for? Did you notice the timing of their healing?

Were they healed as they stood there, asking? No.

Where they cured as soon as they hoped for healing? No.

So, when did they get healed? They were cleansed *as they went*. As they went, the miracle took place. The leprosy left them as they applied some force.

What would have happened if, when Jesus said, "Go!" they had replied, "Lord, we can't go. We're lepers! It's against the law. We can't go into the temple; they'll get mad at us"? What if they had said, "Lord, we can't go. We're hurting and our toes are falling off. Sickness and disease are taking over our lives. What do you mean, 'go'? If we could go, we wouldn't be calling you"?

It's easy to talk about what you can't do. It's easy to give your excuses, rationalizations, and reasons why you can't go, why you can't get moving, why it won't work.

But Jesus said, "Go, and show yourselves to the priests." Thank God, these ten men didn't hesitate! They just started going. And as they went, the miracle was on.

In the same way, as you go—as you apply some force to your faith—God will send the right banker. As you go, God will send the right agent to the negotiations. As you go, the door will open. As you go, the idea will come. As you go, the partner will arrive. As you go, you'll find your destiny.

So *go*!

And as you go, be assured that God helps you and empowers you. God doesn't promise to help you if you just sit back, waiting to see what might happen. But when you go at God's Word, you can run and not be weary, and walk and not be faint.

Apply the force of movement and momentum. Get moving—and watch God do some moving of His own.

13

Using All Your Resources

When I was diagnosed with hepatitis C, immediately I talked and prayed about the situation with Wendy and my children. Then I went to the pastors and elders of our church, and also to several of the doctors who attend our church. I asked them all, "How should I face this? What do you think?" There is safety in a multitude of counselors (Proverbs 11:14).

I didn't talk to *everybody*, of course. Some folks would get scared to hear the news; others would get nervous. But these strong pastors and elders and doctors understood my situation, so I said to them, "How are we going to face this? What are the steps to winning this battle?" During the process of our discussions, I heard a lot of thoughts and varying perspectives.

At one point, one doctor gave me a scripture. You know, it's a good thing when your doctor starts quoting the Bible! His experience and biblical knowledge were an added bonus as I attacked the sickness. I appreciated having a doctor who could stand in faith with me. He quoted to me Proverbs 18:9 in the Amplified Bible: "He who does not use his endeavors to heal himself is brother to him who commits suicide."

"Use every tool you've got: chiropractic care, nutritional care, vitamin supplements, exercise, medicine, prayer, and faith." I felt that was the Word of the Lord for me.

I took his counsel and received that scripture and stood on it. I determined to do everything I could to heal myself with God's help, lest I be brother to him who commits suicide.

FIGHT FOR YOUR LIFE

Sometimes we limit God and even tempt Him by telling Him how He has to work, how He must do something. For instance, when people find out they have a disease, they often say, "Lord, I'm going to go over to the crusade [or the church] and I'm going to get Brother So-and-So to pray for me. When he prays for me, I know I'll be healed."

So they do it. They go to the crusade or to the church and get Brother So-and-So to pray for them—and sometimes they find out they didn't get healed.

What happens then? They get all indignant. They say, "God, I *told* You this was what I was going to do and that's what You were going to do—but You didn't come through for me!"

And when, despite their outburst, they still don't get healed, they get discouraged and upset and they don't care who hears about it: "Well, I prayed, and Brother So-and-So prayed, and nothing happened."

But since when do you tell *God* how it's going to happen? You can't tell God how He is going to work in your life. If you do, you have become God's instructor, His tutor, His counselor. And frankly, the Word of God doesn't think much of such an idea:

Who has understood the mind of the LORD,
    or instructed him as his counselor?
Whom did the LORD consult to enlighten him,
    and who taught him the right way?
    Who was it that taught him knowledge
    or showed him the path of understanding?
Surely the nations are like a drop in a bucket;
    they are regarded as dust on the scales;
    he weighs the islands as though they were fine dust.
Lebanon is not sufficient for altar fires,
    nor its animals enough for burnt offerings.
Before him all the nations are as nothing;
    they are regarded by him as worthless
    and less than nothing.

(Isaiah 40:13–17, NIV)

You don't instruct the Lord on what He needs to do or how to do it. What you do instead is use every tool to fight for life. You use every opportunity to get better, to overcome, and to rise up. That is what I did.

During my conversations with the pastors, elders, and doctors of our church, and after much prayer, it became clear that I would be wise to pursue some medical interventions to help me in my battle against hepatitis C. In the end, my wife and I decided on an experimental course of treatment of double doses of chemotherapy for eleven months. My health care professionals warned me about extreme fatigue, depression, and being physically vulnerable to other illness—and they weren't kidding.

I took pills in the morning, pills at night, and had shots every week. And right away—*bam!*—you talk about headaches, fatigue, nausea, losing weight, and losing hair! Chemotherapy was *very* painful. Every part of my body hurt—even my skin. Just someone touching me would hurt. But I decided not to focus on my problem or circumstances because I'd get frustrated and impatient. I'd start trying to figure out what I could do to fix it. I'd get angry, say something harsh, and make the situation worse. So I said, "All right, Lord, I'm going to follow, obey, and trust You, and I won't compromise."

I was miserable with all that therapy going on—but I used every tool I had, because my goal was to get healed, get clear of the virus, and to live a long, fulfilling life. So I just stayed with it.

Soon I also found out there were some things I could do nutritionally to help me in my battle. I could improve my diet by adding some new things and getting rid of some old things. I could drink lots and lots of clean water, which would help my body fight the disease. Then I discovered there were some supplements and nutritional aids I could get; in all I started taking about five different supplements that would help to heal and cleanse my liver and push hepatitis C out of it. I took them every day.

Next I found out that chiropractic care could help me keep my body healthy in other ways. So I started seeing a chiropractor.

I also made some discoveries on the spiritual side—with more confessions, focusing on Jesus, and meditating on the Word of God—to keep my spirit strong.

I learned there were some additional medical things I could do, besides the chemotherapy. Not every sickness has medical support, but in this case there were some things that my health care professionals felt would help me to deal with the disease. I used every weapon.

Did I feel like doing all this? That's not the point. You have to fight the fight; you must battle your way to victory. I knew I was in a war, so I used every tool I had to win that war.

And you need to do the same thing. What are your options?

I know a lot of folks who say, "Lord, I'm just going to pray and believe that You will heal me," when in fact, if they just did a little research and changed their diet, they wouldn't need a miracle; they'd be feeling better already.

Some people say, "Lord, I know You are going to deliver me in this way, and I'm trusting You," when in fact, if they just got wise counsel, they'd be able to deal with those difficult situations and not have to wait for a miracle.

The point is, don't tell God how He has to do it. You get going and use every tool you have, and then the Lord will be at work as He wills. Do not limit or tempt God, but rather use every tool to fight for life and for destiny.

If you are in a lawsuit, get the best attorneys. I know people who have been in lawsuits; maybe someone filed a suit against them, or maybe it's a divorce case. They say, "Lord, I'm not even going to get an attorney. I'm just going to let You work it out."

But the Lord also gave us a brain, you know, and the Bible commands us to be wise. Jesus told us, "Love the LORD your God with all your heart and with all your soul and with all your mind" (Matthew 22:37, NIV). You don't love the Lord with *all your mind* by turning off your brain and saying, "faith means always doing the irrational thing, the nonsensical thing, the thing that is most opposed to logic and reason and a sound mind." When the Lord tells you to do something wild, of course, you do it; but in the absence of a clear, direct instruction from God that's specific to your situation, the essence of faith is *not* doing the most irrational thing possible...and then blaming God for what happens.

So get an attorney if you need one. If you're sick, explore all treatment options. If you face financial trouble, seek out wise counsel. Do your part. Use your wisdom, use your natural ability, use your understanding, use nutrition, use medicine, and improve your diet. Use every tool you have to fight for life, whether you need medicine or a loan or a counselor or whatever it might be.

It's easy to get negative and pessimistic. We live in a world of "that won't work." But stay optimistic and believe God is working. He is moving in you by His Spirit, He is using medication if you have it, He is using the natural and the supernatural. It's not one or the other with God, it's both. He works in marvelous ways. Don't try to limit Him by telling Him what to do. God will always do things His way.

Remember, if you didn't get healed or can't keep yourself healed, then you'd better start to do *something* you haven't done before. Pray over the medicine; pray for your doctor—but use all the tools you have and keep growing your faith as you go. Don't keep doing what you've always done and hope for different results.

I'm not saying to just run to the doctor or the lawyer and leave God out of the picture. Seek the Lord, listen for His direction, and get wise counsel. If your heart is toward the Lord, you will not leave Him. You'll find a place of balance and wisdom and He will get you through.

GOD HAS A BIG TOOLBOX

Why do we insist that God *has* to work in a particular way? Why do we think there is only one possible way God can work in our lives—especially when throughout history He has made a habit of doing things in all kinds of ways, many of them spectacularly unexpected?

If *you* wanted to start a brand-new nation, would *you* think of using a one-hundred-year-old man and a ninety-year-old woman to have the baby boy who would start things off? And yet, that's what God did with Abraham and Sarah (Genesis 21).

If *you* wanted to lead a nation out of slavery, would *you* think of leading them into a box canyon, with a deep sea on one side, steep mountains on two sides, and a hostile army on the last side? And yet, that's what God did with Moses and the Israelites at the Red Sea (Exodus 14).

If *you* wanted to defeat some well-armed invaders intent on starving out a city, would *you* think of using loud noises in the night to frighten them away? And yet, that's what God did for ancient Samaria (2 Kings 7).

Just think of some of the unusual tools God has chosen over the years to accomplish His purposes: a rib, a bush, a staff, a donkey, a dream, an arrow, a shadow, a hornet, a trumpet blast, a song…the list goes on and on.

Just think of some of the unusual tools Jesus used during His earthly ministry to accomplish His kingdom purposes: wine, a coin in a fish's mouth, a dead fig tree, a funeral, a tax collector, a bright light, a loaf of bread, a young colt, an empty tomb…even spitting on one person.

More specifically, think of the many ways Jesus gave sight to the blind. He touched the eyes of some blind men and said to them, "According to your faith will it be done to you," and immediately they received their sight. He spit on the eyes of another blind man to restore his vision. With another blind man, Jesus merely said, "Go, your faith has healed you," and the man could see—without Jesus ever touching him. With yet another blind man, Jesus made some mud, placed it on the man's eyes, and told him to bathe in a specific pool—only then was the man healed.

Why do we think God *has* to do things our way? Why do we insist on limiting the ways He works? Now, if God likes doing His thing in so many ways—if He has a toolbox that stretches from one end of the universe to the other—then why don't we just thank Him for His creativity and go with whatever He wants to do? Maybe we should remind ourselves of a helpful scripture where God Himself says,

> See, I am doing a new thing!
>> Now it springs up; do you not perceive it?
> I am making a way in the desert
> and streams in the wasteland.

(Isaiah 43:19, NIV)

God has a *big* toolbox, and there's no reason some of those tools shouldn't find a place in our own toolboxes. He invites us to use every tool at our disposal—and so long as those tools come from Him, why wouldn't we?

When I eventually announced my illness to the church—after about three or four months of chemotherapy—right away someone came to me and asked, "Pastor, if you have faith, why are you taking medicine? Doesn't that medicine undermine your faith?"

I responded like this: "What if drinking water would make your skin healthier or make you feel better physically? Would you drink water? Or would you say, 'I'm not going to drink water! I'm just going to believe God and use my faith'?"

Obviously, only a fool would refuse to drink water, if drinking water would help you to get healthy.

What if changing your diet would help you to feel better and live longer? Would you change your diet? Or would you say, "Hey, I'm going to drink soda and eat chips and believe in God for a long, healthy life." What would you be doing? You would actually be tempting God by saying, "God, You gotta do it *this* way while I'm gonna do *nothing*. You have to do it this way if You want me to be healthy."

If you found out that by just improving the way you speak to your wife, you could save your troubled marriage, would you do it? Or would you say, "I'm going to talk the way I want to talk. And God, You save my marriage"?

But the Lord's not taking orders. The Lord is not waiting for you to direct His path.

I understood that, so I said, "God, I'm going to use every tool you provide, every opportunity You give me: nutrition, chiropractic, exercise, attitude, prayer, faith, medicine. I'll use every weapon, lest I be brother to him who commits suicide. I trust that You are the source of all healing, all health, and all life. Thank you, God! You made me whole."

When I first started chemotherapy, the viral count in my blood ran into the hundreds of thousands. Three months after I began treatment, I had another viral count blood test to check on my progress.

"Whoooooeeee!" the nurse said when she called me up to give me the results. "Your tests are negative." The result had clearly shocked her. While the counts of many patients go down in three months, very seldom do they dip all the way to zero. They could find none of the virus in my blood.

"Is that a good thing?" I asked.

"Oh, yeah," she replied. "That's *very* good."

I can't tell you how many people I've talked to who have some form of hepatitis but who are not getting treatment because they heard that the medicine was so harsh. I say the same thing to every one of them:

"Dying is not that much fun, either. Dying and not knowing your grandkids, dying and not fulfilling your destiny, dying and losing years of your life—that's not cool, either. Come on, this is a fight! Use every weapon you have to fight and overcome your problems."

How did I clear the virus? Was it the power of God? Was it the vitamins, the diet? Was it the chiropractic care? Was it the chemotherapy?

Yes! I give God the glory! The means God used doesn't change my testimony at all. It doesn't affect my story at all. I fought the giant and won!

"Did you use the slingshot?"

"Yes!"

"Well, then, it wasn't God."

"Did you use a sword?"

"Yeah."

"Well, then, why didn't you trust God?"

Hey, give me a slingshot, a sword, a tank; a machine gun...got any airplanes? Ballistic missiles? Every time I fire, I'm going to say, "Thank you, Jesus!"

Boom!

"Thank you, Lord! Write a scripture on that bomb!"

It's not either/or. Use every tool. Use every weapon.

Use everything you've got! Trust the Lord to guide you.

PART 4

Overcoming Your Past

14

How to Respond to Disease and Disaster

As you run your race, you are going to hit some hills, some potholes, maybe a storm, maybe suffer a few cramps, a pulled hamstring, or a twisted ankle—but that doesn't mean the race is over.

You can either allow the challenges of life to pull you down, discourage you and stop you from reaching your destiny, or you can use those same challenges to rise up to a higher level of life—like the Word says, to rise up with wings like eagles.

You need to learn to think biblically. Then, whatever happens—the good stuff and the bad stuff, the victories and the failures—will help you grow stronger and do better. So begin to look for what you can get out of every situation.

Instead of asking, "Why does this always happen to me? Why do I have to go through this? Why didn't God heal me?" learn to ask, "What can God do with this that will make me a better person?"

If you get into a negative, unscriptural mindset, then you won't learn. You'll still have the problem, but you won't be learning from it. But if you keep a scriptural mindset, then you'll look for the things that make you better and stronger and wiser and more compassionate. More like Jesus.

When my son Caleb and I climbed Mount Rainier (his first time, my third), I didn't think, *This will be so much fun. Every step will be a joy.* There are parts of the mountain where you're strapped to a rope, inching around a rock, and if you look down, you'll start to wonder, *What the heck am I doing here?* So you don't look down. You look forward and you keep focused and you get through that section, and maybe an hour later you sit and look back and you think, *Wow, we got through that! That's amazing!* Not every part of it is fun, but every part of it is a piece of the journey, helping you to get to the next level and reach your summit. It is exciting, rewarding, fulfilling, but not always fun.

Remember when David, as a boy, went after Goliath, the huge Philistine soldier (1 Samuel 17)? David had a slingshot and he planted a rock right between the giant's eyes. David ran up and stood on top of Goliath. David had no sword because he was a shepherd boy, so he took Goliath's own enormous sword and whacked off the giant's head.

Isn't it amazing that the enemy—that evil, that giant, that problem, that circumstance—became the key to David's kingdom? How he handled Goliath decided his future—and soon the soldiers were singing, "David, King of Israel!"

You may have to slay some giants of your own. It may be a disease, it may be a bankruptcy, it may be a divorce, or it may be a disaster. It's no fun when you're going through it; but boy, to talk about the victory afterward sure is! It's no fun when the diagnosis is cancer or hepatitis or diabetes or some other disease. But it sure is fun when you tell the story about how, with God's help, you overcame it.

How in the world could hepatitis make me a better man? Well, after eleven months of chemotherapy, I have more compassion for people who are diagnosed with cancer or some other disease. I have more understanding of what they're going through when they're on chemotherapy. And I have the sense that "I did it, and you can, too."

I learned a lot of things through the disease that made me a better person, a better Christian, and a better minister. And so I want to make those discoveries in every area of life. When I win, I want to experience the joy of winning and learn how the joy motivates me and encourages me and empowers me. When I lose, I want to learn what lessons I can and get better—and not lose the next time.

So let's learn some useful lessons from the diseases and disasters of life. God has done some things in my life that were great, even awesome. They might have started out on a pretty sour note, but by the end, through faith, God made them sound like a gorgeous symphony. In fact, we probably learn more in the hard times than we do in the good. Don't get down and hurt, look up and see what you can learn.

TEN STEPS TO VICTORY

When you deal with the diseases and disasters of life, you have a decision to make. Are these things going to make you a better person, or are they going to stop you from reaching your destiny?

I faced that decision in 2004, when I first learned I had hepatitis C. That was not a fun year! Yet in the process of those long months, I learned some valuable, and even crucial, lessons.

1. No matter what, stay focused on God's plan for your future.

After you've been sick for a while, you just get so tired of fighting. You're tired of hurting. I know I was. Every day I had a headache and every day I had nausea. All food tasted like I was trying to eat aluminum. I got very weak and lost tons of weight—and I'm not a big guy to begin with. I needed new belts to hold up my pants. I looked like a refugee.

I didn't *feel* like doing anything—but I kept my focus on my future. Every morning, I'd get up, get ready, and take the kids to school. Why? Because I'm a dad, I'm influencing kids, I'm raising kids for God, and I'm going to be around to see their kids and their grandkids. I determined to stay engaged with my vision and my future.

We also continued with plans for building a new sanctuary for our church. Why? Well, just because I got sick didn't mean God stopped the church. Just because I had a battle to face didn't mean God changed my destiny. We moved ahead with our new campus in order to change the spiritual environment of the Northwest. I never hesitated or thought about pulling back.

Don't lose the vision God has called you to! Stay focused.

"Easier said than done," you may say. True—but that doesn't mean it can't be done. So how do you keep focused on your vision, even when you're hurting?

First, you have to recognize that God is not the author of confusion (1 Corinthians 14:33). So God said to Jesus, "I'm sending you to the earth so you can give your life as a ransom for many. Now you're going to have to deal with the Pharisees; you're going to have to deal with Rome; you're going to have to deal with a lot of stuff. But stick with it, and I guarantee you will wind up in the winner's circle." And that's why Jesus set his face like flint. Regardless of what happened,

He knew where He had to go, because that was God's plan for His life (Hebrews 12:2–3).

You have to get that same kind of focus. If God called you to marriage, then despite whatever problems come up—communication troubles, financial difficulties, physical challenges, in-law predicaments—you stick with it. Your troubles don't change the fact that God called you to have a great Christian family.

If God called you to raise up a business, then despite the zoning problems or the banking problems or the manufacturing problems, He has called you to overcome those things through faith and persistence. Fight through them to victory!

It all starts with knowing what God has called you to do, and remembering that He is not a God of confusion. He is not going to change His mind about your destiny or try to stop it when it's only partly finished.

Second, you have to believe that God has a way. *All* things are possible with God. You can overcome the relational problem, the physical challenge, the financial difficulty. You're going to get through this; you're going to find a way. "No temptation [or problem or challenge] has seized you except what is common to man. And God is faithful; he will not let you be tempted beyond what you can bear. But when you are tempted, he will also provide a way out so that you can stand up under it" (1 Corinthians 10:13, NIV). You have to find that "way out." You may not know what it is, but you just know that you will overcome.

Keep your focus, look to Jesus, and stay locked on your vision— because your vision is your future.

2. Stay close to people who will empower you, not discourage you.

People mean well, but sometimes they're not very smart. Some people can bring discouragement to you without even realizing it.

Many people would come up to me and say, "Oh, I heard about the sickness. I feel so bad! Are you going to be okay?" They didn't realize how that kind of exchange never helps.

Others wanted to tell me their stories: "You know my aunt Betsy? She had that same thing, and she died." Well, *now* I'm encouraged. They don't understand that by telling their negative story, they're not helping me win my battle.

I had to decide I was just not going to talk to people who would pull me down. I stuck with those who would encourage and empower me. I loved it when people would tell me, "Man, you are looking *good*," and, "Hey, it's all right, you're doing well. You're getting through this. We're with you. We have your back. We're covering you with prayer." That kind of person helps you stay strong—so hang around those people. Stay with the men and women who encourage you and empower you, not the ones who pull you down.

An athlete in our church had to confront a physical challenge. I didn't call up and say, "What are the doctors saying?" I don't need to know that, as if I were part of his medical team. Instead, I called to encourage him in a positive way.

I don't ever call my buddies and ask, "What are the bankers saying?" I just call and say, "Hey, God's for you; God's with you."

For those fighting sickness, I say, "I'm calling you 'healed.' So far as I'm concerned, you *are* healed and you are whole from the top of your head to the soles of your feet."

Be that kind of friend. Be the friend who encourages and empowers those around you. Don't be the friend they want to avoid.

One last thing: Never talk to people in the waiting room of your doctor's office. I'm not teasing! Proverbs 13:20 says, "He who walks with wise *men* will be wise, / But the companion of fools will be destroyed." So put up your newspaper and don't make eye contact, because they will want to tell you their symptoms, their diagnoses, their pain, and their problems. Remember, you're not there to magnify your sickness; you're there to fight for your healing.

3. Pray without ceasing, especially when negative reports come.

Sometimes we hear a negative report from the doctor, the bank, or the attorney, and in response we say, "Oh, boy, on Sunday I have *got* to get the pastor to pray about this." What we don't realize is that we let that seed take root all week long. We take the negative report and we hold it for days, thinking that sometime in the future, "I'm going to pray about it."

No! Scripture says to pray without ceasing (1 Thessalonians 5:17), so right then, at the moment the doctor brings the bad report, say, "Excuse me, Doc. I'll be right back." Then go over into the next room and say, "Father, I just want to thank You. Your Spirit is working in me. I am healed in the Name of Jesus. You bore my sickness, carried my disease. I just wanted to touch base with You on that."

Then go back to your physician and say, "Okay, go ahead, Doc. What have you got for me?" I don't allow the negative to take root in my spirit. I choose to pray without ceasing.

Or maybe you open your bank statement and realize you don't quite have the month covered. Then you can say, "Father, I'm trusting You. You're Jehovah-Jireh, the Lord who provides. You decided to give me an abundant life, so the report on this financial statement is not the last word. I'm going to stay in touch with You."

Wait on the Lord and He will renew your strength. Don't wait for Sunday! Pray without ceasing.

4. Don't make decisions when you feel fatigued, in pain, or depressed.

Don't make decisions that affect other people or your future when you are in pain, when you're fatigued, or when you feel depressed. When you're hurting, you can't reason clearly, you don't think your best, and you won't make the wisest choices.

I figured out right away when I was on chemo that I shouldn't make important decisions. When a staff member would come to me and say, "We have this issue going on in the children's church," my first thought was, *Do we really need the children's church?* Or when someone would tell me about a challenge with the men's ministry, I'd immediately think, *I don't even want to go to the men's meeting.*

You see, because I was hurting and tired, I would look negatively at everything. But I was smart enough to shut up and say to the staff members, "Would you guys get together, discuss this, and make a decision?" They made the right choices. They worked it out. But if I had stayed involved when I was in pain, I could have messed up my future.

Don't make decisions about your marriage when you're hurting; you may mess up your destiny. Don't make critical decisions when you feel stressed and fatigued; you may miss God's best. Let the people around you support you and help you. Wait until your strength comes back, and then make those decisions.

5. Don't let your environment be controlled or contaminated by your problems.

When a person has been sick for a while, they collect quite a lineup of prescription bottles. You go into their bathroom or kitchen and they have medications and prescriptions scattered all over. You go into the living room and next to the easy chair they have the medical report form, along with the next dose of pills, so they don't even have to get up to take them. Their environment becomes contaminated by their disease.

You see the same thing in people who struggle financially. You go into their office and they have a letter from an attorney right on top of their desk. They have the depressing statement from the bank. They have all this material around them that reminds them of their problems.

I'm not saying that you should ignore or deny the negative. I *am* saying, don't let it become part of your environment.

When I brought home syringes, pills, drugs, and all the other paraphernalia, I had a little place for it where I put it all away. I didn't let it become a part of my home. I didn't want my wife or my children growing up in a sick environment. And it was a funny thing—eleven months of pills every morning and every night, shots all the time, and in the end, someone asked my kids, "When did your dad take his shots?" and they said, "I don't know." They'd never thought about *when* I did it, because they never saw me do it. They knew I did it; I wasn't hiding anything. I just didn't let it become part of our home.

Some of us let our problems—by our conversation, by our attitude, and by the physical things we have around us—contaminate our environment.

Have you ever met somebody who wanted to show you their scars or always tell you their latest diagnosis? I'm amazed that some people (who don't have a medical degree) have learned so much about their disease that they can expound for hours about all their symptoms.

Is it human nature that we want to share our pain when it doesn't help us to do so? I had a friend whose toes had been amputated because of circulation problems. He always wanted to show people his foot, and I refused to look. Eventually he got frustrated with me.

"Why don't you want to see? Does it disgust you?" he asked.

"No, of course not," I replied. "But, I see you as healthy, I see you as whole, and I refuse to see anything else." When I speak like that, I'm not ignoring reality. But, folks, we're fighting for our health here! We're fighting for our lives—and we don't want our environment to be controlled by negative things.

Through the course of my own treatment, my doctors and health care providers would continually tell me about my red blood cells, my white blood cells, my hemoglobin, and all these other things. They would always tell me my something-or-other was at a certain number, and if it went to a certain other number, they would have to lower my dose of chemotherapy. As they explained all these things, in my head I just hummed a tune, because I didn't care. At the end of their statement I would ask, "Do you want me to do anything else? If you want me to do something else, then tell me and I'll do it; but all this other stuff is irrelevant." The whole time I would be thinking, *By His stripes I was healed*.

Don't let your world get controlled by your problems. Don't get to where you want to show everybody your scars and tell them what your doctors said. As much as possible, create a positive environment around you.

6. Don't spend too much time in self-analysis.

After three months on chemotherapy, I was declared clear of the virus—but my doctor told me I needed to continue treatment for eleven months in order to make sure the virus was gone for good. I felt sicker during treatment than when I was walking around with hepatitis C and didn't know it. But I trusted my doctor. I wanted to stop because it was no fun at all, but I went through the entire eleven-month treatment. If I had thought too long about that decision, however, I might have second-guessed myself right into a bigger problem. I might have stopped treatment and the virus could have come back even stronger.

Many people give up too soon, don't finish, don't stay the course, and so they never see what the Lord can really do in their lives. And why don't they continue? Often they stop because they overthink everything they do.

Don't spend a lot of time second-guessing yourself. Don't overanalyze. You will just worry yourself and may even become worse. Instead, stay up and stay positive about what you are doing. Get a checkup and ask, "Am I doing everything I need to do?" Stay faithful to what you said you were going to do, and don't keep wondering if you chose the right track.

Trust what the Word says in Ephesians 4:14 about being tossed to and fro with every wind of doctrine (or in my case, every medical option), and what James 1:8 says about a double-minded man being unstable in all his ways. Be confident in what God says and in His promises. When you consult God, listen to your spirit and don't talk yourself out of wisdom. When thoughts of doubt come (and they will), read the promises of God, who generously gives you wisdom if you ask (James 1:5). If your answer is not apparent to you, consult safe, knowledgeable, mature Christian people for their input (Proverbs 14:6).

7. Don't be afraid to reach out for help.

I remember what Dr. Fred Price said when his wife, Betty, started receiving cancer treatment using chemotherapy and radiation. Dr. Price admitted, "Since we didn't have the faith to *keep* it off of her, we knew we would need some help to *get* it off of her." We often need help from people around us. God made us part of His body. We are not isolated individuals who must handle everything alone. Doctors, counselors, pastors, friends, and family are all part of strong, healthy living.

After almost thirty years of being a Christian, of believing the Word and speaking the Word, I believe in healing. I've prayed for people to be healed and I called myself healed—and yet I still ended up with hepatitis. Yes, I used my faith; but I also used everything I could to support and help my faith.

A lot of people won't go for help when they find themselves in financial trouble. They keep insisting, "I can get myself out." So, let me get this straight: The counsel that got you *into* the problem is now somehow going to get you *out* of the problem? Don't let your ego or pride cause you to hide from others. Be open and humble. The things you need from God may come through other people. Many a cancer patient could have been saved through treatment if they had been diagnosed earlier.

If you didn't have the faith to keep it (whatever "it" is) off you, you are going to need some help to get it off you. That's why the Bible says there's safety in a multitude of counselors (Proverbs 11:14). Matthew 18:19 tells us that when two of God's children agree, it shall be done by our Father in heaven. Get some positive support and stop thinking you have to do it all by yourself.

8. Keep laughing; stay up.

Proverbs 17:22 tells us, "A merry heart does good, *like* medicine." The last thing you want to do if you are in a battle for your health or any other challenge is to watch a bunch of negative, sad, emotional movies. The last thing you want to do if you are fighting sickness and disease is watch horror movies. No!

Get out all the fun stuff, the happy stuff, all those romantic, happy-ending movies. I got together a whole bunch of movies and videos that made me laugh. People would come in and say, "What are you laughing at?"

"I don't know," I'd say, "just some stupid thing—but it's *funny*."

About half of the people on the kind of treatment I went through quit before they finish because of the intense emotional and physiological strain it causes. They would get depressed and try to commit suicide or give up on their health. So when my doctors did a psychological evaluation on me every couple of months, I'd just start making jokes.

"Do you feel like committing suicide?" they'd ask.

"No, but I have a few others I'd like to *shoot—just kidding, Doc.* Hey, Doc, I'm trying to get through this without going crazy—and hanging around you isn't helping."

After a while, they figured out how to deal with me. I was a problem patient. But they did think I was funny.

When the enemy can steal your joy he can steal your faith (James 1:2–3). Stay up and happy in your spirit and you will get through problems better. Don't hang out in the situations that weigh you down; "the joy of the LORD is your strength" (Nehemiah 8:10). A merry heart does good like medicine, Scripture says, so take your medicine and smile up, stay up, and stay happy.

9. Choose to live and not die, choose to prosper and not be poor, choose to overcome and not quit. Don't give up!

God says in Deuteronomy 30:19, "I have set before you life and death, blessing and cursing; therefore choose life." You have to choose life every day.

"Today, I'm going to get up and take a shower. I'm going to go to work. I'm going to choose to live."

"Today, I'm going to smile. I'm going to be nice to my friends. I'm going to choose to live."

"Today, I'm going to believe that God is working on my behalf. I'm overcoming this problem. I choose life. I choose blessing, and I will be blessed. I'm not going to live a struggling, mediocre, halfway, poverty-stricken life. I choose life, and I choose blessing."

You absolutely have to choose it. And sometimes you have to say it out loud:

I choose life!

I choose blessing!

I choose prosperity!

And you must choose it every day.

10. Get in and stay in a good church.

God's house and God's family are His center of healing and strength. Find a place that is happy, teaches the Bible, and is growing. That's where you need to be every week. Go to church every Sunday—at least. The Word says in Proverbs 27:17, "*As* iron sharpens iron, / So a man sharpens the countenance of his friend." The Word also says in Hebrews 10:25 not to forsake "the assembling of ourselves together, as *is* the manner of some, but [to exhort] *one another*." The church is God's institution. He ordained or directed us to be together, to spend time together, *to sharpen each other*. By being out in the world on your own without the church or congregation of people for encouragement and strength you are making life much harder than it needs to be. By utilizing the help and support of others you have a greater chance of success in every realm than if you're trying to live life on your own. We need each other and not being in a church is often a recipe for disaster. The Bible says, "Those who are planted in the house of the LORD / Shall flourish in the courts of our God. / They shall still bear fruit in old age; / They shall be fresh and flourishing" (Psalm 92:13–14).

15

Dream Killers

We all come into the world with the ability to dream big dreams. When you're young, you dream big and you think you can do everything. Boys think they are going to be an NFL player, and when they are done with that, they are going to the NBA. Then they will take on an easy sport, like major league baseball. Then they're going to start a company, and when that's successful, they are going to be a missionary.

Kids just dream big. You did, didn't you? You got through junior high, high school, college, and you had a career plan. You were on your way!

But then you got out into the adult world—and suddenly you ran into a few problems. Maybe you had some relationship breakdowns and got hurt by a boyfriend or girlfriend. Maybe you got into a company thinking it was going to launch you into a great career, but you discovered the boss was a jerk and your coworkers were no fun. So you quit. You tried this and then that, and then a few years down the road, you realized you had let go of your dream. You had given up your destiny.

Now you're just trying to pay the bills.

That's the way the majority of people in America live today. They started out with big visions and exciting dreams, but ended up just trying to survive.

What causes most of us to give up on the dream? What prompts us to forget about destiny in favor of mere survival? Fatigue, stress, and anxiety. These things force many of us to drop out of the race. Jesus understood this well, and so He says to us:

Come to Me, all *you* who labor and are heavy laden, and I will give you rest. Take My yoke upon you and learn from Me, for I am gentle and lowly in heart, and you will find rest for your souls. For My yoke *is* easy and My burden is light. (Matthew 11:28–30)

What burdens are you shouldering today? What kind of labor is dragging you down? What has been making you feel "heavy laden"?

Sometimes we grow up thinking that a life heavy with challenges, difficulties, and problems—burdens weighing us down—is good. We imagine that it means we're important. After all, doesn't it show we are really busy, running around doing a lot of important things?

When someone says, "I have a lot of irons in the fire! My plate is full!" what are they trying to say? They're telling you they're busy. And by that, they really mean, "I'm important. My life must be good, because look how busy I am." Some people are taught that to be spiritual you must be burdened with the weight of the world.

But Jesus says, "No."

Being burdened is *not* good. Being heavy laden is not godly, it's not spiritual, and it doesn't mean you are fulfilling your destiny. Just being busy doesn't mean you are getting anything worthwhile done, nor does it mean you are in God's will or on your way to what the Lord has for you.

Jesus says you need to switch the brand you've been drinking from Burden Heavy to Burden Light, because heavy burdens are going to wear you out. If you keep living under the weight and the burdens of this world, you will faint and you will fall. And eventually you will give up your dreams and forfeit your destiny.

"Take my yoke upon you," Jesus counsels you. That doesn't mean, "Get out of the race!" It simply means, yoke up with Him. Think of the yoke on an ox, the harness that many farmers around the world still use to hook up their plows to their beasts of burden. Jesus says to you, "Get hooked up to God like that. Get in the harness with Him. When you do, He'll help you to pull the cart. He'll help you to plow the field. He'll help you to win your race."

God isn't going to do everything for you, of course. Remember, He invites you to *join* Him under the yoke to receive His help, not dump everything off on Him while you go take a nap. But if you'll come to Him—if you'll wait upon the Lord, if you'll stay involved with God—then He'll keep you going in the race of life. He'll help you to handle those burdens and labors and other responsibilities and challenges that make you feel so heavy laden.

If you continue to do it your own way, however—the normal way the world does it—then you'll just get beat up and beat down. Then you'll get tired and resentful. Soon you'll get bitter and develop an attitude. You'll become a mean, old person—even if you're only thirty-two! That's no fun.

"Take my yoke upon you," Jesus said, "and learn from me."

Learn to walk with God and stay close to Jesus. Why act like the rest of the world? If they want to carry all those burdens by themselves, let them. But you don't have to. Your destiny is far brighter than that. Don't let an urgency addiction—trying to be important by being overworked or trying to do too much—kill your dream.

LOSING YOUR DREAM

Some of us give up the dream and abandon our destiny because we practice what I call *habit insanity*. You get under pressure and you feel stressed. You're superbusy, going through the motions, trying hard and working nonstop—but all the while you are in the grips of habit insanity. You keep doing the same thing, year after year, hoping you'll get different results and wishing things would turn out better... but of course, they don't.

You have to do something you've never done to get something you've never had. It may be something with your kids. Perhaps you had a certain way of disciplining your first child that worked very well. When you disciplined her in this way, she changed her behavior and got the schoolwork done or cleaned her room or whatever it might be. But then the next child came along, and he has a very different response to that favorite discipline—and yet you keep trying it over and over again, each time getting louder and keeping it up longer. When are you going to realize, "Hey, wait a minute! I have a different person here, a different personality with different gifting and a different skill set. Maybe I need to approach him differently"? So rather than do what you always do—only harder, more, or faster—maybe you should try something different.

So how do you free yourself from habit insanity? What should you do in order to move yourself away from this kind of craziness? First, you have to admit the obvious: that what you've been doing hasn't worked in this situation.

There's a lot of truth in the old adage that we need to start working smarter, not just harder. If you work hard enough, I suppose you could chop down a tree with a hammer—but that's not very smart. Get an ax! Get a chainsaw! Get smart!

Habit insanity gets us stuck in thinking that we really are doing the right thing, we just need to do it more—when in fact, we may be doing exactly the wrong thing.

The apostle Paul seemed to be pretty good at avoiding habit insanity. He learned early on to approach different groups of people in different ways. He tried to use whatever he thought might work. "When I was with the Jews," he wrote, "I lived like a Jew to bring the Jews to Christ. When I was with those who follow the Jewish law, I too lived under that law. Even though I am not subject to the law, I did this so I could bring to Christ those who are under the law. When I am with the Gentiles who do not follow the Jewish law, I too live apart from that law so I can bring them to Christ. But I do not ignore the law of God; I obey the law of Christ. When I am with those who are weak, I share their weakness, for I want to bring the weak to Christ. Yes, I try to find common ground with everyone, doing everything I can to save some" (1 Corinthians 9:20–22, NLT). He used whatever worked, and he adapted his approach when working

Many people with a disease settle into a routine of living with it. They have a lifestyle built around being sick, being out of work, being weak. Their favorite chair or bed, TV shows, trips to the doctor and pharmacy all become routine. Don't get sucked into living with your disease or problem. It's your enemy who wants to kill you. Fight it. Get up, get dressed, look your best, go to church, do whatever you can. When you learn to get along with the pain, you'll probably keep going. "And do not give the devil a Foothold" (Ephesians 4:27, NIV).

with various groups so that he could become as effective as possible with each one.

I think we have to do the same thing, whether it's in our career and work life or our parenting or our prayer life. Sometimes what we're doing isn't working, so let's be willing to change. Anything else is just habit insanity—and that's a pretty poor substitute for grabbing hold of your destiny. When was the last time you did something for the first time? Don't get stuck in old ruts. Be willing to change.

Others among us get sidetracked from pursuing their dreams and their destiny because they get trapped in what was. They can't move ahead into a brighter future because they're still living in a dark past.

Like in so many areas of life, you have a choice: either you live with your past, with all its pain and bitterness and hurt, or you go on to your future and to your destiny. You can't do both. You either hold on to your unforgiveness, resentment, stress, and anxiety or you give them up and reach for your dreams and your destiny. Even if we have had success in our past, we can't live on it forever. We need to leave the past and go on to our next success.

A ship in a harbor either leaves its anchor in the water and stays put or the crew pulls up anchor and the ship goes out to sea. In the same way, you can either hang on to your hurt feelings and resentments from the wounds you received in the past or you can give them up in order to go for your destiny. It's your choice.

So what are you going to do? Will you cling to your hurtful past, with all its bitterness and resentment and anger, or go on to something new and better? It's really no choice at all. God's best, God's will, God's destiny—*that* should be your only choice. "Not that I have already attained, or am already perfected; but I press on, that I may lay hold of that for which Christ Jesus has also laid hold of me. Brethren, I do not count myself to have apprehended; but one thing

I do, forgetting those things which are behind and reaching forward to those things which are ahead" (Philippians 3:12–13).

DESTINY KILLERS

While almost all of us start out life with vision, purpose, and big dreams in our hearts, many of us abandon them at some point along the way in favor of a maintenance lifestyle, a survival mentality. Why? Because we allow stress, fear, and worry to stop us from possessing God's best. "[L]et us lay aside every weight, and the sin which so easily ensnares *us*, and let us run with endurance the race that is set before us" (Hebrews 12:1b).

Worry hinders our creativity. Fear stops our faith. Stress drains our energy and anxiety kills our vision. And if you don't get a handle on these killers, it's very possible that you could suffer a heart attack—not just the physical kind, but also the kind that drains your heart of its God-given dreams. I see three primary sources of these destiny killers.

1. Negative Emotions

Envy, unforgiveness, jealousy, pettiness, resentment, and a simmering hostility will all cause your heart to shrink, close, and fail. These are what I call "negative emotions," and if you don't deal with them, they will give you a spiritual heart attack.

A lot of people in our world are carrying around all kinds of negative emotions that do nothing but hurt them. Very often they say things like, "I'll forgive, but I won't forget"—meaning that they haven't really forgiven anything. They'll say, "How can I just let it go? He hurt me! And I'm not going to let him get away with it"—and all the while, the only ones they're really hurting are themselves.

Where do all these negative emotions come from? Most of the time they come from legitimate sources, from real events that cause real pain. It's Mom and Dad's divorce. It's the boyfriend's abuse or the husband's rejections. It's the snub at work. It's the cliques at church. It's the mean salesperson. It's all that stuff. The term "negative emotion" describes all the raw feelings and the hurt that come out of the painful stuff we fail to process biblically.

If we dealt with it scripturally, of course, we would forgive. We would understand. We would not let the sun go down on our wrath. We would deal with it and move on and forget those things that are behind. But unfortunately, we don't always deal with things in a scriptural way—sometimes because of our immaturity, and sometimes because of our laziness. So we start carrying what God never built us to carry...and the negative emotions that result cause our spiritual hearts to feel overwhelmed.

When we have a spiritual heart attack, we no longer feel we can trust God. We no longer can keep the joy of the Lord. We just can't deal with life, so then we either get depressed or drunk or avoid unpleasant situations or deny that they even exist. Our hearts just can't handle the negative emotions that come when we fail to handle the hurts of life in a scriptural way.

When I first got saved, I heard all the typical things: "You're a Christian now, all things are new! You're a brand-new person! God has wiped away your past!"

But a couple of weeks later, after I had experienced a few more problems of life, I started thinking: *Maybe I'm not really saved. I have some of the same negative attitudes, emotions, and feelings. I still feel bad and my life is not fun.*

I quickly discovered that all this negative stuff in my heart that they told me would no longer be there because I had become a Christian was still there. I still vividly remember my sense of fear that I wasn't really saved. *Maybe it didn't work. Maybe I've sinned so much that I can't get saved. You know, I've heard there's something in the Bible called the unpardonable sin. Maybe I did that?*—which, by the way, is the most-asked question in our Wednesday night Bible study at church: "How do you know if you've committed the unpardonable sin?"[1]

Those first few years, as a young Christian I really struggled with how to deal with my own negative emotions.

As I came to better understand Romans 12:2, however—"do not be conformed to this world, but be transformed by the renewing of your mind, that you may prove what *is* that good and acceptable and perfect will of God"—I realized, *Okay, although I'm saved, I still have my past to deal with. God's forgiven it. It's wiped out in terms of how He sees it—but it's still a part of me, and I have to learn and grow and deal with my negative emotions.*

As a more mature Christian, I started dealing with different issues. I don't think I ever worry anymore about losing my salvation or dying; those issues are pretty much settled in my heart. But I do worry about letting people down, about not being able to lead well or get through the process of building the church or finding the

---

[1] I have heard some say that "the unpardonable sin" should really be called "the unrepentable sin." In other words, those who have really committed this sin have no desire to repent of it. They want no part of God and no association with His people. No one will ever come to God saying, "Please, God, forgive me my sins! I am so sorry for what I have done. I need You! I want to live forever in heaven with You!" only to hear God say, "Sorry, kid, but you committed the unpardonable sin. You're out." That will never happen. Bottom line is, if you worry that you have committed the unpardonable sin, then you can be sure that you haven't.

right staff member or handling a problem with the school. I tend to worry about people and problems and issues dear to my heart. I forget these are *God's* people and *God's* church. Jesus said, "*I* will build My church," not, "Casey will build My church."

So when I feel those negative emotions building up, I have to back up in my mind and release them. I have to let it all go. I can't let those negative emotions pile up to the point where I feel paralyzed with worry. I have to keep myself focused on the truths of God, and not on my own anxieties. I just refuse to let my negative emotions keep me from my destiny.

2. Self-Condemnation

So many people worry about what everybody else thinks about them. I have an announcement to make: They are *not* thinking about you. They're more likely worried about what you think about *them*. While we're all sitting and wondering what each thinks about the other, ain't *nobody* thinking about you, because we're all too busy thinking about ourselves.

Low self-esteem, self-doubts, always questioning yourself, wondering if you're good enough, wondering if you've done enough—all of those can bring on a spiritual heart attack. Constant doubts, self-condemnations, and fears are all symptoms of an imminent spiritual coronary.

You know what the problem really is? It's overanalysis. It's good to examine yourself now and then, but don't get caught up in the paralysis of analysis, self-doubt, or self-condemnation. Remember what Paul said: "I care very little if I am judged by you or by any human court; indeed, I do not even judge myself. My conscience is clear, but that does not make me innocent. It is the Lord who judges me" (1 Corinthians 4:3–4, NIV).

We live in a world that constantly magnifies "self." Maybe it's always been that way; maybe every generation deals with the problem in a similar way. We could call it narcissism. It's being caught up in "me" and constantly asking, aloud or silently, "Am I good enough? What do you think about me? Okay, okay, enough about you; what do you think about *me*?"

Part of Christianity is getting beyond yourself. You're not living for yourself anymore. It's not about you. It's not about what you want. It's about God and what God wants. It's about His plan and how you can be an important part of that plan. I really think that's the *only* place you can find joy and a sense of self-worth and value. You'll find it only when you get beyond yourself.

I don't know how many times it's happened to me over the course of my ministry, but I consider it a very telling characteristic of our generation. Some lady comes up to me and says, "I'm leaving my husband. I'm sick and tired of our marriage. I can't stand it anymore! He won't change. He won't listen." And I agree with everything she says. She really is in pain. It's terrible; it's tragic. And then she makes this telling statement: "And doesn't God want me to be happy? A divorce will make me happy, so I'm leaving him."

Well, up to that point I had agreed with everything the lady said. Her husband really *is* a jerk. He really *should* listen. He really *needs* to change. All of that is true—but not that last statement. That wasn't true at all. God's highest purpose isn't that you be happy (or at least, not in the way you think). Yes, He wants you to be happy; but true happiness or joy comes from following Him, not from following your own worldly desires.

If you want to seize your destiny, then you have to get beyond the question, "How can I be happy? What's in it for me?" You have to learn to live for something bigger than yourself.

I realize that's tough, though, because the world constantly promotes self-centeredness. We see it in so many ways. If you're not feeling good about yourself, then you need this antidepressant drug or that face-lift. The idea is something *out there* will make you feel good. Of course, it probably won't work, because after the face-lift you'll want the liposuction, and after the liposuction you'll want the body sculpting...and it just never ends.

Self is never satisfied. Proverbs says the eyes of greed are never fulfilled. And a constant focus on self will always leave you with feelings of self-doubt, self-condemnation, and self-reproach. And when you're filled with that stuff, you have no more room left for your destiny.

3. Unhealthy Lifestyle

Good health is threefold: spirit, soul, and body. And you need to practice a healthy lifestyle in all three areas.

A healthy spiritual life includes things like prayer, Bible reading, a vibrant church life, actively working on your relationship with God, worship, and all the other things the Bible prescribes for what Jesus called an "abundant" life (John 10:10).

A healthy soul life includes pure thinking, feeding the mind with godly thoughts. I like to read books that challenge my mind and inform my worldview. These books aren't necessarily "spiritual," but they keep me thinking hard, thinking godly, and thinking positive.

That's not to say it's mind over matter, or that we need to have a positive mental attitude about everything that happens in life. Some things are *bad* and when we think about them, it's a bummer. But we need to mentally process the stuff of life in a biblical way. We need to think scripturally about whatever thoughts we entertain in our mind.

I think this is as important to soul health as going to church is. Some people believe they can go to church and worship on Sunday, and then read the newspaper every morning and listen to the radio all day, every day, and worry and talk trash and get involved in the "stuff" of the world, without ever guarding their thoughts or ever renewing their minds to the Word of God. And then they wonder, *Hey, I'm a Christian—why am I so depressed?* Well, if you're cramming junk food into your thought life, then you're going to get the same kind of results as stuffing junk food into your physical life. Garbage in, garbage out.

Constantly listening to negative things is the same as eating bad spiritual food. Really, it's bad *soul* food. You just can't live a long, healthy life on chips and soda pop, and feeding your mind junk is just as harmful.

Practicing an unhealthy lifestyle in spirit, soul, or body will bring on a spiritual heart attack. And at the end of your life, you will feel deeply unfulfilled and you will wonder, *What was it all about?*

To feel a genuine sense of fulfillment, satisfaction, and destiny, you have to make a regular meal out of the right spiritual food, soul food, and physical food. That's what it takes to live this life that God has called you to.

ARE YOU HAVING REAL FUN?

Most people in our world aren't having fun. You look at the faces you see on the freeway every morning, and you *know* they are not having any fun. I mean fun in the sense of a deep fulfillment and heartfelt joy of life. You walk through your office or shop any day of the week, and you see a lot of people who are not running their race with joy.

They are just getting by. They're struggling. They are clearly not happy with what they are doing, and they certainly aren't living a full life.

I have heard it said that up to 73 percent of the men and women in America do not like the work they are doing. Yet being unhappy is not motivation enough for most of them to change. Not enjoying what they do is often not reason enough for them to do something about it.

And so they give up on the dream they had as a kid. They drop out of the race. They give up on destiny.

One of our biggest problems is that we rely on ourselves, instead of God. We forget that our greatest joy comes from pursuing the destiny He sets before us. It just won't work to try to get satisfaction from the world. You can concentrate on getting the right job, the right career, and making money, but when you finally rake in the green stuff, you'll still wonder, *What can I get with the money that will make me happy?* At the end of the day there is not enough money in the world to provide fulfillment in the heart.

Have you allowed anything like that to kill your dream? Have you permitted something to force you out of the race? Have you given up on pursuing your destiny?

Maybe you got involved with alcohol and the party scene, and today you just *have* to have a cocktail or a drink. Or maybe you turned to drugs in an attempt to get some different kind of highs. Then it was sex. You tried different men or women, and then you tried men and women.

That's the world, isn't it?

In general, you see a world that's unhappy, that keeps trying a variety of ways to find a little happiness. You can see it in everything from the thrill seeker jumping out of airplanes, to the sexual addict—but basically, we are all looking for the same thing. We're all trying to find something that makes us feel fulfilled and valuable and that gives us a reason to live. We're all searching for a purpose in life.

You, however, already know that God has a purpose for *your* life. He has an amazing destiny for you. He has a dream that He invites you to pursue, a calling that He wants you to fulfill.

Paul says, "I have fought the good fight, I have finished the race, I have kept the faith" (2 Timothy 4:7). You can do that, too.

You don't need to end up unhappy and unfulfilled. You don't need to, because you can avoid the traps and the detours and the dead ends that leave people empty and unfulfilled. God has something much better for you, far better than mere "fun." You can have exactly what King David had long ago. Listen to his expression of wonder in this amazing prayer to God, and see if it doesn't answer your own heart's call:

> You have made known to me the path of life;
> > you will fill me with joy in your presence,
> > with eternal pleasures at your right hand.
>
> (Psalm 16:11, NIV)

That's a lot better than "fun," don't you think?

16

Overcoming the Past

Years ago I knew a Christian woman who, before she was saved, had lived a sexually immoral life. In the years since her conversion, she had become very overweight. She once told me, "I'm not going to lose the weight, because if I get skinny, I'm going to start flirting with men and I'm going to get back into sin. As long as I stay overweight, I can live holy."

Does that sound like a healthy prescription for living to you? Does it sound "spiritual"?

Any number of things can affect how we see ourselves and how we approach our own race toward the destiny God has set before us. One of them is focusing on the past while missing the present and ignoring the future. And anyone will tell you, that is completely backwards—and unhealthy, too.

Back in chapter 5, I talked about how your new family heritage— the one you got when you joined God's eternal family through faith in Jesus Christ—rendered your earthly family background, ancestry, and heritage relatively unimportant in comparison to where you are headed. Now I want to say that the very same thing is true in regard to your past as an individual.

As a member of God's eternal family, you have no reason or right to dwell on your past or to allow your past to hold you back from running the race to the destiny God has for you. If you want to keep running the race, then you simply have to leave the past behind.

Sadly, there are a lot of people today—including Bible-believing, churchgoing Christians—who remain stuck in the past. Either they are trying to live off their "glory days" (those times when they thought they were happiest, most successful, and fulfilled), while others are beating themselves up because of their own "dark days."

Still others tend to focus on the past because they aren't excited about the present or the future. They don't have high hopes for the future, and they certainly don't see the present as anything glorious. So because they don't see today or tomorrow as anything great, they keep thinking about yesterday.

Still others insist on focusing on the past because they see the future at best as unsure, and at worst as frightening. People with this approach get scared when they look through the windshield, so they spend a lot of time looking in the rearview mirror—and that's why they tend to do a lot of crashing and burning.

But whatever the reason people stay stuck in the past, one thing is for sure: you don't have to join them. God wants you to let go of your past, take His hand, and stride confidently into the great future He has planned for you.

A ROAD MAP TO MOVE AHEAD

The apostle Paul provided us with a road map for how a believer should approach his or her past: "I have been crucified with Christ;

it is no longer I who live, but Christ lives in me; and the *life* which I now live in the flesh I live by faith in the Son of God, who loved me and gave Himself for me" (Galatians 2:20).

That is the approach I like to take in regard to my past and what it has to do with where I am today and where I am headed. What I used to be, who I used to be, is dead. I am a new person in Christ. Crucified with Him, nothing from my past can stop me now. The old person—what I used to be—is dead, and the life that I live today, I live by faith in the Lord Jesus Christ, the Son of God (2 Corinthians 5:17).

The past is dead. Don't let something that doesn't matter rule your life. Don't let the divorce, the bankruptcy, the failure define you. You are a new person in Christ. Shed the pain, regret, the shame and move ahead toward God's destiny for you.

The apostle Paul further defined the road map to your future when he wrote, "Brethren, I do not count myself to have apprehended; but one thing *I do*, forgetting those things which are behind and reaching forward to those things which are ahead, I press toward the goal for the prize of the upward call of God in Christ Jesus" (Philippians 3:13–14).

Part of that "pressing on" is learning to let go of your past, learning to enjoy God's love, forgiveness, and healing…and to forgive yourself and let go of your past sins and mistakes while you're at it.

The ninth chapter of Matthew's Gospel shows and tells us that Jesus came to heal and to forgive and to release us from our past, so that we can serve and be all that God has designed us to do and to be.

The first of these stories involves the healing of a paralyzed man— and right away it takes what appears to be a strange turn: "Then behold, they brought to Him a paralytic lying on a bed. When Jesus saw their faith, He said to the paralytic, 'Son, be of good cheer; your sins are forgiven you'" (Matthew 9:2).

When you first read this account, does it seem a little odd, maybe out of place, for Jesus to look at this man and tell him that his sins were forgiven? The man didn't come to have his sins forgiven; he came to get healed. Who asked anything about forgiveness? The man's friends brought him to Jesus on a mat because he couldn't walk. Wasn't it obvious to everyone there—including Jesus Himself—what this man really wanted and needed?

At the scene were some scribes, Jewish religious leaders who were authorities on the Law. Immediately they felt offended at what Jesus had said to the man—so offended, in fact, that they silently called Him a blasphemer. In their minds, God and God alone had the authority to forgive sins, and for Jesus to say what He did was tantamount to claiming deity for Himself.

But Jesus knew what these men were thinking, and He also knew there were some important spiritual lessons to teach that day. He intended to teach everyone in the crowd the connection between forgiveness and healing.

"Why do you think evil in your hearts?" Jesus asked the scribes. "For which is easier, to say, 'Your sins are forgiven you,' or to say, 'Arise and walk'? But that you may know that the Son of Man has power on earth to forgive sins..."

Then Jesus did what the paralyzed man had come there for in the first place. He healed him and told him, "Arise, take up your bed, and go to your house." The man did just that, and the incident amazed all the people who witnessed it.

There are some important things to notice about this story. First, Jesus didn't merely heal this man's body; He also released him from his past—which evidently was a sinful one. Before He did anything else, Jesus told this man that his sins were forgiven, something He didn't say to everyone He healed. In fact, this is the *only* time in the Gospels when Jesus connected His healing of an individual with His forgiving that individual. To no one else in the Gospels did He say, "I'm forgiving your sins so that you can be physically healed."[1]

Jesus knew that something in this man's past—some kind of sin or wrong thinking, skewed beliefs, or ungodly living—had been at least partly to blame for his paralysis. For that reason, before Jesus did anything to heal the man's body, He healed his spirit and his mind.

I need to pause here and point out that not all sickness and disease comes because of individual sin. Yes, *all* death and sickness and infirmity ultimately is a result of the sin of Adam and Eve in the Garden of Eden. But not all of our diseases and disabilities and other physical problems are a direct result of *personal* sin. Some may be (see 1 Corinthians 11:29–30), but not all. Jesus made this clear when He told the disciples that the man born blind was not sightless because of his sin or his parents' sin. No, he had been born blind so that the power of God could be put on display as he was healed (see John 9:1–4).

Still, even from a strictly medical standpoint, we know that many today are sick because of their wrong thinking, wrong actions, and wrong lifestyle choices. My battle with hepatitis C illustrates the point very powerfully for me. In a very real sense, the sins of my youth showed up as a sickness in my adulthood.

What is God's response to someone like me, or to the alcoholic whose liver is failing, or to the sexually promiscuous person who contracts a disease? Some of us might wrongly say that people like us have gotten what we deserved, that our sicknesses are due to our sin and therefore can never be healed.

But we should notice that Jesus never identified this man's sins; in fact, He never even asked. That tells us that it didn't matter to Jesus

---

[1] Although in John 5 Jesus heals a paralytic, and then later says to him, "See, you are well! Stop sinning or something worse may happen to you" (John 5:14, AMP).

what the man had done; all that mattered was that he needed forgiveness and freedom from his past.

The same thing is true for you. It doesn't matter what kind of sins or mistakes you've made in the past. It doesn't matter what has "paralyzed" you—whether it's spiritual, physical, emotional, mental, or relational. God has one response when you come to Him for healing: "Son, your sins are forgiven. Now get up, get out of that sickness, out of that pain, out of that hurt, and get out there and live."

Jesus didn't come to earth so that He could hold your past against you or so that He could withhold blessings and healing from you. And He didn't come to earth to teach you how to "earn" His healing. Jesus' dealings with this paralytic proved that He had come to forgive, heal, and restore, regardless of what caused the sickness and regardless of what kind of sin the man had fallen into. He simply told him, "your sins are forgiven you," and then gave him one final bit of instruction: "Arise, take up your bed, and go to your house" (Matthew 9:6). In other words, Jesus was telling him, "Get on with your life! Rise to a higher level of life and don't let your past hold you down or keep you sick any longer."

So many people today remain paralyzed, infirmed, and hurt because of their past. They struggle with the hurt, with the sickness, with the guilt, and with the physical pain their past actions may have caused them. And all for one reason: They can't forgive themselves. They may be able to forgive the very worst anyone has ever done to them, but they just can't forgive themselves. Instead, they choose to hold their past sins over their own heads.

Jesus came to earth to forgive anyone who comes to Him. So when He declares you forgiven and "clean," you have no right and no reason to think of yourself as anything but right with Him.

Jesus never much worried about what the religious establishment thought of His ways and His teaching. Nor did He fret over their reaction to the kind of people He associated with.

After Jesus had healed and forgiven the paralytic, He again shook up some of the local religious leaders by calling to fellowship a man whose past, in the eyes of most of his neighbors, anyway, was greedy, selfish, and sinful.

Jesus saw a man named Matthew, a tax collector—the very same Matthew who wrote the Gospel that bears his name—and called him to follow. Matthew did as Jesus asked, and that night he hosted Jesus and His disciples, as well as some other worldly friends, for dinner.

A certain group of important religious leaders of the time, the pharisees, had begun to pay careful attention to everything Jesus said and did, many of them hoping to catch Him in some major gaffe. When they saw who He was eating with, they became indignant and asked the disciples, "Why does your Teacher eat with tax collectors and sinners?" (Matthew 9:11).

In order to understand the significance of that question, you need to understand that tax collectors, although Jewish, served as agents of the Roman government. That alone was enough to put them in the "hated" category by most of the Jewish population. But beyond that, most of them handled their business affairs in a dishonest, even unscrupulous way. They earned a reputation as swindlers who collected not just the taxes due, but also exorbitant "surcharges" that they kept for themselves.

In short, Jesus had chosen to hobnob and dine with someone considered by his own people as the worst of scoundrels. And when the pharisees saw what He was doing, they believed they were justified in asking Him why He ate with sinners.

When Jesus heard of the pharisees' question, He said, "Those who are well have no need of a physician, but those who are sick.

But go and learn what *this* means: '*I desire mercy and not sacrifice.*' For I did not come to call the righteous, but sinners, to repentance' " (Matthew 9:12–13).

In other words, Matthew was *exactly* the kind of person Jesus came to forgive, to save, and to use in His own ministry. Jesus came looking for people with messy pasts, not so that He could condemn them, but so that He could reclaim them and change them and give them a new path to follow.

One of the many great things about Jesus is that He hasn't changed. He's the same yesterday, today, and forever (see Hebrews 13:8). He still forgives people and sets them free from their past. He still heals people of every sickness and every disease—and all of that with no thought of how "bad" that past might seem by human standards.

Jesus wants to make *you* whole. He wants *you* to be freed from the negativity of and bondage to your past. And He's not asking you to become "religious" or to hold to any kind of "tradition" in order for that to happen! All He's asking you to do is to believe and to follow Him. And when you choose to do that, He will forgive you, heal you, cleanse you, and make you suitable and able to serve Him—and ready to move ahead toward your great destiny.

DO WHAT JESUS DID

Just a few days after Jesus had completed the mission His Father had given Him, a spectacular scene broke out in Jerusalem, the city where Jesus spent His last week of life on earth. It was the day of the feast of Pentecost, and Jerusalem was bustling with visitors—devout Jews from all over the known world who had come to celebrate.

On that day, 120 of Jesus' followers had gathered in a house to pray. Suddenly and without warning, a sound like a rushing, mighty wind swept through the group. What looked like tongues of fire perched upon each person present, and under the power of the Holy Spirit, they began speaking in languages they didn't even know.

Moments later, those assembled in the house spilled out into the streets, and visitors from all over the globe heard them speaking *in their own languages*. It didn't make any sense! The visitors could see that these people were all Galileans and that there was no way they should be able to speak those languages. Some of the visitors looked and listened to this scene in confusion, while others assumed that the people speaking in foreign tongues must have had a few too many glasses of wine.

Then, a lone figure stood up and started preaching to this diverse crowd. He preached like none of them had ever heard, with extraordinary power, authority, and courage. He explained to everyone that the people they heard speaking in their own languages weren't drunk, but had been filled with God's Holy Spirit, just as had been foretold by the prophet Joel centuries before.

He also told them that the man who had recently been crucified— Jesus of Nazareth, the same man who had performed miracles, signs, and wonders for all of them to see or hear about—had suffered that terrible death only because God had determined beforehand it was to happen. Furthermore, the preacher said, God Himself raised Jesus from the dead as final proof that He was who He said He was: the Son of God, the Messiah, the Savior.

He finished by telling them that the prophets of old had foretold all these extraordinary events, and that God had established Jesus Christ as both Lord and Savior. When some in the crowd heard this, they were touched to their very cores and asked, "Men and brethren, what shall we do?" to which the preacher replied:

Repent, and let every one of you be baptized in the name of Jesus
Christ for the remission of sins; and you shall receive the gift of the

Holy Spirit. For the promise is to you and to your children, and to all who are afar off, as many as the Lord our God will call. (Acts 2:38–39)

From that point on, the church in Jerusalem grew in numbers and in spiritual maturity as that preacher continued to exhort and teach with power, authority, and a courage that seems mind-boggling in light of the fierce opposition that soon came.

Who was that man who preached so effectively and courageously? It was Peter, the same one who had spent three-plus years traveling with Jesus, hearing His teaching, and observing His work. This was the same Peter who, at the moment of truth—as Jesus faced trial and execution—got so frightened about what might happen to him that he denied three times that he even *knew* Jesus.

But that regrettable scene didn't spell the end of Peter's courage! He went on to become one of the fathers of the early church, one of the men who would pick up where Jesus left off and begin taking the message to the world around him, even in the face of fierce and frequent opposition.

What had gotten into Peter? How could a man who had demonstrated such cowardice only weeks before become such a picture of courage under fire?

What happened? Peter was filled with the Holy Spirit. And because he was filled with the Holy Spirit, he was healed and delivered from his past failures. And because of that, he went out and changed the world forever.

Filled with the same Spirit who energized Jesus' earthly ministry, Peter did some of the very same things Jesus had done. He healed the sick (Acts 9:34–35). He raised people from the dead (Acts 9:36–41). And how could Peter manage to do all those things? He did so because he was able to overcome his past failures, move forward in his ministry, and run the race to his own personal destiny.

That is exactly what God wants you to do. He wants you to leave your past where it belongs: in the past! And He wants you to move forward, to help you learn to forgive yourself, and to run your race toward the special destiny He has in mind for you.

The Gospel of Matthew gives us a beautiful "nutshell" description of the earthly ministry of Jesus Christ: "Then Jesus went about all the cities and villages, teaching in their synagogues, preaching the gospel of the kingdom, and healing every sickness and every disease among the people" (Matthew 9:35).

Those are the things Jesus came to do, and He did them perfectly. He taught like no one the people had ever heard, preached very directly the gospel message of salvation, and healed all kinds of sicknesses and diseases.

Right about now, you might be thinking, *Of course He did those things! He's Jesus!* But Jesus called us to do even greater works than He did. In John 14:12 Jesus says, "Most assuredly, I say to you, he who believes in Me, the works that I do he will do also; and greater *works* than these he will do, because I go to My Father."

Returning to Matthew 9:36, the Bible continues with, "But when He saw the multitudes, He was moved with compassion for them, because they were weary and scattered, like sheep having no shepherd. Then He said to His disciples, 'The harvest truly *is* plentiful, but the laborers *are* few. Therefore pray the Lord of the harvest to send out laborers into His harvest'" (Matthew 9:36–38).

In other words, Jesus told His disciples, "Pray that God will raise up people to go out and do the same things I've been doing. Pray for people who want to be like me, who want to do the works I do. Pray for people who have been forgiven to extend forgiveness to others; for people who have been healed to extend healing to others; for people who have put their past behind them to lead others to do the same."

That's what it means to be a Christian! It means being forgiven and healed and putting the past behind you and caring about people. It means lifting others up and out of their sins, their addictions, their problems, their pains, their diseases, and their pasts. It means that, because you know God has not condemned you because of your past, you don't condemn or judge others who are sick, who are in sin, who need the same kind of forgiveness and healing you've received.

You have the opportunity not only to pursue your own God-given destiny, but also to help others find a divine destiny of their own. That's what Jesus did, and that's what He calls you to do, too.

17

Overcoming Poor Self-Esteem

You don't have to look far to see that we live in a world of confusion and despair, a world filled with people who don't think very highly of themselves. And you also don't have to look far to see the consequences of all that negativity: sexual promiscuity; drug and alcohol abuse; reckless behavior that destroys relationships, finances, and careers. People sabotage their lives because of poor self-esteem. They don't think they deserve better or that they can do anything to improve their lives. So they engage in destructive activities, and this kind of behavior only makes them feel worse about themselves.

I don't want to downplay the seriousness of sin as it affects people's spiritual lives or eternal destinations; I just want you to understand that people who don't like themselves, don't like their lives, and don't like where they are headed often remain stuck in a cycle of sin and negativity. And that is a cycle that takes them nowhere but further down.

Think about the people you know who engage in the most

destructive kinds of sinful behavior. Now, ask yourself, "Does he/she have a good self-image?"

More than likely, the answer is a resounding, "No!"

Even in the Christian community, where we are to hold ourselves to higher standards of conduct, many of us struggle with the same issues and sins as the world around us—and much of that struggle is rooted in negative self-esteem.

High rates of divorce, depression, drug and alcohol abuse, and other negative and sinful behaviors within the church demonstrate that we often don't see ourselves in a very good light. Since we don't see ourselves as God sees us, many Christians live far below the way God has called them to live, reach far short of what He has called them to accomplish, and too often miss out on what God has created them to be.

Many with a negative self-image manage to avoid destructive life choices, but they miss out on higher living. Now, don't get focused on the financial aspects of God's blessings and callings and how they relate to self-image (although finances are certainly a part of it). When I talk about higher living, I'm not necessarily talking about the material aspect of living, but rather about a deep peace, a life of joy and love that comes from deep within your soul, body, and spirit when you have a good, positive self-image. I'm talking about enjoying to its fullest this life that God created you for, and not settling for less than what He has for you.

But it's only when you see yourself through God's eyes, and believe what God's Word says you are, that you will be and do all that He has called you to and prepared you for.

A good self-image—seeing yourself as God wants you to see yourself—has nothing to do with your name, nothing do to with your age, nothing to do with where you were raised, and nothing to do with how you were educated. It has everything to do with what you believe about yourself. And it is only as you begin seeing yourself as able, worthy, valuable—in other words, when you have a good self-image—that you will fulfill the calling and purpose God has given you.

How are we going to get good, young preachers out there starting churches? We have to raise them up to believe they can do it. We have to get them believing that God calls them, enables them, and empowers them.

How are we going to get people out there effectively reaching a desperately needy world for Christ? By getting them to the point where they believe that God is with them and leading them where they need to go.

How are we going to get businessmen to go out there and make the money we need to do the work of God, both here and overseas? We need to enhance their self-esteem and get them believing in themselves and believing that God created them to prosper so that they can make a difference in this world.

Only when we see ourselves through God's eyes and believe what God says we are, can we do what God says we can do. Only then will we begin to fulfill our calling in life. But in order to do that, many of us need to overcome what we've been told about ourselves since childhood.

SEE YOURSELF THROUGH GOD'S EYES

Poor self-esteem comes from many places. Family, school, media, and others all play a role. Unhealthy parents can use negative words and actions to cause children to feel bad about themselves. When you spend too much time looking at the media—movies, television, magazines, or Internet, you can think that that is the right way to be and then look at yourself and feel you fall short. In school, teachers have the ability to have tremendous influence over the children in their charge.

My wife, Wendy, tells a story about one particular teacher who told her she couldn't write and would always be just average. Wendy took that as the truth and when we were in Bible school she wouldn't allow me to read one of her essays. She was embarrassed and believed it was not good enough. When she finally let me see it, it was a great paper and there was nothing to be ashamed of. It took her a while to believe me. Anybody who knows Wendy knows she is anything but average, and she is the author of numerous books. That teacher was as wrong as can be.

Remember that the Bible says that life and death are in the power of your tongue (Proverbs 18:21), so take care with the words that come from your mouth. People, especially children, can be vulnerable to a negative word or attitude. Children should be shielded as much as possible from any kind of negative influence; and whenever your child says something that does not line up with God's Word about them, it should provoke conversation.

A negative self-image doesn't only come from these sources. Too many people get their poor self-esteem from religious teaching. They may have gone to church, but they weren't taught what the Bible really says about them. Sure, they heard the message about how they were sinners and that they needed Jesus Christ as their personal Lord and Savior; but they weren't taught that God loves them and enables them to be all He has called them to be.

Far too many churches over the years have taught their people—particularly their young, vulnerable people—to think of themselves as wretches, as lowlifes, as pond scum. These people know they are sinners—boy, do they know it!—but they can hardly imagine themselves as children of God, as coheirs with Christ, as a royal priesthood or a chosen people or a holy nation or any of the other glorious titles that the Word of God actually gives them.

So we are left with a generation of believers who are convinced that it is spiritual and righteous to think poorly of themselves, to believe that if they don't tow the line and do things perfectly, God won't love them or care about them anymore. Those thoughts have been drilled into the minds and hearts of untold numbers of little boys and little girls—and those thoughts can emotionally cripple those children for life.

But I am happy to tell you that God's thoughts about you are higher and far more positive than anything you may have heard as a child or as an adult. Speaking through the prophet Isaiah, God said, " 'For My thoughts *are* not your thoughts, / Nor *are* your ways My ways,' says the LORD. / 'For *as* the heavens are higher than the earth, / So are My ways higher than your ways, / And My thoughts than your thoughts' " (Isaiah 55:8–9).

When we start to think God's thoughts, we start to learn God's ways and start to see ourselves as He sees us. No longer do we see ourselves through the lens of a negative self-image thrust upon us by our families, by those in authority over us, by others we've known, or by negative religious teachings. When we lose our focus on those negative influences, we are able to look in the mirror every morning and speak God's thoughts about ourselves as they are recorded in Scripture.

Then, instead of saying, "I'm a nothing," we can say, "I'm created in the likeness and image of God."

Instead of saying, "There's nothing good in or about me," we can say, "I'm crowned with glory and honor."

Instead of saying, "I'll never amount to anything," we can say, "I've been created to take dominion."

But we need to understand that agreeing with God and having a positive self-image—and speaking as I've just illustrated above—isn't arrogance. And it isn't, as the apostle Paul might put it, "thinking more highly of ourselves than we should" (see Romans 12:3). It is simply recognizing who you are in Christ, what you are created to be, and what your purpose in life really is. It is, in fact, making God's thoughts your own, which are far higher than the negative, self-abasing, low thoughts that come from anywhere but heaven.

THE PROBLEM OF BEING "JUST GOOD ENOUGH"

Recently I was talking to a young friend of mine at church who, about ten years ago, started working in a business, and he started where so many young people start out: at the very bottom. But he worked hard, persevered, and continued believing that God had a plan for his life. He sought that plan and dedicated his life to his vision of his destiny. Because of that, God raised him up, and today he's making hundreds of thousands of dollars a year.

This successful young man has a brother about the same age. They grew up in the same home with the same mom and same dad, went to the same schools, and attended the same church—but the brother has a very different story. The two siblings have hugely different standards of living. While one travels first class, the other goes coach. One day, the more successful brother asked the other, "Why do you live like this?"

It's a good question. But it didn't get a good answer.

"Well, this is good enough," the other brother said.

Thinking of yourself in negative terms will certainly keep you from enjoying God's very best for yourself, but so will engaging in "good enough" thinking. God hasn't saved you, filled you with His

Holy Spirit, and given you your very own spiritual gifts so that you could be "good enough." No, in every area of life, He wants you to be the very best you can be—in ministry, in personal relationships, in business, in any endeavor you take up.

I was not raised in a Christian home, but it was a good home. My mother and father loved me, provided for me, and gave me a good life. But one of the things I took away from my upbringing and from the model my parents presented me was that you grow up and you go out and get a job in which you just get by financially and in life in general. You never think about making enough money to give away to others or to save for a good retirement or to leave your children an inheritance.

Sometimes "good" is the enemy of "better," and almost always of "best." Sometimes "good" isn't what God has for us. God calls us to live our destiny, to be light in a dark world, to change and impact our world.

When the apostle Paul writes, "Whatever you do, do all to the glory of God" (1 Corinthians 10:31), do you suppose he means, "Whatever you do, do it in a more-or-less passable way"? It's hard to see how. Since when is the phrase "glory of God" a synonym for "good enough"? Or when Paul writes, "Whatever you do, work at it with all your heart, as working for the Lord, not for men" (Colossians 3:23, NIV), do you suppose he really means, "Whatever you do, work at it just hard enough so that you don't get fired"? It just doesn't make any sense.

Changing your self-image very often means jettisoning that paradigm of "good enough" thinking for something else. Since "good enough" thinking so often comes out of what was pounded into your head as a child, and sometimes beyond, it can be a difficult task. But the glorious news (and I mean "glorious," not "uh, pretty good") is that it's possible to change that thinking, to infuse yourself with a self-image that doesn't settle for "good enough" but dares to reach out for God's very best.

Sometimes the thing that keeps me going in ministry is that every so often, I see someone get out of "good enough" thinking, learn to have a good self-image, and start pursuing his or her destiny. That excites me! And it gives me the confidence that all of us can do it, if we simply learn to stop listening to the voices of the past that hold us down and start listening to the voice of a God who says we are worthy of something far more than "good enough."

God has gifted you and set you apart to be something more than average, more than just "good enough." And in order to do that, you need to have a healthy, positive self-image that comes from knowing His Word, believing His Word, and living His Word.

CHANGING YOUR SELF-IMAGE

There is nothing the devil would like more than to have you dwelling on the negatives in your life. He wants you to focus on the ideas that led you to a negative self-image or to self-condemnation.

You need to get your mind off of what the devil's doing and saying about you, as well as what people in the past have done and said, and instead get your mind on what God is doing and saying and wanting. And you don't do that by telling yourself not to think about the wrong things that have been said, done, or thought, but by focusing on the *right things*—on the things that cultivate good, positive self-esteem.

Have you ever tried to forget something by telling yourself *not* to think about it? It didn't work, did it? That is like trying to make your sore back feel better by saying over and over, "I believe my sore back is healed in the name of Jesus. So I'm going to just go to work and not focus on my sore back. I'm not going to think about my sore back or let my sore back stop me from doing what I need to get done today. No, sir, my sore back will no longer be a sore spot for me anymore, praise Jesus." In trying to get your mind off of your sore back, you only remind yourself that you are in pain. Probably you will end up needing a strong painkiller.

It is not possible to forget something by resolving in your mind to *not* think about it. The only way you can banish a stubborn thought from your mind is to focus on something else, so that the negative thought gets squeezed out. In the case of that sore back, for example, you might want to focus on your work, on the telephone call that needs to be made, on that client who needs attention, on that project that is due tomorrow—all those things you do when you're not in pain. When you do that, you might get all the way to the end of the day before you think about your back.

So instead of trying to tell yourself, "I will have a better self-image," or "I won't be so self-critical," or "I won't think about the unhelpful, unkind words spoken to me," or "I'm *not* incapable," you focus on what God thinks of you, what you know you do well, the good things you've heard said, and the fact that you are more than able to do everything God has placed before you. Focus on what the Word says about you. Such as 2 Corinthians 5:17, "Therefore, if anyone *is* in Christ, *he is* a new creation; old things have passed away; behold, all things have become new." Philippians 4:13, "I can do all things through Christ who strengthens me." Romans 8:37, "Yet in all these things we are more than conquerors through Him who loved us."

Unfortunately, negative thoughts will still be with us and, most of the time, negative thoughts that come to us have an origin outside of ourselves. In my experience, people tend to struggle with seven "seed thoughts," thoughts that take root in our hearts and grow into negative perceptions that manifest themselves as low self-esteem. They get down on themselves and run into trouble because they never come to grips with these seven lies from the pit.

I believe that *all* negative self-thinking is rooted in at least one of these seed thoughts I've listed below. I also believe that you can combat and defeat them, if you apply the truths and principles of God's Word.

1. I'm isolated and I feel all alone.

Solution: Build new, godly relationships.

When you feel as though you don't have any friends, that nobody cares about you, that you are all alone in this world, it becomes easier to dwell on your shortcomings and flaws. Focusing on your own loneliness leads to feelings of isolation—and that is fertile ground for low self-esteem.

What should you do about it? There is no grand spiritual remedy for loneliness; it's just a matter of getting out there and making some friends. Getting involved in your local church is a good place to start—and when I say get involved, I don't mean just taking up space in the pews. Find a group appropriate for you and get yourself "plugged in." Take your focus off of yourself and learn to introduce yourself to Christian brothers and sisters. "Those who are planted in the house of the LORD / Shall flourish in the courts of our God. / They shall still bear fruit in old age; / They shall be fresh and flourishing" (Psalm 92:13–14).

The Bible tells us, "A man *who has* friends must himself be friendly" (Proverbs 18:24). That means that if you want to fight off those poisonous feelings of loneliness and isolation, you have to make an effort to be a friend.

2. I'm too depressed and discouraged.

Solution: Focus on God's strength.

Nothing will grow the seeds of low self-esteem like the twin brothers of discouragement and depression. When you start to focus on things that aren't working for you, it becomes easy to feel discouraged. And when you start thinking nothing will work, you become depressed. When that happens, it is difficult to simply "try something else," when what you had tried didn't work. You feel that nothing works for you, that life is too hard and not fair. You throw a pity party, and you don't need to invite anybody else to come because you are doing a good job all by yourself.

When those feelings of discouragement come, it's time for you to refocus, to take your eyes off of the discouragement and on to some courage. Focus on the truth that "all things work together for good to those who love God, to those who are the called according to *His* purpose" (Romans 8:28)—and that includes the difficult things, the things that don't make sense or don't seem right or fair. Remember, you are an overcomer! Jesus Christ, who lives in you, is greater than the devil, who is in the world (1 John 4:4)!

"This Book of the Law shall not depart from your mouth, but you shall meditate in it day and night, that you may observe to do according to all that is written in it. For then you will make your way prosperous, and then you will have good success. Have I not commanded you? Be strong and of good courage; do not be afraid, nor be dismayed, for the LORD your God *is* with you wherever you go." (Joshua 1:8–9)

3. I'm not as good as everyone else.
Solution: Stop making comparisons.

Nothing good comes out of feeling inferior to others or out of making comparisons between yourself and others. When you make comparisons between yourself and others, you do one of two things: You believe you are better than they are; you believe you are not as good. Either way, it is unhealthy.

Comparing yourself with others leads to a negative self-image because it causes you to take your eyes off of what God has made you to be and to do and instead places them on who and what others are and what they are doing.

The apostle Paul wrote, "For we dare not class ourselves or compare ourselves with those who commend themselves. But they, measuring themselves by themselves, and comparing themselves among themselves, are not wise" (2 Corinthians 10:12).

Comparing your looks to others, your intelligence to others, your income to others, your wife and family to others, your ministry to others—you name the comparison—is unhealthy and unwise, simply because it causes you to strive to be something God never intended you to be. It also stops you from being what He meant for you to be, which is, the best *you* possible.

4. I'll never get it right and I'll never be happy.

Solution: Remember God is working in you.

We all know people who just seem to have an air of negativity and pessimism about them. They say things like, "I'll never get out of debt," "I'll never be healed and healthy," "I'll never be able to afford to buy my own home," "I'll never have a happy marriage." *I'll never* ____ (fill in the blank).

What is sad about people like this is that their *I'll never*'s more often than not become self-fulfilling prophecies. Remember, the Bible tells us that as a man thinks in his heart, so is he (Proverbs 23:7—and the same thing is true for a woman, by the way). This is more than the power of positive thinking; it's the truth of the Word of God. And if you dwell on thoughts and keep speaking words that say "I'll never," then you can be sure that you won't.

If you have found yourself falling into negative and pessimistic thinking, then it's time again to refocus, to turn your thinking completely around. Say to yourself, "I can do all things through Christ who strengthens me," and that, "I am more than an overcomer through Christ." Take that small step of faith, and it will set you on your way to being a positive and optimistic thinker and talker instead of a negative and pessimistic one. "[Not in your own strength] for it is God Who is all the while effectually at work in you [energizing and creating in you the power and desire], both to will and to work for His good pleasure and satisfaction and delight" (Philippians 2:13, AMP).

5. I'll never get out of debt.

Solution: God will bring you more than enough.

One of the things that will keep those in dire financial straits (or those who live in lack or poverty) right where they are is their focus on their present situation and not on what they really want it to be.

I can tell you in all certainty that if you fix your focus on your poverty and lack, you'd better learn to enjoy it, because you're going to have it for the rest of your life. But if you focus on what you can do and how God wants to bless and prosper you, then you will be blessed and prosperous. "The thief does not come except to steal, and to kill, and to destroy. I have come that they may have life, and that they may have *it* more abundantly" (John 10:10).

We live in the greatest, most prosperous nation in the world, a nation that affords us the greatest opportunities for abundance in history. Yet so many people get focused on and talk about their own poverty and lack.

Read Bible verses and passages that tell you how God wants you to prosper. Read books and listen to tapes—biblically based, of course—that talk about success. Hang around and talk to successful people. When you do those things, you'll start to change your thinking, and you'll move toward success yourself.

6. The future scares me. What if I mess up?

Solution: Fear not—your steps are ordered of the Lord.

Some people are afraid of everything. They're afraid to change, afraid to try and fail, and, worst of all, afraid to succeed. All of those fears are grounded in the fear of changing how they live and how they think.

If you want to improve your self-image, you need to stop dwelling on your fears. You need to starve those fears and feed your faith, and soon you will find that your fear has been replaced with courage, your timidity with boldness.

Remember, "God has not given us a spirit of fear, but of power and of love and of a sound mind" (2 Timothy 1:7). Fear is not of God, but power and love are. You must choose to receive His gift of power and love and learn to walk daily in those things.

7. I just don't think I can do it.

Solution: Doubt your doubts—believe your beliefs.

If you were to read the Bible from cover to cover, you'd probably see that nothing offends God more, keeps us from enjoying all that He has for us, or limits us more than doubt and unbelief. "So Jesus answered and said to them, 'Have faith in God'" (Mark 11:22).

Some people get so focused on their own shortcomings, flaws, and limitations that they just can't focus on what God has called them and equipped them to do. If that describes you, it's time to change your focus from yourself to the truth of God's Word and what it says about you. The apostle Paul wrote, "faith *comes* by hearing, and hearing by the word of God" (Romans 10:17).

When you receive God's Word, you receive faith; and when you receive faith, you begin believing what He says about you. When you do that, over time your self-image changes for the better. "But without faith *it is* impossible to please *Him,* for he who comes to God must believe that He is, and *that* He is a rewarder of those who diligently seek Him" (Hebrews 11:6).

PART 5

Finishing Your Course

18

Run to Win

To run the race of life and win, we need the Holy Spirit to guide and empower us. The *only* way we'll keep running all the way to our destiny is by depending upon the Holy Spirit of God to give us what only He can provide. Without Him, we're lost. But with Him, we'll finish our race to destiny and make it all the way to the winner's platform.

Jesus gave us many fantastic promises while He walked this earth alongside His disciples; it's hard to think of a better one than the one recorded in John 16:13. It says:

> However, when He, the Spirit of truth, has come, He will guide you into all truth; for He will not speak on His own *authority*, but whatever He hears He will speak; and He will tell you things to come.

That's an awesome promise, isn't it? God says the Holy Spirit will come to you and that He will teach you and guide you. He will show you things to come. Do you believe that? Do you count on that? Do you live as though it's true?

Some portions of the Bible we *really* believe; other portions we tend to ignore or think won't work for us. I'm not sure why we do that, but we can't afford that here, in regard to the Holy Spirit. We need to believe the truth, that He's teaching us and guiding us.

Some people, when presented with some challenge, exclaim, "Oh, I can't do that. I have *never* been able to. I *will* never be able to. I'm not good at that and have never been good at it." Such a person is really saying, "I can't be taught. The Holy Spirit can't teach me. I've learned all I'm ever going to learn, and not even the Holy Spirit of God can change that." So the person locks out the source of higher potential in his or her life and can never quite believe that God can take him or her *beyond*.

God says that if you will believe in the Holy Spirit and depend upon the Holy Spirit, He'll teach you and guide you. The Bible says the Holy Spirit will show you "things to come." That doesn't mean He's going to announce every event that is going to happen on the earth. And I certainly don't mean He'll get you into tarot cards, the horrible-scope, or mixing with psychics! No, He will show you things you need to know about *your* life, *your* calling, and *your* career.

For example, when Wendy and I were first married, we sensed the Holy Spirit directing us about our lives. It gave us a sense of divine purpose. We were not trying to just get through life! The Holy Spirit was and still is guiding us along every part of the journey, showing us "things to come." In Greek, the original language of the New Testament, the phrase "things to come" literally means "He announces in detail things to come."

Don't merely accept the Holy Spirit as a doctrine. Don't be satisfied with the knowledge that He exists. I want to encourage you to actively partner with the Holy Spirit. Put that at the forefront of your mind. Realize, accept, and embrace what the Holy Spirit wants to do in *you*.

Remember the words of Psalm 37:23 that we briefly looked at

earlier? That verse tells us, "The steps of a *good* man [or woman] are ordered by the LORD." That is what the Holy Spirit does in your life. He directs your steps and guides your life.

Notice that the Bible doesn't say, He "maybe" will guide you or "might" direct you or "could sometimes" guide you or "if you're lucky" He'll guide you. It says, He *will* guide you, teach you, and show you things to come.

Do you believe that? Are you sensitive to that? Are you aware of that? Are you allowing the Holy Spirit to guide you?

If you have been struggling through life is it because you have been ignoring the Holy Spirit? Could it be that you have been doing it your way and therefore haven't been doing it His way? It is time to allow the Holy Spirit and ask the Holy Spirit to guide you where He wants you to go.

So does that mean you should neglect to make wise plans? Not at all. A scripture says, "The plans of the diligent lead to profit / as surely as haste leads to poverty" (Proverbs 21:5, NIV). Make your plans—but then let God use them as He wills. Place all your plans in His hands, and then let Him fulfill them, alter them, or scrap them, as He sees fit. God wants to use your plans to help you step out in faith, to dare to do great things for God, to pursue the destiny He has for you.

You see this pattern in the life of the apostle Paul. He made his plans, but he always made room for the guidance of the Holy Spirit. Consider the following example:

Now when they had gone through Phrygia and the region of Gala-tia, they were forbidden by the Holy Spirit to preach the word in Asia. After they had come to Mysia, they tried to go into Bithynia, but the Spirit did not permit them. So passing by Mysia, they came down to Troas. And a vision appeared to Paul in the night. A man of Macedonia stood and pleaded with him, saying, "Come over to

Macedonia and help us." Now after he had seen the vision, immediately we sought to go to Macedonia, concluding that the Lord had called us to preach the gospel to them. (Acts 16:6–10)

Do you see what happened here? First, Paul made plans to preach the gospel in Asia. Sounds like a good plan, doesn't it? And yet, the Holy Spirit somehow made it clear to him, "No, you're not going there today."

So then Paul shifted to plan B. He looked at the nearby region of Bithynia and said to his colleagues, "Okay, if we can't go to Asia, then let's bring the Good News to the people in Bithynia." But then again, for some reason the Bible does not explain, "The Spirit did not permit them."

If you had been Paul, would you be getting anxious by now? Would you wonder what in the world was going on? Apparently, it didn't faze Paul. And that night, the Spirit gave Paul a vision that the apostle and his companions "concluded" was the leading of God to take the gospel to Macedonia. So that's what they did, and that's where Paul and his coworkers reaped a great harvest. (And where, by the way, they also experienced some real persecution. Remember: Just because the Spirit leads you somewhere to do something, it doesn't mean you won't face stiff challenges!)

Make your plans with God's help, and then trust God to lead you wherever He wants you to go. That's the surest route to your destiny.

THE HOLY SPIRIT NOURISHES

The Holy Spirit guides and directs you as you walk with God, but He does more than that. He has to, or you'll never finish your race!

In fact, you need at least two things from the Holy Spirit to keep you running your race to destiny. The first is refreshment.

A marathon runner has to prepare for a race of 26.2 miles, which equals hours out on the road. The best in the world can probably do it in two hours and some minutes; for you and me, it would take eight hours or more.

If you ever watch these races, you may have seen times where a runner starts dropping back and the announcer says, "It looks like he's dehydrated." The next thing you know, the athlete is sitting on the side of the road, trying to straighten his legs, which have begun to cramp up, and he can't finish his race.

I believe we have a population of believers with spiritual cramps, because they are spiritually dehydrated. If you want to finish strong, you have to be full of the Holy Spirit and His energy. You just won't make it without His refreshment.

John 4 describes how Jesus went to a community well, where he met a woman. "Give Me a drink," He said to her.

"How is it that you are talking to me—you are a Jew and I am a Samaritan," was basically her answer.

"If you knew the gift of God, and who it is who says to you, 'Give Me a drink,'" Jesus replied, "you would have asked Him, and He would have given you living water" (v. 10).

Notice how Jesus used the illustration of water to describe the presence of God, the life of God, salvation, and the Holy Spirit. "You are talking about natural water," He was telling the woman, "but I'm talking about living water, spiritual water."

The woman objected that He had no bucket.

It was just the opening Jesus wanted. "Whoever drinks of this [natural] water will thirst again," He said, "but whoever drinks of the water that I shall give him will never thirst. But the water that I shall give him will become a fountain of water springing up into everlasting life."

According to Jesus, in the natural realm you drink water, but soon get thirsty again. In the spiritual realm, however, if you get born of the Spirit and filled with the Spirit, God installs a fountain inside of you that will renew your strength and increase your stamina. It will keep you spiritually hydrated so you can run your race and win. The Holy Spirit is a fountain springing up on the inside of you.

Have you ever watched volunteers on a marathon course standing on the side of the road holding out cups of water for the runners? About ten miles out, the runners start to get dry, so as the runners race by the volunteers, the competitors grab a cup and keep going.

Have you ever tried to drink and run at the same time? Running is hard enough, but these athletes are drinking while they run. Why go through all that? Because they know that if they don't stay hydrated, they will cramp up and not finish their race.

A few more miles down the road, they need a drink again. Why? Because they know if they don't stay hydrated, they can't run their race. They will start to cramp up and lose their strength. And soon they will be sitting on the side of the road.

The saddest thing in the Olympics is seeing runners who look as though they'll have to drop out of the race. You see them staggering into the stadium, looking disoriented. Some of them are not running straight; they can barely stand up. Although they trained their entire life for this race and gave it everything they had, the heat and the humidity or some other conditions were so harsh that they just couldn't keep enough water in them.

It's no different for you in the spiritual realm.

No matter how much you want to have a good marriage; no matter how much you want to win your race; no matter how much you want to prosper, be healthy, have good kids—if you don't keep the water of life, the Holy Spirit, flowing like a fountain in your life, then you're going to get stuck on the side of the road. And you won't finish your race to destiny.

How often do you stop and pray with the Spirit, listen to the Spirit, and plug into the Holy Spirit? If it is once a week, I guarantee that you are dehydrated. If it's only on Sunday, I guarantee that you are dehydrated.

Some folks are always praying for the Holy Spirit to come down when they are in trouble. When they feel empty, they say things like, "Lord, come down and touch me. Lord, I need more power! Oh, God! Please send the Holy Spirit!" They read the story of Elisha in the Old Testament and how he said, "I want the double portion." So they say, "Lord, could I get a *double portion* of your presence?"

What do they want, two Holy Ghosts?

Jesus said, "I want to put power *in* you. You will *become* the temple of the Holy Spirit. You will have a well of living water *inside* you, a fountain of life continually springing up in your soul."

So when you feel empty, say instead, "I know You live in me, God. I am born of the Spirit and I am filled with the Spirit. Holy Spirit, spring up within my soul. Spring up and make me whole!"

We need that refreshing water of the Holy Spirit if we are going to run the race to win and so fulfill our destiny.

Acts 1 and 2 describe how the Holy Spirit came in power at Pentecost. He's been poured out on all flesh, and now we can drink and be full. We don't have to wait for anything. Out of our bellies flow rivers of living water. In other words, God is telling you, "There's more than enough. You will never have to wear out. You never have to burn out. You never have to get down and you never have to get spiritually exhausted." You may get tired physically, but emotionally and spiritually, you don't have to feel drained.

Some time ago on a return trip from Hawaii, I started observing people on the airplane. Everybody had on their leis, T-shirts, flowered shirts, and shorts. They were saying things like, "Oh, I wish I had another week! How soon are we coming back?" "Well, we've already made our reservations for next year."

Most of the conversations centered around how good the vacation was, but how they needed more of it. What were they saying? They were still thirsty. They came to drink, but the mai-tai didn't help much. They came to sip some liquid refreshment, but the beach didn't do it.

I'm not saying you shouldn't take vacations; they are good, physical things that you need in order to have a balanced lifestyle. But in order to have the life God wants for you, Jesus said, "Come to *Me* and drink."

Get the Holy Spirit working in your life! Don't relegate Him to one hour a week at church. Make Him a part of your life and let the living water keep you hydrated, so you don't cramp up on the side of the road of life and so you don't drop out of the race. Stay in the race and run to win.

Your spirit can be renewed every day. You can have a new attitude every day. You can love the same wife after thirty, forty, fifty years and longer, every day with a fresh heart, a fresh spirit, and a fresh attitude. Or you can keep trying new wives and never feel refreshed.

Take the vacation and do all the things that are healthy for you physically—but remember you had better get refreshed spiritually, too. And the only way to do that is to stay involved with the Holy Ghost.

Pray with the Holy Spirit. Some people say, "I don't believe in that tongues stuff. Who needs that? What is that all about? That sounds crazy to me!"

I understand—but if you want it, if you're thirsty, if the world can't satisfy you, then come to Him and drink and begin to pray with Him. The Holy Spirit will guide you, teach you, and renew your

During chemotherapy I learned some important things about hydration and dehydration. In the first couple of weeks, I got really down, both physically and emotionally. I told one of my friends who had just gone through the same treatment, "If I have to feel like this for eleven months, I don't know what I am going to do."

"How have you been drinking the last few days?" he asked.

"What do you mean?" I replied.

"How much water have you had?"

"I don't know."

"There's your problem."

The medication had dehydrated my system, and so by not having extra water, I had become very dehydrated. And then what happens? You get tired, your attitude gets bad, you start feeling down, and you think you are depressed—but in fact, you're just dehydrated.

It works exactly the same way in the spiritual realm. Stay filled with the Holy Spirit.

strength. He will be like a fountain of living water, springing up on the inside of your spirit and soul.

Isaiah 12:3 says, "with joy you will draw water / From the wells of salvation." The Bible shows us again and again how the Holy Spirit and His work in our life is the supernatural water we need to stay hydrated.

YOU NEED POWER

Besides drinking a lot of water, runners also eat various types of nutrition bars for strength. These bars have a lot of simple carbohydrates, protein, and a little bit of fat. The runners have to get carbs and protein into their system, because if they don't keep up their energy, they can't run any longer and so they can't make the distance.

It's the same with the Holy Spirit. Spiritually speaking, He brings power to our lives.

"[F]or John truly baptized with water," Jesus said, "but you shall be baptized with the Holy Spirit not many days from now" (Acts 1:5). And then He promised, "you shall receive power when the Holy Spirit has come upon you" (Acts 1:8).

So you drink living water from the Holy Spirit *and* you feast on Holy Spirit's nutrition bars to get power as you pray with the Spirit and listen to the Spirit. Don't relegate Him to Sunday morning. Don't just push Him off into a corner until you really need Him. Stay plugged in with the Holy Ghost and tap into His limitless power.

As our church grows, we're building buildings, I'm talking to bankers, I'm thinking about how we are going to accomplish all our goals—despite the challenges, the building department, the city politicians, the finances, and the budgets. So I say, "Holy Ghost, I need some power. I need some help here, because I can't do this by myself."

You may look at your own job, your bills, your kids, your schedule, the family needs, the economic needs, and you start to think, *This is overwhelming.* However, when you start feasting on the power of the Holy Ghost, suddenly you discover you can deal with and handle situations that seemed impossible before.

I told you earlier that, when I was younger, I raced bicycles. A road race lasts anywhere from three to six hours. You get really hungry during a road race, so you have to take food with you on the bike. In the Tour de France, you see people handing riders food from the side of the road, just like they do with cups of water; but we had to take our own food with us because we were kids. So we often took nutrition bars.

It was the same when I climbed Mount Rainier a while back. We needed to eat something—we had to get protein, carbs, and fats into our systems—in order to have the energy to complete the climb. But we had to remind ourselves to eat. We were working so hard and focused so intently on our goal that nutrition wasn't at the forefront of our minds. But if we didn't remember to eat until our bodies signaled that we were running out of energy, it would be too late. We would be tired, our muscles would be fatigued, and we would start getting really cranky as our blood sugar dropped.

I think that's often what happens to Christians. We go to work, one kid has soccer, another has piano, we have to go to the grocery store, then to the gas station, then to a meeting—we cram so much stuff into our lives that we forget to eat from the power of the Holy Spirit. We forget to pray and let the Holy Spirit empower our lives. So what happens? We get down, we lack fuel, and we start to run out of gas. Then we start thinking, *What's wrong? Why is this happening?*

It's just that we haven't tapped into God's power to enable us to keep going. We haven't waited on the Lord and on the Holy Spirit.

WHAT DOES IT MEAN TO WAIT?

To wait on the Lord doesn't mean do nothing, as if you're just supposed to sit around, twiddling your thumbs. No, the Word says, wait *on* the Lord—like a waiter or waitress waits on customers in a restaurant.

Servers are there to take your order. They are paying careful attention and listening.

"May I help you? I'm ready to take your order."

"Is there anything else I can get you?"

"Do you know what you want?"

"Would you like something to drink?"

"Can I add anything else to that?"

"Would you like me to refill your drink?"

You like it when you find a good waiter or waitress at a restaurant, don't you? But what about when you go to the restaurant, someone sits you down—and then nobody comes back for forty-five minutes? You're thinking, "Hel-*lo*, I'm here! I'd like to place an order! *Somebody?*"

I think that's the way God is with us. We come to the Lord, we get saved—and then He doesn't see us again for a long time. God says, "Hey, I have more for you! I have some good ideas for you. I have some good plans for you. I have an abundant life for you. Come on back and take the order."

But we're not waiting on the Lord. We're involved with other things; we get caught up with the world. Maybe it's time we remember what Isaiah says to us: "But those who wait on the LORD / Shall renew *their* strength; / They shall mount up with wings like eagles, / They shall run and not be weary, / They shall walk and not faint (Isaiah 40:31).

You, or somebody you know, may be dealing with cancer or be on chemotherapy right now. Or maybe they're just going through some challenge, difficulty, disease, or financial disaster. Stuff happens! Economies change, markets fluctuate.

Maybe you had a growing, thriving business, and then the market shifted. The thing that was selling, or the service that was working and was so profitable last year, or for the last five years or ten years, has all dried up. Now you're in a bad spot and you are trying to catch up, pay the bills, and not go bankrupt. Stuff happens—physically, economically, financially, and relationally.

Maybe you had a business partner who was 100 percent with you. Suddenly the man went south or the woman took off. And you're left thinking, *What happened? Why did that happen?* It's simple: Things happen in this world.

But even in the midst of those challenges, we can learn, we can grow, we can improve. When we tap into the power of the Holy Spirit, we don't have to get bitter; we can get better.

And you don't have to do it all on your own strength. You don't have to figure it all out using your own wisdom. In fact, you can't.

The apostle Paul accomplished an awful lot in his day, but he never saw it as what *he* did. In fact, he once wrote, "I will not venture to speak of anything except what Christ has accomplished through me in leading the Gentiles to obey God by what I have said and done— by the power of signs and miracles, through the power of the Spirit" (Romans 15:18–19, NIV).

Those words from Paul echo what God said through Zechariah the prophet many centuries before: " 'Not by might nor by power, but by my Spirit,' says the Lord Almighty" (Zechariah 4:6, NIV).

Anything good and lasting that you accomplish in your life, you will accomplish only by tapping into the wisdom and power of the Holy Spirit. Paul wrote, "It is God who works in you to will and to act according to his good purpose" (Philippians 2:13, NIV). You can't reach your destiny through your own strength and wisdom, nor does God expect you to or want you to. It is *God* who works in you, energizing and creating in you the power and desire to do His will.

If you do it God's way—if you wait on God—He'll show you how to run this race. If you wait on the Lord, you can run and not be weary. If you look unto Jesus, you can run with endurance and win. The Word of God says that by waiting on the Lord, you can run this race and win the prize of life. You can have the fulfillment, satisfaction, joy, and abundant life that God wants you to have.

All you have to do is continually drink from the fountain of life, the Holy Spirit, who lives inside you. He offers you the water of life, right at this moment. Won't you drink?

19

Champions Endure

Life and a marathon have a lot in common. They're both about endurance, consistency, and long-term thinking.

You might be able to sprint for a day, but how will that change your life? Just because you have one good day doesn't mean you have changed your long-term outlook. You can have one great week where everything works, but if the rest of your weeks are lousy, then something's not working. You have to start thinking long-term.

The fact is you are going to have days when things are neither good nor fun. There will be days when you feel awful—and yet that may be the day that God does more in your life than ever before.

But how will you make that discovery if you give up before reaching the finish line? Part of success in life is just staying in the race, never giving up, and outlasting the devil.

Since the apostle Paul has been such a reliable mentor for us so far, it only makes sense that he has some helpful counsel about endurance. In 2 Corinthians 4:7–9, he writes:

But we have this treasure in earthen vessels, that the excellence of the power may be of God and not of us. *We are* hard-pressed on every side, yet not crushed; *we are* perplexed, but not in despair; persecuted, but not forsaken; struck down, but not destroyed.

A little later, in verse 16, he adds, "Therefore we do not lose heart. Even though our outward man is perishing, yet the inward *man* is being renewed day by day."

Enduring means not quitting, refusing to give up. Every day is not going to be fun, no matter how right with God you are. So you endure. You endure some days in marriage, you endure some days on the job, and you endure some days in dealing with your physical body. Difficult stuff may be happening on the outside, but you can stay strong on the inside. You may be old enough to go to IHOP for the senior discount, but on the inside you're being renewed day by day. And that's how you're able to endure.

I'm only in my fifties, but on days when I'm with my son, who's in his twenties, I find myself thinking, *Gosh, it sure would be nice to be twenty-one again.* When we climbed Mount Rainier a while ago, he more or less ran to the top of the mountain. It's a two-day trek to 14,500 feet—the tallest peak in the continental United States—so it's a bit of a climb. Caleb, my son, is at the top saying, "Okay, what do we do now?" And I'm thinking, *Sheesh, I just endured this mountain.*

You have to endure some things if you're going to get where God wants you to be. But that's what running the race is, and that's what living for God is all about.

THE LORD WILL DELIVER ME

I admit that it's hard to endure the tough times if you're not sure you're going to make it. If it's a toss-up whether you're going to succeed or fail, advance or retreat, win or lose, then it gets much harder to "set your face like flint" like Jesus did and just keep on keepin' on.

Things get much easier, though, if you know you have an almighty helper on your side who is committed to getting you to the finish line.

At the very end of his life, Paul felt more than a little perplexed and persecuted. A lot of things had come against him and a lot of people had abandoned him. In this dark time in his life he wrote to Timothy, his young protégé:

> But you have carefully followed my doctrine, manner of life, purpose, faith, longsuffering, love, perseverance, persecutions, afflictions, which happened to me at Antioch, at Iconium, at Lystra—what persecutions I endured. And out of *them* all the Lord delivered me. (2 Timothy 3:10–11)

Paul knew all about suffering. He knew all about persecution. He knew all about afflictions. And yet, because he also knew all about love (since he was a child of the God of love) and faith (since he lived by faith), he knew all about perseverance. He knew how to endure. He knew how to keep going. And he tells you that, no matter what comes against you—difficulties, challenges, hard times—you must believe that the Lord will deliver you from them all.

I simply can't define every way God is going to deliver every person. It's the old story of the guy standing on the roof of his house as a flood comes. The guy prays for deliverance, and soon a boat comes along and the people inside offer to pick him up. "No, I'm fine," he

> When I got saved, I prayed for years, "I am healed, I am whole in the name of Jesus." And yet, after I'd been a pastor for twenty-five years, I was diagnosed with hepatitis C. I had to do something different from what I had always done.
>
> Some people counseled me to trust God, to believe God, and to refuse to take medication. "He'll deliver you," they said.
>
> Well, God did deliver me, but He used medicine and diet and faith and a lot of other means to do it. Sometimes we put God in this box of what His deliverance must be, and so we miss out on some of the other things He might want to do in our lives. God delivers in many ways. Don't get stuck in one place. Seek out the options that you have to receive God's best.

says. "The Lord's going to deliver me." And he keeps on praying. A little while later a helicopter comes by to rescue him, but again he refuses, giving the same reason. As he continues to pray, the waters keep rising, and finally the guy drowns. In heaven he approaches the Lord and says, "Lord, how come you didn't deliver me?" And the Lord replies, "I tried! I sent the guy in the boat and I sent the helicopter, but you told them to go away. What were you *thinking*?"

Many of us want God to respond like a wizard. We want God to be our own personal magician. But the Lord is *not* your magician. He's *not* your wizard. He is your Lord, and He says there are some things that you'll just have to endure. There are some things you'll have to persevere through. Even so, His promise remains the same: "out of them *all*" the Lord delivers you—even if His deliverance doesn't look like you thought it would.

I'd be less than honest if I didn't admit that Paul's final word on the subject is not "out of them all the Lord delivered me." In the last chapter of his last book, in fact, just a few verses from the very end, Paul writes, "I was delivered out of the mouth of the lion. And the Lord will deliver me from every evil work and preserve *me* for His heavenly kingdom" (2 Timothy 4:17–18).

He said this even though he knew his death was right around the corner. He had just told Timothy, "I am already being poured out as a drink offering, and the time of my departure is at hand" (2 Timothy 4:6), so he knew his days were numbered. He could probably guess that, this time around, the Romans were going to slice off his head. There would be no saving earthquake, as there had been in Philippi (Acts 16:26). There would be no protection from the venomous snake, as there had been in Malta (Acts 28:5–6). Paul knew he was about to die.

And yet, he says, "the Lord will deliver me from every evil work and preserve me for His heavenly kingdom." What could he mean? He clearly didn't think God was going to deliver him from the sword of the Roman executioner. So what did he mean?

I think he must have meant something like this: When in faith we entrust our lives to God, He will certainly deliver us from every lion that threatens us, all the way to the final moment when we finish our race and fulfill our destiny. And at that moment, it's time for God's final work of deliverance, to deliver us to heaven itself.

The Romans meant to end Paul's life, but in fact, they had acted merely to "deliver" Paul into God's "heavenly kingdom." They weren't Paul's executioners; they were merely God's delivery boys. And God had preserved his servant Paul all along the way. The worst that can happen is we go to meet the Lord in heaven. "We are confident, yes, well pleased rather to be absent from the body and to be present with the Lord" (2 Corinthians 5:8).

To make it to the end of his race, to reach his destiny, Paul realized he had to endure. He had to persevere through difficulties and challenges. All the bad stuff didn't go away at the snap of a finger. He couldn't pull out his magic wand and say, "*Abracadabra, hocus pocus, make the devil lose his focus* (on me)."

Neither can you. So is that bad news? Not really. God is a lot better than magic, because His deliverance doesn't depend on knowing the right incantation or the proper spell. His deliverance depends on His character, which never changes; on His wisdom, which is infinite; on His power, which has no limit; and on His love, which He has set upon you for all eternity.

At the end of the day, we simply cannot define ahead of time what God's deliverance is going to look like. The best thing we can do is to stay faithful to Him, through faith, and glorify Him in whatever happens.

Through the years people have come up to me at church and said, "Wow! Have you ever thought you would have a church like this? Can you *believe* what the Lord has done? It must be amazing, when you look around and see all the people coming to church. You probably never thought it would be like this, did you?" I always give them the appropriate answer: "Yeah, praise God. We're just grateful." But many times, I've thought, *Yeah, it's great; but I thought it was going to be like this fifteen years ago. I've been struggling for a long time to get to this point. What's taken You so long, God?*

I just don't think we can define all these things or tell God how it has to happen. We just have to go with the flow and keep our faith working and trust that He's working everything out. Because He is. Even if it takes a *looooong* time.

STAY IN THE RACE

Have you ever been to a really bad movie? You sit there and sit there and wonder how much longer the thing will drag on—and it's only been eight minutes! But when the movie is good, it's suddenly over and it feels as if you've been watching for only twenty minutes instead of two hours.

Time is one of the things that makes life hard. When things are not going well, time seems to slow down. It always seems to take longer than it should to turn around a bad situation. Why is that? When we're having fun, time moves right along. But when we're not having any fun, time seems to slow to a crawl. Hebrews 10:35–36 says, "Therefore do not cast away your confidence, which has great reward. For you have need of endurance, so that after you have done the will of God, you may receive the promise."

We all need patience and endurance to live the life God has called us to. God doesn't follow our clocks or timetables. We are to be like wine—we get better with time. But this goes against the modern mentality. We want fast food, fast money, fast love...Anything that is truly valuable takes time to develop. Anything that is of God will take time to grow and it will stand the test of time. Man can make a cubic zirconium stone in a few hours, but it takes many years to make a real diamond.

There are many areas in life that require effort. Isn't it interesting that you seldom hear of a marathon runner using performance-enhancing drugs? Sprinters always seem to be getting busted for using steroids and amphetamines. They have to last only about ten seconds, so some choose to use drugs to help them for those few seconds—if they think they can get away with it. The marathon guy, on the other hand, has to be out there for hours. If you try to run twenty-six miles on drugs, you are going to die! The marathoner *can't* cheat. He has to eat right. He has to keep his weight right. He has to be prepared for all twenty-six miles. It's the only way he'll endure.

As Christians, anytime we try to cheat, it's because we're thinking short-term. We're thinking only about the next one hundred meters. We're thinking only about the next few moments—and we're forgetting that this life is an endurance race.

It's not about having sex now (and we'll talk about getting married later).

It's not about how I can get a pile of money now and wait till later to figure out how to have a good career.

It's not about how I can buy the whole city with zero money down.

How foolish to think that everything from a healthy body to money in the bank can come quickly and easily! We get deceived—it's a lot like the runner trying to cheat with steroids. And at the end of the day, we're the losers.

Don't look for an easy way or a get-rich-quick scheme. Walk with God and His principles. Just do what it takes to endure. Do what it takes to stand the test of time. Do what it takes to get through the challenges and difficulties of life.

It probably won't happen as fast as you wish it would, and probably not as soon as you want it to happen; but you have to decide that your life is not about how fast you can sink into the easy chair; it's about doing what God has called you to do.

Hebrews 12:1–4 says,

> Therefore we also, since we are surrounded by so great a cloud of witnesses, let us lay aside every weight, and the sin which so easily ensnares *us*, and let us run with endurance the race that is set before us, looking unto Jesus, the author and finisher of *our* faith, who

for the joy that was set before Him endured the cross, despising the shame, and has sat down at the right hand of the throne of God.

For consider Him who endured such hostility from sinners against Himself, lest you become weary and discouraged in your souls. You have not yet resisted to bloodshed, striving against sin.

Lay aside the *weight*, He said. What is a weight? A weight is that negative emotion, that bitterness, resentment, unforgiveness, fear, or stress, that makes you feel heavy and down, that causes you to lose your spark and your sharpness. Eventually it causes you to lose your sunny personality because you are just trying to keep up and make it through.

God said, "Lay aside your burdens, negative emotions, fears, worries, defensive living, and hurt—lay them all aside."

"Well, I'm just going to ask the Lord to take them."

Bad move. He doesn't want them! Nor will He take them. He won't carry all that stuff; that's why He tells you to lay it aside. It's a choice, a decision. You have to say, "I'm not going to stay angry. I'm not going to stay hurt."

I admit, I can get freaked out over my teenager driving to school, or over issues at the church, finances, staffing, and so on. Or I can choose to lay all that aside and say, "You know what? That's real stuff, but I'm not going to let it weigh me down. I'm just not going to let it make me sad and make me mad."

I was standing in the boarding line at the airport recently when a lady in front of me asked to change her seat. By this point, she'd already been through the ticketing process and had checked in her baggage. But now she wanted a different seat. The young lady checking boarding passes said, "My understanding is that this flight is sold out, so at this point I don't think that's going to be possible. We're boarding the airplane."

Well, that's not what the lady wanted to hear. She got all upset and started yelling and made a real spectacle of herself. Obviously, that lady was carrying some burdens and some weights. And this young airline employee had to stand there and take the heat for all the drama in this unhappy lady's life.

After the red-faced woman had finished screaming and yelling, she finally boarded the aircraft. Then I stepped up to the young employee, handed her my ticket, and said, "It's one of those days." She winked at me.

You just have to decide that you're not going to let the stuff of this world make you a mad, sad, angry person. You have to make that choice.

A lot of times we don't make that choice because of our perspective. I've found that so much of how we react to life depends upon how we look at things.

If I said to one guy, "Let's go climb Mount Rainier," he might say, "Great! When are we going?" If I said the same thing to another guy, he might look at me and say, "Are you *crazy?*"

The mountain is the same. What's different? How each guy looks at it.

It's not the job; it's not the kids; it's not the traffic; it's not the money; it's not the budget; it's not the world. *It's how you look at it.*

The mountain is always there. The race is always there. One person runs the race with difficulty, angrily, struggling, with an attitude, cursing every step, while the other person runs quietly in the rest and the strength of the Lord.

If you're going to stay in the race of life, you have to do it God's way, not the world's way. And that means you need to lay aside the weights.

God also told us to lay aside the sin. When we sin, we violate God's Word and live contrary to His will. Why do we do it? Well, because sin feels good...for a while. Hebrews 11 gives an interesting testimony about Moses. Verse 24 says, "By faith Moses, when he became of age, refused to be called the son of Pharaoh's daughter."

Who wouldn't want to be called the son of Pharaoh's daughter? Who wouldn't want to live in a palace, have the best clothes, the finest food, the top servants, and be recognized as the Pharaoh's own grandson? So why did Moses turn all of that down? Verse 25 explains: "choosing rather to suffer affliction with the people of God than to enjoy the passing pleasures of sin."

Sin really does offer some pleasure. Adultery is fun...for a minute. Fornication is fun...for a little while. Getting drunk is fun...that night. The next morning is when it catches you. Sin feels good for a while, but very soon the pleasure passes and then you start reaping the terrible consequences.

You know, when they invite you to the casino, they never say, "You're guaranteed to lose, sucker."

When they sell you the beer, they never say, "You're going to be a drunk and a loser."

When the world invites you to sin, it never says, "Remember, these pleasures are temporary."

They really ought to put a little label on every liquor bottle and every blackjack table in the world that says, "Have fun quick, because it won't last long."

Never tell kids that sin isn't fun, because they will find out you lied. It *is* fun to sin—but not for very long. Very soon the addictions, the habits, the losses, and the negative results start catching up. Some of us already know that.

Moses gave up the pleasures of his royal position not because he was against fun or pleasure, but because "he looked to the reward" (v. 26). He reasoned that God knew how to reward His people far better than Satan knew how to pay his. God's reward lasts; the devil's doesn't. God's is real treasure; the devil's is nothing but cheap trinkets.

I've been a Christian for over thirty years, but I can still go get drunk tonight or go pick up a prostitute, if I so choose. I've seen it happen with others—but I know such a choice won't help me run my race. It won't help me win. And I'm after destiny, not just cheap thrills.

When people hear my testimony of drug abuse as a teenager, they often come up to me afterward and say, "Pastor Treat, I'm just like you."

"Really?"

"Yeah, I'm on drugs and I know you know what I'm feeling."

I always want to say to them, "Listen, I was a drug user as a teenager. That was thirty-some years ago!" That's not what I actually say, though. I usually just answer, "Yeah, I feel your pain."

"Do you ever feel like going back?" they ask.

I always try to be gracious and supportive and say, "Here's what I've done and here's how I've kept going."

The fact is I've laid aside the sin because I realize it isn't going to get me where I want to go. I tried the drugs, the alcohol, the sex, the world—all that stuff. I know what it is and I know it's not going to get me where I want to be, so I choose to lay it aside.

Just like Moses, we have to make the choice to lay aside the sin that so easily besets us. We have to choose to run the race that God sets before us.

Are you struggling with laying aside some sin? If you are, maybe it's because you don't know where you really want to go. I'm glad I settled that issue a long time ago. My eyes are on the prize. I'm choosing destiny! And if you're smart, you will, too.

We also turn to sin because we think it will help us somehow—to relieve our stress or some bad feeling. So we have sexual relations outside of marriage, or drink to relax, or use drugs to forget our problems. Rather than waiting on the Lord and coming to Jesus to have our strength renewed, we just take a pill to try to ease the pain.

But whenever you sin, you violate God's plan—and the thing you want, you lose. Every time you sin, you compromise what is right; and any time you compromise to gain, in fact you always lose.

"Don't I have the right to feel good, have some fun?"

Yes, you have that right—*after* the victory. But when you're in the midst of the race, you don't, no. Once you cross the finish line you get to have a little celebration, but you can't sin. In the meantime, you just have to endure.

"Well, I just can't take it anymore. I'm going to go smoke some pot."

All right, go ahead. But just remember that whatever you compromise to gain, you always lose.

"I just hate my marriage and my wife is stupid. Don't I have the right to have some womanly affection?"

Don't forget, whatever you compromise to gain, you always lose. Remember that when you're sitting in the attorney's office. Remember that when you write the alimony check.

"I'm in too deep. I'll just file bankruptcy and get out of here." You can get out if you want to, but let me assure you that you won't get to where you want to be. As soon as you start looking for the quick and easy way out, you compromise. Don't forget! *Whatever you compromise to gain, you always lose.*

I know it's not our nature to trust God and turn away from what seems to be the easy way out of our troubles. That's not the way we do things. "Give me that steering wheel, Lord! I'll get things going around here." And three crashes, four tickets, and ten disasters later, we end up saying, "Okay, God, You go ahead and drive." But by then you're all beaten up. Why not let Him do it from the start?

First John 4:16 says, "And we have known and believed the love that God has for us. God is love, and he who abides in love abides in God, and God in him." Maybe the reason we start compromising, cutting corners, and looking for the quick and the easy is because we don't know and believe the love that God has for us. We start thinking, *I better start taking things into my own hands, because I'm not sure God has my back.*

What if you truly trusted Him? What if you genuinely counted on the love of God? What if you sincerely believed in the love that God has for you? Could you relax and say, "Okay, I'm not going to get nervous. I'm not going to speed things up or try to take things into my own hands. I'm not going to compromise. I'm going to trust the love that God has for me"?

FIX YOUR EYES ON JESUS

I'll never forget many years ago when we did the RAMROD. RAMROD stands for Race Around Mount Rainier in One Day. You bicycle up Mount Rainier twice—one time up to Paradise, then back down around the other side to White Pass. Then you climb back up and then down into Buckley.

The morning I started, I felt terrible. I must have eaten too many energy bars or something, because I felt awful. A bunch of us were riding together and I just wanted to go somewhere to throw up. For the first couple of hours, all I could think was, *I'll never make it.* One hundred seventy-five miles—*twice* up the mountain? There was just no way.

But then something happened; somehow, I forgot to think about feeling bad. I started talking to the guys on the team. I started looking at the scenery around me. I got focused on the mountain ahead of me and I just started climbing. I got into my rhythm and I got into a pace. Before I knew it, I was riding over Paradise on my way down the backside of the mountain, ready to come back up the other side. And the next thing I knew, I was back sitting at the truck in Buckley, talking about how "bad" we were. We talked about how much fun the ride was, and how it wasn't that hard, and how we did it without a problem.

What happened? I got my mind off myself.

How do you make it through the tough times? How do you overcome adversity? How do you deal with those times of stress and pressure and challenge? Hebrews 12:2 gives the answer. It tells you to do it by "looking unto Jesus."

Look unto Jesus and follow His example. He's the author. He's the finisher. He's the Alpha. He's the Omega. He's the Beginning. He's the End. Don't focus on your pain. Keep your eyes on Jesus.

How many times have our marriages paid the price because we became so focused on what we didn't like about our spouse? That made it easy to say, "Forget it, I'm out of here. I'm done with this." Of course we could have come through. We could have made it. We could have lasted. We could have endured—but we had our eyes on the wrong thing.

I wonder how many times we lost the career that the Lord brought to us. "But there were people there who were not nice!" I'm not saying they were. But you focused on what you didn't like and became upset about what was wrong—and so you walked away from a blessing. What would have happened had you just stayed focused on the Lord and looked unto Jesus? He would have brought you through. He would have changed the hearts of those people or He would have moved them out, one or the other.

Our job is to endure, and we do it by staying focused on the Lord.

Look not at the things that are seen, but at the things that are not seen. Remember, the things that are seen are temporary and subject to change, while the things that are not seen are eternal.

So that's what I'm looking at. Jesus isn't going to change! His promise isn't going to change! His Word isn't going to change! His will isn't going to change! And when I'm looking unto Jesus, the bright future He's promised me isn't going to change, either.

I'll never forget when I was twelve years old and my brother, Dale, was ten. My mom and dad decided we were going to Arizona. We had a Ford pickup truck with a canopy—not a camper, a canopy. So they threw some blankets and sleeping bags into the back of the truck, along with this canopy they had bolted down. It was a two- or three-day drive.

After we'd driven about half an hour, I started banging on the truck cab, trying to get Mom and Dad's attention. "How far till we stop? How far till we have dinner?" After a while they stopped the truck and told me, "Do not ask us 'how far' anymore. Play your games. Get your mind on something else. You are not going to drive us crazy for three days asking, 'When will we get there?'"

Isn't that the way we are?

"How soon are you going to deliver me, Lord?"

"When am I going to see the miracle, Lord?"

"When is my spouse going to change?"

"How fast are you going to turn this circumstance around?"

And God says to us, "You know what? Y'all better just get busy looking unto Jesus and quit worrying about your problem, because the longer you focus on it, the longer it's going to take." The more you look unto Jesus and let your faith and patience work, the more God can move you through those circumstances and toward your destiny.

Notice what else the writer of Hebrews said about Jesus: "for the joy set before Him." It certainly is no joy being nailed to a cross! So where was the joy? It was in Jesus' expectation of soon sitting down at the right hand of the Father. He looked beyond the cross and saw the joy. He looked across the pain and saw the blessing.

You and I are going to have to do exactly what Jesus did.

You need to say, "I'm going to look beyond this season of trial in my finances. I can't get the bills paid and I'm struggling—but I am going to look beyond that, because I know there's a day when God will bless me financially and my bank account will grow. Bills will be paid and I will be prospering. So I'm going to look to that joy as I'm going through this. That's how I'll endure the cross."

Keep your focus on the joy, because you know the Lord is going to get you through this and leave you with a great testimony. You will be able to let everyone know what the devil did, what the Lord did, and how you won in Jesus' name.

Have you ever read James 1:2? He adds another dimension to all this. "My brethren," he says, "count it all joy when you fall into various trials."

Oh, great!

Well, he didn't say you'd necessarily *feel* joy. You need to make the choice to be joyful when you fall into various trials, tests, challenges, and difficulties of life. Why? Verse 3 gives the reason: "Knowing that the testing of your faith produces patience."

All right, so you're in a test to see what kind of resolve, what kind of faith and patience you really have. You'd better decide right now if you're going to pass this test or flunk out. And don't miss what happens when you pass! Verse 4 says, "But let patience have *its* perfect work, that you may be perfect and complete, lacking nothing."

Now, *that's* the place where you're trying to get! Lacking nothing! You want to be healthy, with a healthy marriage, a prosperous company, paid bills, and money in the bank. And how do you get to that "lacking nothing"?

You go back to that *count it all joy* stuff, coupled with patience.

Allow your faith and your patience to get you to the place where you *count it all joy*. Get to that place where you are looking unto Jesus—because He is the author and the finisher of your faith.

RECEIVE THE PROMISE

Very often, the way you start is nothing like the way you finish. You can start feeling weak or feeling down, but if you focus on the Lord, you can endure and end up triumphant. However, if you get focused on the negative feelings, you may never finish at all. You have to decide, "My eye is on the prize. My focus is on the Lord. I am seeing His will, His purpose, His plan. I don't care about anything else in between. I'm going to finish. I'm going to keep the faith. I'm going to win."

Hebrews 10:35–36 says, "Therefore do not cast away your confidence, which has great reward. For you have need of endurance, so that after you have done the will of God, you may receive the promise."

Now, isn't that something? It's possible to have done the will of God, to have done everything God wanted you to do, and yet...

"God, what else do you want me to do?"

"Nothing."

"Come on, give me *something*."

"Okay—endure."

"Uhhh, how about giving me something else?"

After you've done the will of God you have need of endurance so you'll receive the promise.

We tend to give up too quickly, don't we? We don't want to wait. We don't want to endure, so we compromise—we give up. We move on...and so we miss what God has for us.

You have need of endurance, so that after you've done the will of God, you won't miss the promise. You did all *that* for the Lord, so you might as well hang in there. Don't quit now!

The passage goes on to say, *"For yet a little while, / And He who is coming will come and will not tarry. / Now the just shall live by faith"* (vv. 37–38). Notice the writer didn't say, "the just shall try a couple of days by faith." No, he said, *"live* by faith."

Come on! Keep that faith and patience.

Come on! Don't quit. Don't give up. Don't draw back. Keep on believing until you receive the promise—and that's a lot easier to do when you realize that *God is more committed to your success than you are.* That's an important truth! God is not only more committed to your success than you are, He's also more committed to your healing, to your prosperity, to your marriage, and to every other part of your life.

Do you really believe you are going to get yourself farther down the road of life than God can get you? Do you really believe you can get yourself a better life than God can get you? Maybe if you just let Him do His thing, at the end of the day your challenges or problems will begin to shrink in the shadow of His presence.

I think I'll just slide on over to the passenger seat and quit worrying. In fact, I think I'll just take me a nap and let the Lord do the driving.

20

Jesus DID So Can YOU!

This book has been about successfully running a race—the race to the destiny God has for you personally regardless of whatever present difficulties you face. I've done my best to explain that God wants every one of us to learn what it takes to claim His promises for ourselves, and thus claim what He has set aside for us—both in this world and in the world to come.

Now I want to close by showing that you can run your race successfully only because Jesus completed His own race to destiny. As you become more and more like Jesus every day by exercising your faith, then you, too, can successfully run your race to destiny.

But maybe you're still saying, "I can't!" Maybe you're saying:

- I can't overcome my addiction.

- I can't overcome my temptation.

- I can't deal with the problems in my life.

- I can't believe what God says about me.

- I can't claim the promises God has made to me.

Those are all lies. You most certainly *can*, and you can because God has called you to do it. And as I've said before, He will never call you to do something He doesn't also equip you to do.

There's no question that He's calling you to be what the apostle Paul called an "imitator of God" (Ephesians 5:1). That's good news, indeed—but even better is the fact that God has given you His very own Son, Jesus Christ, as your chief example.

Near the end of His earthly ministry, Jesus said to Thomas, one of His disciples, "I am the way, the truth, and the life. No one comes to the Father except through Me. If you had known Me, you would have known My Father also; and from now on you know Him and have seen Him" (John 14:6–7).

At that point, the disciples weren't quite tracking with Jesus, so Philip said, "Lord, show us the Father, and it is sufficient for us" (v. 8). Jesus answered, "Have I been with you so long, and yet have you not known Me, Philip? He who has seen Me has seen the Father; so how can you say, 'Show us the Father'?"

God the Father sent God the Son, Jesus Christ, to be one of us so that we could learn to live like Him; and the only way we can learn to live like Him is to connect with Him, to know Him in a personal, intimate, real way. As we get to know Him better, God enables us to become more and more like Jesus in every way.

Jesus faced every earthly challenge we face now, including the temptation to sin. The writer of the epistle to the Hebrews tells us, "For we do not have a High Priest who cannot sympathize with our weaknesses, but was in all *points* tempted as *we are, yet* without sin" (Hebrews 4:15).

Jesus is your example of how to overcome temptation and repel the advances of the devil. While the tempter did everything he could to sidetrack Jesus from His mission, Jesus simply answered, "It is written..." In saying that, Jesus set a perfect example for you. You overcome by the Word of God.

Christianity is about two things: connecting with God in a real, relational way and having a model to follow in Jesus Christ. None of the other things we do in church are nearly as important as these two. None of our arguments or debates about the fine points of theology and religious issues really mean that much in the big scheme of things.

When you get to heaven, God won't ask you about your theology or how you conducted yourself in worship services. All He will concern Himself with is whether you connected with Him through Jesus Christ and whether you lived your life with Jesus as your model in everything you did.

YOU *WILL* HAVE TRIBULATION, BUT...

While Jesus came to take away the eternal effects of sin on those who would put their faith in Him, He did not immediately remove the negatives sin has brought into our world. In fact, I would say that He didn't change the world itself, only those who would believe in Him. That is why He told His disciples, "In the world you will have tribulation; but be of good cheer, I have overcome the world" (John 16:33).

Some believers don't know how to handle it when bad things happen to them. Too many of us tend to turn to God and ask "Why?" whenever the negative things hit us. But as we have seen, our physical bodies have to reside in this fallen and cursed world, and that means they often get smacked with the negative things that go on in it. That is why even genuine believers deal with fatigue, sickness, and other problems. It's also why our flesh can so often want the wrong thing. Your mind and your spirit may say, "No, this is not right for me," but your flesh says, "Yes, I want to enjoy this." You and I live under that negative influence of the world, and Jesus did not remove it. Though there will come a day when Jesus will remove all those consequences and influence (see Revelation 22:3), in the meantime—in the here and now, where we live—we're going to have to deal with suffering, pain, and misfortune.

Nevertheless, we can also be cheered by the fact that if we follow Jesus faithfully, we *will* overcome this world. That is what the apostle Paul wanted some Christian friends to understand when he wrote:

Yet what we suffer now is nothing compared to the glory he will give us later. For all creation is waiting patiently and hopefully for that future day when God will resurrect his children. For on that day thorns and thistles, sin, death, and decay—the things that overcame the world against its will at God's command—will all disappear, and the world around us will share in the glorious freedom from sin which God's children enjoy. (Romans 8:18–21, The Living Bible)

While you and I are spiritually free, the whole world still struggles under the burden of the curse. There will come a day when Jesus will come back, lift the curse, and raise to life those who have died believing in Him; but in the meantime, we will have to endure until the earth is reborn:

And even we Christians, although we have the Holy Spirit within us as a foretaste of future glory, also groan to be released from pain and suffering. We, too, wait anxiously for that day when God will give us our full rights as his children, including the new bodies he has promised us—bodies that will never be sick again and will never die. (Romans 8:23, TLB)

First John 5:18 tells us that the wicked one, the devil, does not touch the one who has been born of God. Once you are saved, Satan can do nothing to touch your spirit. Obviously, however, he's quite good at touching people's bodies. The flesh is the house that God gave us to live in while we live here, but it's also the vehicle through which the enemy and the world influence us. And that means we have a battle to fight.

Even the apostle Paul wrote, "For the good that I will *to do*, I do not do; but the evil I will not *to do*, that I practice. Now if I do what I will not *to do*, it is no longer I who do it, but sin that dwells in me.... O wretched man that I am! Who will deliver me from this body of death?" (Romans 7:19–20, 24).

That's what we struggle with today—but there's coming a day when even our bodies will be born again, when our flesh will be made righteous and glorified, when no more curse will hound this earth. Until then, however, we deal with the challenges.

Jesus didn't remove everything that has to do with the curse, but He transformed *you*. So when bad things happen, you should never say, "Why me? I thought I was a child of God! I thought He was taking care of me!" He *is* taking care of you, of course, but "in the world you will have tribulation."

Despite all of this, you can be encouraged, knowing that Christ has overcome the world, overcome the enemy, and overcome the curse. And because He has overcome all these things, you also get to live life as an overcomer.

YOU STILL WIN

Jesus came to earth, in part, to show you how to successfully live the kind of life God wants you to live, even as you navigate a fallen world. He did just that as He claimed victory over the devil and over the world's corrupt and cursed systems. As John wrote, "You are of God, little children, and have overcome them, because He who is in you is greater than he who is in the world" (1 John 4:4).

The devil is still out there in the world, trying to harass you; but the Bible tells you that the One in you is greater—more powerful—than the devil or any of the world's systems. So, no matter what the devil throws at you, no matter what this world may bring your way, *you still win!*

You don't win because you're more religious. You don't win because you haven't missed Sunday school in seven years. You don't win because you're well educated or intelligent. You don't win because you put the biggest offering in the plate every Sunday. You win, you overcome, because Jesus Christ who lives in you is greater than he who is in this world.

So as the world looks and says, "How sad! You have cancer," or "Oh, no! You've lost your job!" or "I'm so sorry that you are going

> Many things in the world are against you, but remember God is for you. He and His church are for your success in every realm of life. He wants you healed, whole, and blessed. Focus on that, never forget that. When I was at my worst, I knew God did not want me to stay there. He was pulling me through and He is pulling you, too!

through troubles in your marriage," you can confidently and peacefully look through your circumstances and know that the One you know is greater than any of your problems.

That is how you learn to win in life and how you cultivate the attitude of an overcomer. As I've frequently pointed out in this book, it's a matter of focus. And if your focus is on Jesus and on being like Him in everything you say and do, then you will victoriously run your race to destiny.

The apostle John described what it takes to be a child of God when he wrote, "Whoever confesses that Jesus is the Son of God, God abides in him, and he in God" (1 John 4:15). Notice that he didn't say, "Whoever joins the church" or "Whoever is religious" or "Whoever serves as a deacon." The one condition for being invited into the family of God is to confess and believe that Jesus is the Son of God—and if you have done that, then your eternal destiny has been settled.

But your eternal destination isn't the only thing that gets settled when you confess Jesus Christ. John insists there is much more to being one of God's children:

> And we have known and believed the love that God has for us. God is love, and he who abides in love abides in God, and God in him.
>
> Love has been perfected among us in this: that we may have boldness in the day of judgment; because as He is, so are we in this world. (1 John 4:16–17)

As He is, so are we in the world. But what is Jesus in the world? What did He look like as He walked this earth? How do you work on being like Him?

It's not in thinking that you *are* somebody—although He makes you somebody—but in the fact that you *know* Somebody. And because you know Him, you can know that if sickness or poverty come against you, you are as He is in this world.

Disasters? Problems? Opposition? Disappointment? Those things happen in this world, but they didn't take Jesus down—not until He chose to give Himself up to die. And neither will they take you down. Why not? Because *as He is, so are you in this world.*

So what, exactly, was Jesus in this world? And what, exactly, are you because of it? And what will that do for you? Since you want specifics, let me give you five.

1. Jesus lived His dream, fulfilled His destiny, and overcame every challenge.

Jesus is your example in that He came into the world and did everything His Father sent Him to do. He loved people, healed people, blessed people, preached to people, and gave Himself up as a sacrifice for our sins.

Jesus fulfilled His destiny in that He lived out the full will of God the Father. He's healed! He's blessed! He's full of peace and joy. As He is, so are you. Jesus is successful, victorious, overcoming, powerful, and now seated at the right hand of God; and as He is now, so are you in this world. You are called to live your dream, fulfill your destiny, and overcome every challenge on the way to becoming what God wants you to be and do.

2. Jesus didn't bow to the religious or popular controllers of his day.

Jesus faced opposition from the religious establishment of His time—the pharisees, the sadducees, the scribes—and from the Roman government. These groups opposed what He was trying to do. Yet when He didn't bow, they didn't know what to think, what to say, or what to do. He was here under the authority of His Father, and He obeyed Him perfectly in every way.

In our day, you face opposition from the media, from popular culture, and from what is considered politically correct. As Jesus didn't bow to the forces of opposition in His day, neither should you bow to the opposition in yours. You should never worry much about what is socially acceptable or politically correct. If Jesus is into it, then you're into it. If it's not like Jesus, then you're not like it.

3. Jesus encouraged and embraced the downtrodden and defeated.

If ever there was someone for the "little guy," for the individual the world wouldn't accept or embrace, it was Jesus.

One day, the religious leaders brought a sexually immoral woman to Jesus, a lady caught in the very act of adultery. "The Old Covenant law says we should stone her," they insisted. "But what do you say? What should we do with her?" As He so often did, Jesus answered this loaded question with an answer that immediately stumped them. "Whoever is without sin"—read that again, *whoever* is without sin"—"throw the first stone." Suddenly, these religious leaders realized how wrong and how silly they were.

Jesus defended someone who was down that day. He didn't endorse or excuse her sin. In fact, He told her, "Go and sin no more." All He did was love her, embrace her, and accept her.

That is how you are to be. You are to love and support people. You are to reach out to the defeated and the downtrodden. You are to love the alcoholic and the drug addict and say, "Come on, we want you with us in our church. You are one of us!" You are to say to the divorced, "We are with you because we've all been through tough stuff, too."

Jesus loved and accepted people, so you must, too. You don't have to endorse their sin, but you accept and love the sinner and help him or her to rise above it—just as Jesus has done for you and me.

4. Jesus refused to be a victim of circumstances.

Jesus faced storms, both figuratively and literally. He faced political and religious pressure. Bad things happened to him, unfair things, but He refused to be the victim. Instead, He approached everything that happened to Him as what it really was: Part of His Father's plan to bring salvation to the world.

Likewise, you should never play the part of the victim or look for ungodly ways to make your life easier. Instead, take responsibility, allow God to use whatever comes your way, and rise above it all. In every way, Jesus was a victor and not a victim. You can do as He did, in every area of your life.

5. Jesus prospered in every way to change the world He lived in—one person at a time.

Jesus came into the world to change it, not to leave it the way He found it when He first got here. You can do the very same thing in your own corner of the world.

When you follow the example of Jesus, when you make being like Him your focus, you can't help but change things and change people. When you follow the example Jesus set, you aren't religious and condemning, but peaceful and loving.

Jesus told His disciples, "If you abide in Me, and My words abide in you, you will ask what you desire, and it shall be done for you. By this My Father is glorified, that you bear much fruit; so you will be My disciples" (John 15:7–8).

Abide in Me. That means remaining in Jesus, clinging to Jesus, living in Jesus, no matter what happens. It means continuing to know and grow in Him every day and in every way. And when you abide in Him, you don't bother arguing religious doctrine, traditions, and things of men. When you abide in Him, you don't live under condemnation and guilt or worry that you're not good enough. Instead, you live with His peace, His joy, and His love. And when you do that, you bear fruit—just as Jesus did.

Most importantly, when you abide in Him, you can successfully obey His final command to His disciples: "And Jesus came and spoke to them, saying, 'All authority has been given to Me in heaven and on earth. Go therefore and make disciples of all the nations, baptizing them in the name of the Father and of the Son and of the Holy Spirit'" (Matthew 28:18–19).

LOVE AS JESUS LOVED

Mere hours away from His ultimate earthly destination, the cross, Jesus got His disciples together to hand out some final instructions. Among those instructions was the following commandment, which may be the greatest Jesus ever spoke:

> This is My commandment, that you love one another as I have loved you. Greater love has no one than this, than to lay down one's life for his friends. You are My friends if you do whatever I command you. No longer do I call you servants, for a servant does not know what his master is doing; but I have called you friends, for all things that I heard from My Father I have made known to you. (John 15:12–15)

Christianity is all about relationship, intimacy, personal involvement, and friendship with Jesus Christ—all of which makes us sons and daughters of God the Father, as well as brothers and sisters with

294

one another. That's the life He's called you to live, and it's the basis for running the race to your personal destiny in Him.

Know His purpose, His plan, His passion, His place, and His power in your life! When you know Him, you live with His love, His peace, and His joy. And when you live with those things, you are well on your way to being all He has made you to be, called you to be, and prepared you to be.

In short, even when you're feeling your worst, you'll be at your best—and that means you'll be running your race to destiny.

Note to My Friends

I have received many letters regarding my diagnosis and treatment for hepatitis C. Since every person is different, I suggest seeking treatment specific to your own needs and not attempting to follow the pattern that was prescribed for me.

I was diagnosed with hep C, genotype 1, stage 2. I was treated at the University of Washington in Seattle in an experimental program with double doses of ribavarin and interferon for eleven months. In addition to chemotherapy, I consulted a physician specializing in nutrition and natural medicine who developed a program specific to my needs. I also received treatments from a chiropractor.

A year after ending chemotherapy, I received a clean bill of health from my health care providers. I am considered cured of the virus.

In addition to this book, the teaching series I suggest are How to Do Your Best When You Feel Your Worst *and* Heart of a Winner.

There is also a DVD entitled Overcoming Hepatitis C. *They are available at www.caseytreat.com.*

The scripture I used to help decide my course of treatment was Proverbs 18:9 (AMP), "He who is loose and slack in his work is brother to him who is a destroyer and he who does not use his endeavors to heal himself is brother to him who commits suicide."

I hope this information helps you or a loved one who has been diagnosed with hepatitis C or any other disease, or who faces any kind of affliction or difficulty. God bless you.

Casey Treat

Casey Treat

Scripture Reference

Unless otherwise noted, all Scripture references are taken from the New King James Version (NKJV) of the *Bible*. Copyright © 1982 by Thomas Nelson, Inc., Publishers.

Scripture quotations marked as

AMP are taken from the *Amplified Bible*, copyright © 1954, 1958, 1962, 1965, 1987 by The Lockman Foundation. Used by permission.

KJV are taken from the King James Version of the Bible, copyright © 1979, 1980, 1982 by Thomas Nelson, Inc., Publishers.

TLB are taken from *The Living Bible*, copyright © 1971. Used by permission of Tyndale House Publishers, Inc., Wheaton, Illinois 60189. All rights reserved.

NIV are taken from the *Holy Bible*, New International Version, copyright © 1973, 1978, 1984 International Bible Society. Used by permission of Zondervan Bible Publishers.

NLT are taken from the *Holy Bible*, New Living Translation, copyright © 1996, 2004. Used by permission of Tyndale House Publishers, Inc., Wheaton, Illinois 60189. All rights reserved.